Lith. of Ed. Weber & Co. Balto.

STATE HOUSE AT ANNAPOLIS IN 1789

ANNALS OF ANNAPOLIS.

ANNALS *of* ANNAPOLIS

COMPRISING

SUNDRY NOTICES OF THAT OLD CITY

FROM THE PERIOD OF

THE FIRST SETTLEMENTS IN ITS VICINITY IN THE

YEAR 1649, UNTIL THE WAR OF 1812:

TOGETHER WITH

VARIOUS INCIDENTS IN THE HISTORY OF MARYLAND,

DERIVED FROM

EARLY RECORDS, PUBLIC DOCUMENTS,

AND OTHER SOURCES:

WITH AN APPENDIX,

CONTAINING A NUMBER OF LETTERS FROM

GENERAL WASHINGTON, AND OTHER
DISTINGUISHED PERSONS,

WHICH LETTERS HAVE NEVER BEEN PUBLISHED BEFORE

Compiled and Edited by
David Ridgely
Librarian of the State Library

HERITAGE BOOKS
2019

HERITAGE BOOKS
AN IMPRINT OF HERITAGE BOOKS, INC.

Books, CDs, and more—Worldwide

For our listing of thousands of titles see our website
at
www.HeritageBooks.com

A Facsimile Reprint
Published 2019 by
HERITAGE BOOKS, INC.
Publishing Division
5810 Ruatan Street
Berwyn Heights, Md. 20740

Entered according to the Act of Congress, in the year 1840,
by David Ridgely,
In the Clerk's Office of the District Court of Maryland

Originally published
Baltimore:
Cushing & Brother
1841

— Publisher's Notice —
In reprints such as this, it is often not possible to remove blemishes from the original. We feel the contents of this book warrant its reissue despite these blemishes and hope you will agree and read it with pleasure.

International Standard Book Numbers
Paperbound: 978-0-7884-4748-8
Clothbound: 978-0-7884-8086-7

DEDICATION.

TO THE

CITIZENS OF ANNAPOLIS,

THIS LITTLE VOLUME

IS RESPECTFULLY DEDICATED,

BY

THE AUTHOR.

INTRODUCTION.

The author of the following pages entertaining the belief, that their publication might be acceptable to his fellow-citizens, has committed them to the press, in the hope that his readers may derive something of interest and entertainment from their perusal. In taking this step, he has had many misgivings. Diffident of his ability to invest his subject with the interest that belongs to it, he would have been loath indeed to give 'The Annals of Annapolis' publicity, had it not been for the absence of any such publication.

It must not be supposed by his readers, that this work is intended to supply the place of biography. The lives of eminent citizens form a part of the history of the times in which they acted and flourished, but that minuteness of detail which belong to such efforts is neither within his reach, nor within the scope of this design. Eminent men are occasionally mentioned, when they are necessarily associated with the annals of the city, but, at the same time, many citizens of learning, parts and patriotism, must escape particular mention in such a work as this.

He has gathered his *materiél* from the records and documents within his reach. He is greatly indebted for much of it to 'Bozman's' and 'McMahon's Histories of Maryland,' 'Henning's Statutes at Large of Virginia,' 'The Maryland Gazette,' a series of essays under the caption of 'The Annapoliad,' 'Bacon's Laws of Maryland,' and 'Eddis's Letters from America,' and to a late venerable Lady of Annapolis, for many traditionary reminiscences.

He bespeaks for this publication the clemency of a generous public.

PREFACE.

The original design in collecting and arranging the materials contained in this volume, was merely to give some outlines of the Annals of Annapolis, but so limited were the records and documents on that head, that it was from necessity partially abandoned. In those periods where nothing immediately connected with Annapolis was found, incidents in relation to the history of the Province and State of Maryland, have been introduced.

The labour in doing this was greater than the compiler anticipated. But if any reader shall find entertainment, or be gratified by its perusal, the Author will not be disappointed.

The authorities and documents from which these pages have been compiled, are generally acknowledged. It would be difficult, and perhaps unnecessary, to name particularly every source from which information has been obtained. For the use of that rare and valuable file of papers, *The Maryland Gazette*, acknowledgments are here tendered to Jonas Green, Esquire, the descendant of the first venerated and venerable printer of Maryland.

Many defects will doubtless be apparent in the style of this work, but when it is remembered that no claim to skill in literary composition is made (and fortunately but little or none was required in this undertaking) the generous and the learned will overlook all such deficiencies as may meet the eye of the critic, and do justice to the intention and object of this collection.

Being in possession of some original letters from general Washington and a few other distinguished men of his day, which it is believed have not hitherto been published, they are placed in an Appendix to this volume, and perhaps will form the most interesting part of it.

Fearful that the importance of the facts that are detailed, may be overlooked, from the want of skill in setting them forth, this volume is now given to the public for what it is worth; even a small tribute to the history of his native State, will, he trusts, be acceptable to his fellow-citizens.

ANNAPOLIS, *Dec.* 1840.

CONTENTS.

Chapter I.

Cecilius, Lord Baltimore, prepares for sending out a Colony—Appoints his brother to conduct it—They depart from Cowes—Arrive in the Chesapeake—Sail up the Potomac—Fix upon St. Mary's for the first settlement—Reception by the Natives—Father Andrew White—Town of St. Mary's—The Capital of the Province—An Assembly called—Act of Virginia against dissenting Ministers—The Puritans leave Virginia—Take refuge in Maryland—And settle at Providence, now Annapolis—Oath of Fidelity—Mr. Thos. Greene appointed governor in the absence of Governor William Stone—He proclaims the Prince of Wales—The inhabitants of Providence prefer the dominion of the Commonwealth—Governor Stone returns—Calls an Assemby—The Puritans refuse to attend—Governor Stone visits Providence—Returns Burgesses to the Assembly—They attend—Providence organized into a county, called Anne Arundel—Murders committed by the Indians—Susquehanock Indians—Preparations against the Indians, ... 13

Chapter II.

Tranquility of the Province—Governor Stone visits Providence—Appoints Mr. Edward Lloyd commander of Anne Arundel county—Appoints Commissioners—The Puritans at Providence again refuse to send Delegates to the Assembly—Bennett and Claiborne reduce the Colony of Maryland—Governor Stone retained in office by them—Is soon deprived of his office by them—The Colony submits to the Commonwealth of England—Governor Stone reinstated—Cromwell proclaimed in the Province—Governor Stone declares the Puritans at Providence to be enemies of Lord Baltimore—The Province again reduced—Governor Stone rebuked by Lord Baltimore for resigning his Government—Governor Stone re-assumes his office and powers as Governor—Organizes a Military Force—Seizes the Provincial Records—Secures the Arms and

Ammunition of the Province—Governor Stone makes preparations to reduce Anne Arundel to submission, and marches towards the Severn—Arrives at Herring Creek—Appears in the River Severn—The Golden Lion—Governor Stone's party land on Horn Point—Captain Fuller, at the head of the Puritans of Providence, marches to meet them—Battle on Horn Point—Governor Stone condemned to Death—The Soldiers refuse to execute him—Others executed—The Property of Governor Stone and his party sequestered—Lord Baltimore restored to his Rights by the Lord Protector—Appoints captain Josiah Fendall Governor—The Puritans acknowledge the authority of Lord Baltimore—Acknowledgment, 40

Chapter III.

Contempt of Assembly—Trial of Edward Erbery—Condemned and Whipped—Witchcraft—Condemnation of John Cowman—And pardoned—The Quakers remonstrate against taking Oaths—Proceedings of the Assembly thereon—Indian Affairs—Protection of the Indians by the Colonists—Hostility of the Susquehanocks—Causes of—Treaty with them—Murders committed by the Indians—Expedition against them—Five Chiefs of the Susquehanocks murdered—Impeachment of Major Thomas Truman—His Trial and Conviction—Proceedings of the Assembly thereon—Controversy between the Lord Proprietary and the Lower House of Assembly upon the Act for calling Assemblies—Extracts from the Rules of the Lower House of Assembly—Annapolis erected into a Town, &c.—Commissioners appointed to survey and lay out Annapolis—Annapolis becomes the Seat of Government—Governor Nicholson causes the Records to be removed from St. Mary's—Public Ferry—First Corporation of Annapolis—Mr. Richard Beard makes a map of the Town—A Market and Fair—Proposition for a Bridewell—Improvement of Annapolis—A Church proposed to be erected—King William's School established—*William Pinkney* a Student of it—Governor Nicholson projects a Library for Annapolis—A State-House built—Roman Catholics—Persecution of, , . . . , 55

Chapter IV.

Dispute between Governor Nicholson and the Lower House of Assembly—They become reconciled—Governor Nicholson leaves this Province to preside over Virginia—Petition of Mr. John Perry—James Crawford, a Delegate, killed by lightning—First public Jail—State-House burnt down—A new one erected—Described—Improvement of the town—A plot for burning of Annapolis, discovered—Bounds of Annapolis—Annapolis chartered—Description of Annapolis—Delegates from Annapolis to receive only *half wages*—Improvements—Mr. James Stoddart appointed to lay off anew the city—Mr. Wm. Parks appointed to compile the Laws of the Province—Improvements—Appropriation to build a Government-House—Mr. Jonas Green appointed Printer to the Province—His character—Editor of the Maryland Gazette—The first public horseracing—Aurora Borealis—South River Club—Military movements at Annapolis—Anniversary of George the Second—Trade and Commerce of Annapolis—The first Ship-Yard—Brig Lovely Nancy—Notices of some of the oldest houses of the town—The old Episcopal Church—Indians—King Abraham and Queen Sarah—*A Hiccory Switch*—A Jockey Club formed—Races—The first Theatre built—The first Lottery drawn in the Province—Governor Sharp arrives at Annapolis—The military march from Annapolis against the French on the Ohio—General Braddock and other distinguished persons arrive at Annapolis—Doctor Charles Carroll, his death—Annapolis entrenched—Hostilities of the French and Indians—Small-pox, ... 101

Chapter V.

Forts on the Border Country—Fort Frederick—Reduction of Quebec—A Company of Comedians at Annapolis—Stone Wind-mill erected—Collection for the sufferers by fire at Boston—Ball-room—Cold winter—Stamp Act—Proceeding at Annapolis on—Maryland Gazette—Sons of Liberty—Repeal of the Stamp Act—A new Theatre opened—Gov. Eden arrives at Annapolis—His character—Death and burial—Articles of Non-importation, &c.—Arrival of Brig Good Intent—Resolute course pursued by the Association—Its results—Mr. Wm. Eddis—Annapolis described—Whitehall—Governor Sharpe—His character—Appropriation to build the present State-House—Commissioners appointed—The Foundation laid—Incident—Dimensions of the building—The Architect—Anniversary of the Proprietary's birth—Rejoicings at Annapolis—Ladies of Annapolis—Saint Tamina Society—Their Proceedings—Theatre opened—Trustees appointed by the Legislature, to the Theatre—Theatre pulled down—Causes which led to it—Mr. Dunlap—Trustees appointed to build a new Church—Meeting of the Citizens of Annapolis—Their proceedings on the Act of Parliament for blockading the Harbour of Boston—Some portion of their Resolves dissented from by many Citizens—Proceedings of the Dissentients—Burning of the Brig Peggy Stewart—And the tea on board—The Proceedings had thereon, ... 131

CONTENTS.

Chapter VI.

Tea Burning in Frederick County—The Citizens of Annapolis organized into Military Companies—Proceedings of the Baltimore Committee of Observation—The ship Totness, with salt on board, burnt just below Annapolis—General Charles Lee—Massachusetts' Colony—Lord Viscount Barrington—Addresses—Gen. Burgoyne—And Gen. Lee—Council of Safety—Chart of the Harbour of Annapolis—Appropriation to fortify the City—Fortifications—Slaughter Houses—Certain Citizens ordered to leave the City—Colonel John Weems before the Committee of Safety—Their proceedings thereon—Captures in the Chesapeake, by Capt. Nicholson, of the ship Defence—Offers Battle to Otter Sloop of War—Balls prohibited throughout the Province—A Declaration of the Delegates of Maryland—Meeting of the Associations of the City of Annapolis—Their Proceedings—Maryland Troops leave Annapolis for Philadelphia—Letters from Philadelphia—Appeal to Maryland—Responded to—Battle on Long Island—Maryland Troops—Major Gist—Maryland Officers made prisoners at Long Island—Thomas Johnson, jr. Esq. Governor of Maryland—British Ships of War pass up the Bay—Gov. Johnson's Proclamation—Mr. Griffith—Baltimore Troops—Battle of Brandywine—General Smallwood—Colonel Smith—Fort Mifflin—Surrender of General Burgoyne—Count Pulaski—Battle of Monmouth—Letter from Commodore Grason to Gov. Johnson—Battle at the Capes—Winter of 1780—Chesapeake crossed by carts and carriages—Baron de Kalb—Battle of Camden—The Baron wounded—His death—Congress voted a Monument to his memory—To be erected in Annapolis—Inscription for the Monument—Extracts of Letters relative to the Battle of Camden—Maryland Troops—Battle of the Cowpens—Col. Howard—Maryland Troops—British Sloops of War off Annapolis—General Lafayette drives them down the Bay—Meeting of the citizens of Annapolis—To consider the Acts of Assembly—For the Emission of Money Bills—Their Proceedings—Militia Assembled at Annapolis—British Fleet arrives before York—Troops landed—Maryland Regiment marches from Annapolis to join the Southern Army—The Recruiting Service—Gen. Smallwood—The Fourth Maryland Regiment marches from Annapolis to join the Marquis de la Fayette—The French Fleet, &c. at Annapolis—From the Head of Elk—The French Army arrives from the North about the same time, on their way to Virginia—Battle of Eutaw—Extract of a Letter from Camp—Col. Howard—Maryland and Virginia Troops—Officers killed and wounded at Eutaw—Surrender of Lord Cornwallis—Rejoicing at Annapolis, ... 163

Chapter VII.

General Washington arrives at Annapolis—Public Dinner—Ball—The Citizens address him—His Answer—He leaves the City—The Birth of a Dauphin celebrated at Annapolis—Count Rochambeau arrives at Annapolis—Embarks for France—Cessation of Hostilities—Public Rejoicing—Public Dinner—Toasts on the Occasion—State-House Illuminated—Ball—Peace—General Greene arrives at Annapolis—Corporate Authorities of the City address him—General Greene's Reply—The Society of Cincinnatti for the State of Maryland formed in Annapolis—Officers of the Maryland Line—Congress in Session at Annapolis—General Washington arrives there—Is entertained by the Citizens—Corporate Authorities address him—His Reply—General Washington resigns his Commission into the hands of the Congress—Proceedings of Congress thereon—General Washington again visits Annapolis accompanied by General Lafayette—They are entertained by the General Assembly—General Lafayette—Addressed by the Governor and Council, and by the Legislature—His Answers—The General Assembly naturalizes General Lafayette—St. John's College—The President of the United States arrives at Annapolis—His Reception—Annapolis—Baltimore—Citizens of Annapolis address the President of the United States—The President's Reply—Defence of Annapolis—Tribute to the Memory of Washington—General Tureau, arrives at Annapolis—His Reception—*William Pinkney* arrives at Annapolis—His Reception—Public Dinner—Officers and Crew of the Frigate Philadelphia—Meeting of the Citizens of Annapolis—Frigate Chesapeake—Proceedings of the Citizens—Piracy in the Chesapeake Bay—Pirates Captured—Conclusion, 200

Chapter VIII.

City of Annapolis—Its Population—Shipping—Its Site—Its Advantages—Naval Academy—The Round Bay—Rail Road—Its proximity to the seat of the National Government—Its Harbour—The Treasury—The Government-house—St. John's College—Episcopal Church—Roman Catholic Chapel—Methodist Church—African House of Worship—The Farmers' Bank of Maryland—Court-house—City Hall—City Hotel—Ball-room—Theatre—The Garrison at Fort Severn, ... 230

A list of the Governors of the Province and State of Maryland, from the First Settlement in 1633 to 1840, ... 249

APPENDIX.

Letter from General Charles Lee to the President of the Council of Safety of Maryland, ... 251
Letter from the Hon'ble John Hancock to the Convention of Maryland, ... 254
Letter from the same to the same, ... 256
Letter from Colonel Smallwood to the President of the Convention, ... 256
Letter from General Washington to Thomas Johnson, Jr. Governor of Maryland, ... 263
Letter from the same to Daniel of St. Thomas Jenifer and William Fitzhugh, ... 264
Letter from the same to Governor Lee, of Maryland, . . 265
Letter from the same to the same, ... 265
Letter from the same to the same, ... 266
Letter from the same to Philip Schuyler, John Matthews and Nathaniel Peabody, Committee of Co-operation in Congress, 267
Letter from the same to the same, ... 269
Letter from General Washington to the Committee of Co-operation in Congress, ... 269
Letter from the same to the same, ... 270
Letter from General Washington to Governor Lee, of Maryland, 272
Letter from the same to the Committee of Co-operation in Congress, ... 272
Letter from the same to George Plater and William Bruff, . 275
Letter from the same to Governor Lee, ... 275
Letter from the same to the same, (*Extract,*) 276
Letter from the same to the same, ... 276
Letter from the same to the same, ... 278
Letter from the same to the same, ... 279
Letter from the same to the same, ... 280
Letter from the same to the same, (*Extract,*) . . . 281
Letter from General Greene to Governor Lee, ... 282
Letter from Colonel Armand to the Governor of Maryland, (*Paca,*) 282

ANNALS OF ANNAPOLIS.

CHAPTER I.

Cecilius, Lord Baltimore, prepares for sending out a Colony—Appoints his brother to conduct it—They depart from Cowes—Arrive in the Chesapeake—Sail up the Potomac—Fix upon St. Mary's for the first settlement—Reception by the Natives—Father Andrew White—Town of St. Mary's—The Capital of the Province—An Assembly called—Act of Virginia against dissenting Ministers—The Puritans leave Virginia—Take refuge in Maryland—And settle at Providence, now Annapolis—Oath of Fidelity—Mr. Thos. Greene appointed governor in the absence of Governor William Stone—He proclaims the Prince of Wales—The inhabitants of Providence prefer the dominion of the Commonwealth—Governor Stone returns—Calls an Assembly—The Puritans refuse to attend—Governor Stone visits Providence—Returns Burgesses to the Assembly—They attend—Providence organized into a County, called Anne Arundel—Murders committed by the Indians—Susquehanock Indians—Preparations against the Indians.

1632. CECILIUS CALVERT, Lord Baron of Baltimore, having succeeded to the proprietary rights of his father, George Calvert, and having obtained possession of the charter* for the government of the province of Maryland, made his preparations for planting this colony. These preparations were begun in June, 1632.

* The royal grant was given on condition that 'two Indian arrows of those parts' should be delivered at Windsor Castle, every year, on Tuesday, in Easter-week: and also, the fifth part of all the gold and silver which might be found within the province.

The difficulty of procuring and furnishing a sufficient number of colonists, with the necessary conveniences to enable them permanently to form their colony, caused some delay before their departure from England.

1633. It was not until this year that the colonists were ready to embark on their voyage, and Lord Baltimore, who had originally designed to accompany them in person, changed his mind, and appointed his brother, Leonard Calvert, Esquire, to go in his stead, in the character of governor, or lieutenant-general.

On the 22d of November, 1633, they sailed from Cowes, in the Isle of Wight, and on the 24th of February, 1634, arrived off Point Comfort in Virginia.

1634. After entering the Potomac and sailing up that river about fourteen leagues, they came to an island called 'Heron Island,' and anchored under another neighbouring isle, to which they gave the name of 'St. Clements.' Here the governor landed, and setting up a cross, in the Roman Catholic manner, took formal possession of the country; 'for our Saviour and for our sovereign lord the king of England.' But the governor on reflection thinking it would not be advisable to settle so high up the river, in the infancy of the colony, determined to seek for a settlement further down. He, therefore, returned down the Potomac, taking captain Fleet with him. They proceeded to a small river on the north side of the Potomac, within four or five leagues of its mouth, which the governor called 'St. George's river.' Sailing up this river about four leagues, they came to an Indian town, called by the natives *Yoamaco*, from whence the tribe here inhabiting, was called *Yoamacoes*. The governor having landed here, entered into a treaty with the Werowance, or chief of the tribe—who, with the natives, agreed to leave the whole town to the English, as soon as they could gather their corn; and which they faithfully performed. The governor then, on the 27th of March, 1634, caused the colonists to land, and according to the agreement, took possession of the town, which they named '*St. Mary's.*'

Being thus favourably received by the Indian inhabitants, whose affections they had the good fortune to conciliate by the liberality of their conduct, they were soon enabled to purchase extensive tracts on the most moderate terms, and to settle their lands to the best advantage, without fear of molestation from the original possessors.

The following interesting article, '*The Pilgrims of Maryland,*' taken from the '*Metropolitan Catholic Almanac,*' for the year 1840, is here given for the gratification of the curious antiquarian. It is considered not to be out of place here to state that the general assembly of Maryland, at its December session of 1836, made a liberal appropriation for the purpose of procuring from Rome a transcript of the *Narrative of Father Andrew White*, which is deemed important to the elucidation of the early history of our state; and that the services of a distinguished gentleman of the order of the Jesuits, now in Rome, are kindly promised to obtain it for the library of the state.

THE PILGRIMS OF MARYLAND.

The student of American history must ever regret that so little has been done to furnish the particulars of the first settlement and early transactions of Maryland, by such as having been actors in those scenes, could have supplied the loss of the early records, destroyed in Ingle and Claiborne's rebellion, about ten years after the landing in 1634. Had Maryland been equally fortunate with her sister colonies, in the possession of her early records, she had not wanted an enlightened and impartial historian to present to the world the enterprizing and honourable actions, as she has with a masterly pen exhibited the just and liberal principles which distinguished the founders of this province.

Mr. McMahon, with a taste and industry worthy of his genius, has culled from the mouldering and neglected records in the archives of the state, all that they possessed of interest on this subject. The subsequent publication by the State, of the history of Maryland from its settlement to 1660, by Bozman, exhibits that patient and laborious scholar, after having devoted years of toil to his favourite work, unable to elucidate many important events, or to pourtray the characters of conspicuous individuals, for the want of authentic materials.

A gleam of hope remains that among the letters of the missionaries of the society of Jesus, who first preached the gospel in Maryland, may be found much interesting matter for a history of the early days of that state.

Enlightened scholars of every nation and creed have long appreciated those charming volumes, *Lettres Edi-*

fiantes et Curieuses, which by their communications on civil and natural history, geography, astronomy, &c. &c. have added so much to the stores of learning, while their edifying accounts of religion have delighted all who esteem true virtue and admire the heroism of the soldiers of Christ.

A young American clergyman,* of the society of Jesus, while pursuing his studies at Rome, found in the archives of that distinguished body, various letters similar to those collected in *Lettres Edifiantes,* written by *Father Andrew White,* and other priests, who accompanied the first settlers of Maryland. He brought with him copious extracts from these documents, which having been accidentally seen by John Bozman Kerr, Esquire, an active member of the house of delegates in this state, and an accomplished scholar, that gentleman proposed that the legislature should take measures to procure all the information on the early history of Maryland, which might be found in the archives of the Jesuits. A resolution was adopted, which, it is hoped, will result in producing important materials for the future historian.

The following abridgment of the extracts from Father White, contains many particulars, which, though not of great importance, are interesting to the curious, having never before been published. His descriptions of various countries and their productions, which are very particular in the original, are in most cases omitted here. The paper from which these extracts were made, is in Latin, in the archives of the society of Jesus, at Rome. It appears to have been written from the city of St. Mary's, within about a month after the

---

*The late Rev. William McSherry.

arrival of the first vessels, probably in April, 1634. It is entitled,

'*A Report of the Colony of the Lord Baron of Baltimore, in Maryland, near Virginia, in which the quality, nature and condition of the country and its many advantages and riches are described.*

' There is a province near the English colony in Virginia, which, in honour of Maria his queen, his majesty the king of England wished to be called Maryland, or the land of Mary.'

'This province his majesty, in his munificence, presented to the lord Baron of Baltimore, in the month of June, 1632. This distinguished nobleman immediately resolved to settle a colony, with the particular intention of establishing the religion of the gospel and truth in that and the neighbouring country, where, as yet, the knowledge of the true God had never existed. He was encouraged in his enterprize by the favourable account of the country left by his worthy father, whose testimony, founded upon actual observation, was worthy of the utmost confidence, and was corroborated by the reports of others who had visited the same region, as well as by the published narrative of captain Smith, who first described it.' After alluding to the liberal conditions of settlement proposed by Lord Baltimore, Father White continues:

' The interests of religion constituted one of the first objects of Lord Baltimore, an object worthy indeed of christians, of angels, of Englishmen; than which, in all her ancient victories, Britain never achieved any thing more honourable.

' Behold those regions waiting for the harvest. They are prepared to receive the fruitful seed of the gospel.

Messengers have been sent to procure suitable persons to preach the life-giving doctrine, and regenerate the natives in the sacred waters of baptism. There are those now living in this city, (St. Mary's) who saw ambassadors from the Indian nations to Jamestown in Virginia, sent there for the purpose of effecting these objects. May we not suppose that many thousands were brought into the fold of Christ in so glorious a work.'

After a glowing and minute description of the country, with its trees, fruits and other productions, its rivers and the various kinds of fish, he proceeds to give the

'NARRATIVE OF THE VOYAGE TO MARYLAND.

'On the 22d of November, being St. Cæcilia's day, under the gentle influence of an eastern wind, we dropped down from the Isle of Wight.

'Having placed our ship under the protection of God, the Blessed Virgin Mother, St. Ignatius, and all the guardian angels of Maryland, we had progressed but a short distance, when we were obliged for the want of wind, to cast anchor off the fortress of Yarmouth, where we were welcomed by a salute. While lying here we were not without some apprehensions from our sailors, who began to murmur among themselves, alleging that they expected a messenger from land with letters: and because none arrived, they seem disposed to create delays. A kind providence put an end to our fears; for during the night a strong but favourable wind sprang up, and our pinnace,* which appre-

---

* The pinnace appears to have been a sloop of forty tons, and was called 'The Dove.'

hended an attack from a French brig, that kept within a short distance of her, took advantage of the wind and put to sea. We, not willing to lose sight of her, followed her with all speed, and thus frustrated the evil designs of our sailors; this was on the night of St. Clement's day, 23d of November. On the next morning, about 10 o'clock, after receiving a second salute from the fort at Hurst, we were carried beyond the breakers at the extremity of the Isle of Wight, and narrowly escaped being driven on shore. Taking advantage of a strong fair wind on that day and the next night, we left the western point of England, slacking sail, lest running ahead of the pinnace, she might fall into the hands of the pirates and Turks who then infested these seas. On the 24th of November, we made great headway until evening, when a violent storm arose, and our sloop being diffident of its strength, being only of 40 tons burden, hove to, and informed us that in case of danger, she would carry lights at her mast-head. We were in a well built ship* of 400 tons, as strong as iron and wood could make her, and our captain was one of great experience. The storm was so violent that we gave him the choice of returning to England or pursuing the voyage. His intrepidity and confidence in the untried powers of his ship, induced him to choose the latter. But in the middle of the night, in a boiling sea, we saw our sloop at a short distance from us, showing two lights at her mast-head. Then, indeed, did we fear for her, and on losing sight of her we all supposed she had been swallowed up in the stormy sea. Six weeks elapsed before we again heard from her. But God had preserved her. Fear-

* 'The Ark.'

ing that she could not survive the storm, she changed her course, and took refuge in the Scilly Isles. She afterwards sailed in pursuit of us, and we met at the Antilles. On the 27th and 28th, we made but little progress. On Friday 29th, a most dreadful storm arose, that made the most fearless men tremble for the result. Among the Catholics, however, it made prayer more frequent, vows were offered in honour of the B. V. Mother, and her immaculate conception, of St. Ignatius, the patron Saint of Maryland, St. Michael and all the guardian angels. Each one prayed earnestly to expiate his sins through the sacrament of penance. For having unshipped her rudder, our vessel was tossed about at the mercy of the winds and waves. At first, I feared that the loss of our ship and death awaited me, but after spending some time in prayer and having declared to the Lord Jesus, and to his Holy Mother, St. Ignatius, and the protecting Angels of Maryland, that the purpose of this voyage was to pay honour to the blood of our Redeemer, by the conversion of barbarians, I arose with a firm confidence that through the mercy and goodness of God, we should escape the dangers that seemed to threaten our destruction. I had bowed myself down in prayer, during the greatest rage of the tempest, and, let the true God be glorified! Scarcely had I finished, before the storm was ceasing.

'I felt myself imbued with a new spirit, and overspread with a flood of joy and admiration at the benevolence of God to the people of Maryland, to whom we were sent. Blessed forever be the merciful charities of our dear Redeemer. The remainder of the voyage, which lasted three months, was prosperous; our captain affirmed that he never witnessed a more pleasant and happy one. The period of three months included the time we spent at the islands of the Antilles, but we were in fact only seven weeks and two days at sea.

'In sailing along the Spanish coasts we were apprehensive of falling into the hands of the Turks, but we never met them. Having passed the pillars of Hercules and the Madeira islands, we were able to scud before the wind with full sail. The winds are not variable in those regions, but always blow in a southwest direction, which was our exact course. At the distance of about three leagues from us we descried three sail of vessels, the smallest of which appeared to be larger than ours. Fearing they were Turkish pirates we were careful to avoid them, though we prepared our vessel for action. But as they showed no disposition to engage us, we concluded they were merchantmen, bound for the fortunate islands, and as much afraid of us as we were of them.'

Father White, after some philosophical reasoning to account for the trade winds, some interesting descriptions of the tropical birds, and the flying fish, &c. &c. seen on their passage, remarks that, 'during the entire voyage no person was attacked with any disease except that at Christmas, wine having been freely distributed in honour of that festival, several drank of it immoderately; thirty persons were seized with a fever the next morning, of whom about twelve died shortly after; of these two were Catholics, namely, Nicholas Fairfax and James Barefoot.'

The route taken by the pilgrims is described to have been by the Azores, and to Barbadoes, at which latter island they landed on the 5th of January, 1634, new style. Instead of the hospitable reception which they expected from the governor and inhabitants, who were English, Father White says, 'the governor and inhabitants plotted together to exact unreasonable prices for provisions and other necessary supplies.' From the great abundance of potatoes in the island, they received a wagon load gratis. At the time of the arrival of our pilgrims the slaves had rebelled, and determined to seize the first vessel that should arrive, but being discovered, the ringleaders were executed; and, says the narrator, 'our vessel being the first that touched the shore, was the destined prize, and the very day we landed we found eighty men under arms, to check the startling danger.'

After describing the island of Barbadoes and its productions, the writer says, 'on the night of the 24th of January we weighed anchor, and passing the island of St. Lucia at noon on the following day, we arrived in the evening at an island inhabited by savages only. A rumour had been caught by our sailors, from some Frenchmen who had been shipwrecked, that this island contained an animal in whose forehead was a stone of uncommon brilliancy, called a carbuncle.' Father White dryly remarks, 'its author must answer for the truth of this report.' At dawn on the following day they reached Guadaloupe, and at noon arrived at Montserrat, inhabited by Irishmen driven from Virginia, on account of their profession of the Catholic faith.

Thence they sailed to another island, where they spent one day; thence to St. Christophers, where they remained ten days, by the friendly invitation of the English governor and two captains, 'who were Catholics.' The governor of a French colony in the same island also welcomed them warmly. Father White continues: 'having at length weighed anchor hence, we pursued our voyage until we reached a point on the coast of Virginia, called 'Comfort,' on the 27th of February. We were under a good deal of dread from the unfriendliness of the English inhabitants of Virginia, to whom our colony had been an unwelcome theme. We brought, however, letters from the king and the high constable of England to the governor of the province, which contributed very much to appease their feelings, and to procure us future advantages. After receiving kind treatment for nine or ten days we set sail, and on the 3d of March, having arrived in the Chesapeake bay, we tacked to the north to reach the Potomac river, to which we gave the name of St. Gregory. We called the point which stands on the south St. Gregory,* that on the north St. Michaels,† in honour of the choir of angels. A larger and more beautiful stream I never have seen. The Thames compared with it is but a rivulet. Bounded on the sides by no marshes, it runs between solid and rising banks. On either side are splendid forests, not overgrown by weeds or briars; you might drive a four-horse carriage, with the reins loose in your hands, through them. We found the natives armed at the very mouth of the river. That night fires were blazing throughout the country, and as they had never seen so large a ship as ours, messengers were sent around to announce the arrival of a *canoe* as large as an island, and numbering as many men as the trees in a forest. We passed on to the Heron Islands, so called from immense flocks of those birds. We touched at the first of them, which we

* Smith's Point.   † Point Lookout.

called St. Clements, on which, owing to its sloping banks, we could only land by fording. Here the maids who had landed to wash the clothes, were almost drowned by the upsetting of the boat. I lost a large portion of my linen—no small loss in this part of the world. This island abounds in cedar trees, sassafras, and all those herbs and flowers entering into the class of salads, and the walnut tree with a heavy shell, and a small but very delicious kernel. A scope of four hundred acres did not appear sufficient for our new plantation. We desired a place which might preclude the commerce of the river to strangers, and also the possibility of their infringing on our boundaries. This was the most narrow crossing of the river.'

'On the day of the annunciation of the B. V. Mary, (25th of March,) we first offered the sacrifice of the mass, never before done in this region of the world. After which, having raised on our shoulders an immense cross, which we had fashioned from a tree, and going in procession to the designated spot, assisted by the governor,* commissary, and other Catholics, we erected the trophy of Christ the Saviour, and humbly bent the knee in reverence during the devout recitation of the litany of the holy cross. Our governor, however, having understood that the great chief of Piscataway was obeyed by many petty chiefs, determined to visit him, to explain the objects of our coming; that having conciliated his good will, our settlement might be more favourably regarded by the rest. Having, therefore, joined to our pinnace another, which he had procured in Virginia, and leaving the ship at anchor off St. Clements, retracing his course, he sailed up the

* Leonard Calvert.

southern bank of the river. Finding the savages had fled into the interior, he proceeded to the village, which taking its name from the river is yet called Potomac. Here he found Archihu, the uncle and tutor of the king, who was yet a boy. The regency was in prudent and experienced hands. Father Altham, who accompanied the governor, (for I was detained with the baggage,) explained, by means of an interpreter, the truths of the Christian religion. The chief listened to him willingly, after acknowledging his own faults. Being informed that no hostile motives had brought us among them, but that feelings of benevolence prompted us to impart to them the advantages of civilization, and to open the path of Heaven to them, and to the more distant regions, he expressed himself not only well satisfied, but very grateful at our arrival. The interpreter was from the Protestants of Virginia. As the Father could not explain every thing at once, he promised to return in a short time. 'I think,' said Archihu, 'that we should all eat of the same table; my young men will visit the hunting grounds for you, and all things shall be in common with us.' From hence we went to Piscataway, where all immediately flew to arms. About one hundred, armed with bows, were drawn up with their chief at their head. On learning our pacific intentions, laying aside his fears, the chief stepped into the pinnace, and on understanding our benevolent views in their regard, gave us liberty to settle in any part of his kingdom we might select. In the meantime, while the governor was on his journey to the emperor, the savages at St. Clements becoming more bold, mixed familiarly with our sentries. We were accustomed to keep up a patrol day and night, to protect our woodcutters, and our vessel, which was now undergoing repairs, from any sudden attack. The natives expressed their surprise at the size of our vessel, and wondered what part of the earth produced a tree large enough to make such a boat; for they thought that it, like an Indian canoe, was hewn out of the trunk of a single tree. The report of our cannon struck them dumb with fear.'

'In his visit to the emperor, our governor carried with him as a companion, one Henry Fleet, a captain among the settlers in Virginia, a man much beloved by the natives, and skilled in the knowledge of their language and settlements. In the beginning he was very obliging to us, but being seduced by the malicious counsels of a certain Claiborne, he became very hostile, and in the most artful manner inflamed the minds of the natives against us. However, while he was our friend, he pointed out to our governor a suitable place for a settlement, than which a more heavenly and lovely spot Europe could not furnish. Having proceeded from St. Clements about nine leagues to the north, we glided into the mouth of a river, to which we gave the name of St. George.* This river flows from south to north about twenty miles before it loses, like the Thames, the salt water taste. In its mouth are two harbours, in which three hundred ships of the line could ride at anchor. We placed one of them under the protection of St. George, the other, more interior, under that of the B. V. Mary.'†

'On the left side of the river was the settlement of Yaocomico. We ascended on the right side, and hav-

* Now called St. Mary's river.
† This harbour must be either the mouth of what is now called St. George's river, or the entrance to St. Inigoe's creek.

ing halted about a thousand paces from the shore, we selected a site for the city, to be designated by the name of St. Mary. And to avoid all imputation of injury and occasion of enmity, having given in payment hatchets, axes, hoes, and some yards of cloth, we bought from the king about thirty miles of that part of the country now called Augusta Caroline.'*

'A fierce and warlike nation of savages called the Susquehannahs, particularly hostile to king Yaocomico, made frequent incursions into his territory and devastated his settlements. The inhabitants, through fear of these savages, were forced to seek other homes. This was the cause of our having so promptly obtained possession of that part of his kingdom: God, in his goodness, opening a path for his law and eternal light by these means. The natives emigrate here and there daily, leaving behind them the fields and clearings that surrounded their homes. It amounts almost to a miracle that savages, who but a few days before arrayed themselves in arms against us, should now with the meekness of the lamb throw themselves on our mercy, and deliver up every thing to us. Here the finger of God is evident, and doubtless Providence has some good in store for this nation. A few have been permitted to retain their dwellings for one year, but the lands are to be delivered free into our hands the next year.'

'The natives are tall and handsome in their persons, their skin is naturally of a copper colour, but they daub it over with red paint mixed with oil, to protect them from the flies.† This practice, which is decidedly more of a convenience than an ornament, gives them a hide-

---

* Now St. Mary's county.   † Moschettoes.

ous appearance. They daub their faces with other colours, at one time sky blue, at another red, and occasionally in the most disgusting and terrific manner. Being deficient in beard, at least until late in life, they draw painted lines from the corners of their mouths to the ears, in imitation of it. The hair, which is generally black, is tied around with a fillet, and drawn in a knot to the left ear, with the addition of any ornament in their possession which they consider valuable. Some wear as an ornament a copper plate with the figure of a fish engraved upon it, placed upon the forehead. Others wear necklaces of glass beads; beads are esteemed of less value by them, and do not answer the purposes of traffic so readily. They are dressed generally in deer skins, or something of that nature, which hangs from the back in the fashion of a pallium, and is bound round the naval like an apron; the rest of the body is naked. Boys and girls move about perfectly uncovered; they tread on thorns and thistles, without sustaining injury, as if the soles of their feet were horn. Their arms are the bow and arrow, two cubits long, pointed with a piece of buckhorn, or sharp edged flint. They shoot these with such dexterity, as to transfix a sparrow at a considerable distance. Their bows are not very tightly strung, and they are unable to strike objects at a very great distance. By the use of these arms, however, they secure a sufficient quantity of food, as squirrels, partridges, turkeys, &c. of which there is a great abundance. They live in huts of an oblong and oval form, nine or ten feet high; an opening of a foot and a half in size, through the roof, admits light and allows the smoke to escape. They construct a fire on a pavement in the centre, and sleep in a circle around

3*

it. The kings and principal chiefs have each a hut of his own, and a bed made by driving four stakes in the ground and laying poles over them. A tent of this description is allotted to my companion and myself, in which we are comfortably enough accommodated until a better house can be erected. *This may be considered the first chapel in Maryland;* it is, however, furnished in a more becoming manner than when it was inhabited by the Indians. In our next voyage, should Providence smile on our undertaking, we shall be supplied with all that is necessary for furnishing houses generally. The disposition of the tribe is sprightly and ingenious; their taste is very discriminating, and they excel the Europeans in the senses of sight and smell. Their food consists of certain preparations of corn, which they call *pone* and *ominy,* to which is added fish and any thing that they have caught in hunting or in their snares. They have neither wine nor spirits, nor can they be easily induced to taste them, except such as the English have infected with their vices. As to their deportment, it is extremely modest and proper. In neither male nor female have I seen any action contrary to chastity. They come voluntarily and mingle with us daily, offering us, with a joyful countenance, what they have caught in hunting or fishing, and partaking of our food with us, when invited by a few words in their own language. As yet we are able to converse with them very little except by signs. Many of them have wives, and preserve their conjugal faith unsullied. The countenances of the women are sedate and modest. The natives seem possessed of most generous dispositions, and reciprocate liberally any acts of kindness. They decide on nothing rashly, nor are they affected by any sudden impulse of feeling; but when any thing of importance is submitted to their consideration, they reflect on it in silence, as if anxious to be governed entirely by reason; then having formed their determination, they express it briefly, and adhere to it most obstinately. If they were once imbued with the principles of Christianity (for which indeed nothing seems to be wanting but a knowledge of their language) they would certainly become examples of every moral and Christian virtue.'

'They are much pleased with the courteous language, as well as the dress of the Europeans, and would now be clothed in our manner, if the avarice of our traders did not prevent it. Our ignorance of their idioms has hitherto prevented us from learning accurately their opinions on religion. We have, however, through the aid of interpreters, (not always to be relied on,) caught these particulars: They acknowledge one God of heaven, whom they call our God. They pay him no external honours, but endeavour in various ways, to propitiate a certain evil spirit whom they call *Ochre*, that he may not injure them. I understand they worship also grain and fire, as deities very benevolent to mankind. Some of our men say they saw the following ceremony in the temple *Barcluxen*. On a certain day, all the men and women of all ages, from many villages, assemble around a large fire; the younger ones are in advance, nearer the fire; then having thrown some deer's fat on the fire, they raise their hands aloft and cry out with a loud voice, 'Taho! Taho!' During an interval, some one holds out a large bag, which contains a pipe, similar to those we use for smoking tobacco, though much larger, and some powder which they call *potu*. The bag is then carried around the fire, followed by boys and girls singing alternately in an agreeable voice, '*Taho, Taho.*' The circuit being finished, the pipe and the powder are drawn out of the bag. The potu being distributed to each one standing around, and lighted in the pipe, each person present smokes it, and consecrates every member of the body by blowing it over them. We are not yet in possession of other facts, except that they seem to have some knowledge of a flood in which the world was destroyed, on account of the sins of mankind.'

'We have been but one month here: the remainder must consequently be reserved for another voyage. I can, however, assert that the soil is especially rich. The earth, soft and black to the depth of a foot, is overspread with a fat and reddish coloured clay, covered every where with widely spreading trees, of great value and surpassing beauty, except here and there a small patch of cultivated ground. The land is also refreshed by abundant springs of excellent drinking water. The only quadrupeds we have seen, are the deer, beaver, and squirrels which equal in size the European rabbit. The flocks of birds are innumerable, such as eagles, herons, swans, geese, ducks and partridges. Hence, you may suppose there is nothing wanting here which may minister to the necessities or the pleasure of its inhabitants.'

The town of Saint Mary's became the capital of the province; and the first legislative assembly of the province was called and held there, about the commencement of the year 1635—(to wit, on the 26th of February, 1634-5, old style.)

Having stated these preliminary facts of the settlement of St. Mary's, and not intending to connect the history of the province with the 'Annals of Annapolis,' further than what may appear to be necessary, we will now turn to some of the causes which eventuated in the settlement of the present capital of the state.

1642. In this year, the assembly of the province of Virginia, passed an act to prevent dissenting ministers from preaching and propagating their doctrines in that colony. Under this act, the governor and council of Virginia issued an order that all such persons as would not conform to the discipline of the church of England, should depart the country by a certain day.

Notwithstanding the laws against the puritans in Virginia, they continued to keep up a conventicle of their members for some years, which had in the year 1648, increased to one hundred and eighteen members.

1648. At this period the government of that colony caused a more vigorous execution of the laws to be enforced against them.

Their conventicle in Virginia was therefore broken up, and the members of it being driven out of that colony, were dispersed in different directions. The pastor (a Mr. Harrison) went from thence to Boston, in New England, in the latter end of this year—and the elder (a Mr. Durand) took refuge in Maryland.

1649. This is stated by one of their own members, to have taken place in the year 1649, but at what time of the year, we are no where informed. Most probably they did not leave Virginia in a body, but gradually in small numbers, in the course of the spring and summer of this year. It is stated by Mr. Leonard Strong, in his *'Babylon's Fall,'* &c. that they were not invited into Maryland by governor Stone; but by a friend of the governor's, that they were only 'received and protected.' These people seated themselves at a place by them called *'Providence,'* but afterwards *'Proctors,'* or *'The Town Land at Severn.'* Later still, *'The Town at Proctors;'* then *'The Town Land at Severn where the town was formerly.'* After that, *'Anne-Arundel Town,'* which was subsequently changed into *'The Port of Annapolis.'* And finally, under its charter in 1708, was established as the *'City of Annapolis,'* as will be shewn hereafter in its proper chronological order.

It is alleged by the advocate of the puritans who thus settled at *Providence*, (Leonard Strong, before recited,) that 'an oath to the Lord Baltimore was urged upon this people soon after their arrival, which if they did not take, they must have no land, nor abiding in the province.' The oath here alluded to was the oath of fidelity, as prescribed by his lordship, and annexed to his 'Condition of Plantations,' of 1648.

They were made acquainted by captain Stone before they came here, with that oath of fidelity, which was to be taken by those who would hold any land here from his lordship; 'nor had they any objection to the oath, till they were as much refreshed with their entertainment there, as the snake in the fable was with the countryman's beast; for which some of them were equally thankful. But it was deemed by some of these people, too much below them to take an oath to the Lord Proprietary of that province, though many protestants of much better quality, had taken it.'

Although these people had thus with the permission of the Lord Proprietary's government, seated themselves within the province of Maryland, yet it does not appear that they had immediately thereon subjected themselves to the proprietary government at St. Mary's.

The peninsula or neck of land whereon Annapolis stands, was probably uninhabited by any Europeans before their arrival; and, thus secluded from the rest of the inhabitants of the province, it is probable that, according to the usage of the congregational church of New England, a branch of which church they were, a sort of hierarchical government was established by them, similar to that which had been practised by the first colonies of Plymouth, Massachusetts, and Connecticut.

Neither does it appear that any grants of land or territory were made to these people, either collectively or individually, either prior to or subsequent to their arrival in Maryland, until the latter end of July, 1650, when their settlement was organized as a county, under a commander and commissioners of the peace, as the Isle of Kent had been before.

In this year, (1649) when Charles the First was beheaded, Mr. Thomas Greene, who was now governor of Maryland, in the absence of governor Stone, caused the Prince of Wales to be proclaimed in the province, as 'the undoubted rightful heir to all his father's dominions,' on the fifteenth day of November of this year.

Another proclamation was also issued of the same date, 'to further the common rejoicing of the inhabitants upon that occasion,' declaring a general pardon to all the inhabitants of the province, for every offence before committed.

It appears, however, that the puritans who had just settled on the Severn, did not join in the 'common rejoicing;' but preferring the rule and dominion of the commonwealth of England, just established in the mother country, to that of the declared succession of their late sovereign, Charles the First, desired to be exempt from the common privilege of causing the shores of their beautiful Severn to re-echo with their 'rejoicings' on this occasion.

1650. In January of this year, governor Stone having returned to the province and resumed the functions of his office, convened the legislature by proclamation, to meet at St. Mary's on the second day of April ensuing.

On the day appointed the assembly accordingly convened—but as no returns were made, nor any appearance of the freemen or burgesses, from Providence, 'the governor adjourned the house till Friday next, the fifth day of the same present month.'

In the meantime it appears that governor Stone visited the new colony at Providence; probably with a view of reconciling in an amicable way the refractory puritans to the proprietary government. For it seems that they consented to send two burgesses to the assembly, and the governor himself made the return thereof as follows:

'By the lieutenant, &c. of Maryland. The freemen of that part of Maryland, now called Providence, being by my appointment duly summoned to this present assembly, did unanimously make choice of Mr. Puddington and Mr. James Cox for their burgesses, I being there in person at that time.'

Accordingly, on the 6th of April the assembly met,

and after choosing Mr. *James Cox* speaker, and Mr. William Britton their clerk, proceeded to business. We may remark here, that this choice of the speaker seems to indicate the growing strength and influence of the infant colony that had settled at Providence.

The puritans who had founded Providence, formed, at this early period of their settlement, a considerable population. And having sent, and been represented by their burgesses or delegates at this last assembly, and so far submitting to the proprietary government, an act was passed at this session, entitled, 'an act for the creating of Providence into a county, by the name of *Anne Arundel County.*' The tenor of this act was, 'that part of the province of Maryland, on the west side of the bay of Chesapeake, over against the *Isle of Kent,* formerly called by the name of Providence, by the inhabitants there residing, &c. shall from henceforth be erected into a shire or county, by the name of Anne Arundel county, and by that name be ever hereafter called.'

It was probably so called from the maiden name of Lady Baltimore, then late deceased—Lady Anne Arundel, the daughter of Lord Arundel of Wardour, whom Cecilius Lord Baltimore had married.

No boundaries were assigned by this act to the county. As the population of that part of the province was detached from the other inhabited parts, and like *Kent Island,* was insulated from the rest of the province, such population constituted its limits in fact, until in process of time other counties being erected adjacent thereto, defined its boundaries.

This detached colony had its inconveniences and difficulties to contend with, incident to all newly-settled places. It became thereby not only more obnoxious to the Indians, but more liable to alarm, and more easily assailed by these aborigines.

Some acts of assembly, made at the last session of assembly, indicated considerable uneasiness existing at this period among the colonists, on account of some recent murders and captures committed upon them by the natives. It appears that two of the inhabitants of Kent and Anne Arundel counties had been lately murdered in a most cruel and barbarous manner by certain Indians.

It is most probable, that the Indians who committed the above-mentioned murders, were the *Susquehanocks*, a powerful and warlike tribe, who inhabited all that part of Maryland which lies between the Patuxent and *Susquehanough* rivers, on the western shore, and all that portion of country from the Choptank to the *Susquehanough*, on the Eastern Shore.

This assembly, in addition to this cautionary measure of preventing a repetition of such murders by the Indians, thought it necessary that some more effectual remedy to check such conduct of the natives, should be applied, and accordingly enacted, 'an order providing for a march upon the Indians,' as follows: 'Whereas, certain Indians, this last year, have most wickedly and barbarously murthered an English inhabitant of the county of Kent, and another inhabitant likewise since, in Anne Arundel county, *Be it therefore ordered*, That the governor, with the advice of the council, or the major part of them, shall have power, in case such Indians, who have committed such barbarous and wicked murthers, shall not be sent in, after demand made of them, to the government here, to receive such punishment as is due for such offence, to press men, and to appoint such allowance for their pay, and to make war upon these nations of Indians refusing to deliver up those offenders as aforesaid, as in his and their best discretion, shall be thought fit; the charge of which war to be laid by an equal assessment on the persons and estates of all the inhabitants of this province.'

It would appear, however, notwithstanding all this preparation for an Indian war, that a considerable *trade* was still carried on, either with these hostile Indians, or more probably with some other tribe or tribes, who remained in a state of peace with our colonists.

CHAPTER II.

Tranquility of the Province—Governor Stone visits Providence—Appoints Mr. Edward Lloyd commander of Anne Arundel county—Appoints Commissioners—The Puritans at Providence again refuse to send Delegates to the Assembly—Bennett and Claiborne reduce the Colony of Maryland—Governor Stone retained in office by them—Is soon deprived of his office by them—The Colony submits to the Commonwealth of England—Governor Stone reinstated—Cromwell proclaimed in the Province—Governor Stone declares the Puritans at Providence to be enemies of Lord Baltimore—The Province again reduced—Governor Stone rebuked by Lord Baltimore for resigning his Government—Governor Stone re-assumes his office and powers as Governor—Organizes a Military Force—Seizes the Provincial Records—Secures the Arms and Ammunition of the Province—Governor Stone makes preparations to reduce Anne Arundel to submission, and marches towards the Severn—Arrives at Herring Creek—Appears in the River Severn—The Golden Lion—Governor Stone's party land on Horn Point—Captain Fuller, at the head of the Puritans of Providence, marches to meet them—Battle on Horn Point—Governor Stone condemned to Death—The Soldiers refuse to execute him—Others executed—The Property of Governor Stone and his party sequestered—Lord Baltimore restored to his Rights by the Lord Protector—Appoints captain Josiah Fendall Governor—The Puritans acknowledge the authority of Lord Baltimore—Acknowledgement.

AFTER this last session of assembly, the affairs of the province seem to have subsided into apparent peace and quiet. The puritans of Providence appear to have acquiesced in, and submitted to the proprietary government at St. Mary's.

In July of this year, governor Stone visited the settlement at Providence for the purpose of organizing it into a county; and while there, he issued a commission directed 'to Mr. Edward Lloyd, gent.' appointing him 'to be commander of Anne Arundel county until the Lord Proprietary should signify to the contrary,' and to

Mr. James Homewood, Mr. Thomas Meares, Mr. Thomas Marsh, Mr. George Puddington, Mr. Mathew Hawkins, Mr. James Merryman, and Mr. Henry Catlyn, 'to be commissioners of the said county, with Mr. Edward Lloyd, for granting warrants and commissions, and for all other matters of judicature,' &c.

This commission bears date on the 30th of July, 1650, at Providence.

Mr. Puddington had been one of the Delegates at the last session of assembly.

The names of these gentlemen, thus commissioned, are given principally with a view of gratifying the reader, who may be a native of Maryland, that he may know the names of those who were the principal men among the puritans who first settled on the Severn, and from whom many respectable families in this state now deduce their descent.

1651. Governor Stone, it seems, agreeably to annual usage, had called an assembly, to meet at St. Mary's, in March of this year. But from strong circumstances, it is to be inferred that the puritans of Providence (or Anne Arundel) refused or neglected to send any delegates or members to attend this assembly; and Mr. Lloyd, as it appears, acting most probably in conformity to the wishes of those over whom he presided as commander, returned some message 'to the general assembly then sitting at St. Mary's,' which gave considerable displeasure to the government there, or at least to Lord Baltimore, in England, when he came to be informed of it, who expressed his resentment at the message somewhat warmly in a letter to the assembly.

What this message was, is not now to be exactly

4*

ascertained, no copy of it remaining on record. We are authorized, however, in collecting from what his lordship wrote upon the subject, that the purport of Mr. Lloyd's message was, that the inhabitants of Anne Arundel county, which they themselves called Providence, had come to the resolution of not sending any burgesses or delegates to the general assembly at St. Mary's, notwithstanding the summons for that purpose.

This stand was, without doubt, taken with a view to the expected dissolution of the proprietary government, and was probably meant by them as a prompt manifestation of their willingness and desire, that Maryland should be reduced to the obedience of the commonwealth of England.

1652. As soon as the triumph of the commonwealth cause was consummated by the death of the king, and the results which followed it in the mother country, the Parliament directed its attention to the subjugation of the American colonies which had been disaffected to that cause.

Governor Stone, having contended against the authority assumed by Bennett and Claiborne, commissioners appointed by the parliament for the reduction of the province of Maryland, but finding any opposition useless, at length effected an arrangement with the commissioners; by which he was permitted to retain and exercise his official powers, which appear to have been administered with fidelity to the commonwealth. Yet, notwithstanding these acts of submission, and professions of allegiance, he was soon after charged by the commissioners above named, with disaffection to the protector's cause.

They demanded of governor Stone the Lord Baltimore's commission to him, which he showed them ; thus getting the commission in their hands, they detained it, and removed him and his lordship's other officers out of their employment in the province under him, and appointed others to manage the government of Maryland, independent of his lordship.

Thus was the province of Maryland completely reduced to obedience to the parliament of the commonwealth of England, and all authority and power of the Lord Baltimore within the colony which he had planted at so much cost, and reared with so much care, entirely taken out of his hands, with the probable prospect, that it would never again be restored to him.

After the commissioners had made a temporary settlement of the government in Maryland, they returned to Virginia, of which province Bennett was made the governor, and Claiborne the secretary of state.

Bennett and Claiborne having thus provided for themselves honorable, and perhaps profitable stations in Virginia, returned to Maryland about the latter end of June, to make a more satisfactory settlement of the government of that province also. Finding that governor Stone had acquired, by his highly correct conduct in his office, great popularity with the inhabitants of the province, and moreover that it was the manifest 'desire of the inhabitants, that governor Stone should re-assume his former place of governor ;' arrangements were accordingly made, and he was reinstated by proclamation of the commissioners, bearing date the 28th of June, 1652.

1653. Contrary to the common usage of the colonial trade to the Chesapeake, 'no English shipping,' it seems, had arrived within the province of Maryland during the spring and summer of this year. Consequently, as governor Stone states, he had received no instructions or intelligence to direct him in the government of the province, no act by the colonial government was passed, directly affecting the interests of the settlement at *Providence*.

1654. In 1654, receiving certain intelligence of Cromwell's elevation to the protectorate, governor Stone recognized and proclaimed him as protector, on the 6th day of June, in this year.

This same year, governor Stone, by proclamation, charged the commissioners, Bennett and Claiborne, and indeed the whole puritanic party mostly of Anne Arundel, with 'drawing away the people, and leading them into faction, sedition and rebellion against the Lord Baltimore.'

Induced by this proclamation, the commissioners again returned to Maryland, and with the assistance of the puritans at Providence, by force of arms, turned out governor Stone and the Lord Baltimore's other officers, and put others in their places.

After a short resistance, governor Stone, in July of this year, again submitted to the authority of the commissioners' government.

1655. Early in 1655, it appears that governor Stone received written instructions from Lord Baltimore, in which he blames him for 'resigning up his government into the hands of the lord protector and commonwealth of England, without striking one stroke.'

Being thus instigated by the Lord Proprietary, to attempt the recovery of the proprietary government, he now re-assumed his office of governor under his former commission.

After such a rebuke from his lordship, governor Stone determined to resist the authority set up by the commissioners; and to make one more struggle for that power and authority which he had held from, and exercised under the Lord Proprietary's commission.

In virtue of his official authority, he proceeded to issue military commissions to officers, and to organize an armed force in the county of St. Mary's, for the purpose of taking possession of the government.

Of these he despatched a party to the house of Mr. Richard Preston, situated on the river Patuxent, where the provincial records had been deposited on the revolution in July last, and caused them to be seized and brought to St. Mary's. On the information of this seizure of the records arriving at Providence, (now Annapolis,) captain Fuller and his council, in whom the government of the province had been invested, sent two messengers with letters to governor Stone, 'in a way of peace and love,' desiring him to make it known by what power he surprised the records, and desiring an answer thereto. Governor Stone returned only a verbal answer—that ' he would shew no power, but affirmed that he acted by a power from Lord Baltimore; and that the Lord Protector had confirmed the Lord Baltimore's power.' The messengers were thereupon dismissed and went home.

Soon after this, governor Stone issued a proclamation for the purpose, it would appear, of quieting the minds of the people of Patuxent, on his resuming the government of the province, and his seizure of the records, protesting therein, that it was not his intention to use any hostile proceedings either against them or the people at Providence. As Mr. Preston's house on the Patuxent had been used since July last, as the seat of government for the province, where the provincial records had been kept, a considerable quantity of arms and ammunition, as it appears, had been there also deposited. Governor Stone, as a further precautionary measure, thought it proper to secure these arms and ammunition, and accordingly sent an armed party of twenty men for that purpose, under the command of William Eltonhead and Josias Fendel. They seized upon such arms, &c., as they could find, not only in Preston's house, but in others in the neighborhood, which it is stated they searched, and brought the same to St. Mary's.

Soon after these transactions, governor Stone began to make preparations for reducing the puritans of Anne Arundel to a submission and obedience to Lord Baltimore's government. Having collected together and armed about two hundred of the yeomanry of St. Mary's county, who were willing to follow him, he set out with his little army, about the 20th of March, 1654, O. S. towards Providence. He had collected, also, about eleven or twelve vessels, probably such as are now called *bay craft*, for the transportation of some of his forces, part of them marching along the bay coast, and the vessels serving to ferry them across the mouths of the rivers.

Before they had arrived at Herring creek, (sometimes called Herring bay,) in Anne Arundel county, they were met by messengers in a boat, who had been sent by the government at Providence with a letter to governor Stone, remonstrating against his proceedings, and desiring to be informed not only of his authority and power in so doing, but whether 'he were resolved to come to no parley or treaty,' protesting, in the said writing, 'that, by the help of God, they were resolved to commit themselves into the hand of God, and rather die like men, than live like slaves.' No answer to this message appears to have been given by the governor, as may be inferred from the fact that 'these messengers were apprehended, and their boat seized ;' but three out of the six persons on board the boat, contrived to make their escape, and carried back to the government at Providence the intelligence that Stone and his army were on their march towards them in hostile array.

On the arrival of governor Stone and his troops at *Herring creek*, they found there, it seems, one of the commissioners, to whom the government had been intrusted in July last, by Bennett and Claiborne. This gentleman they caused to be kept under guard: and either at this place or at a little further on his march, governor Stone deputed Doctor Luke Barber and Mr. Coursey to go on before them to Providence, with a proclamation addressed to the people of Anne Arundel. Of the contents of this proclamation, thus sent by Doctor Barber, we are not informed, except so much of it as is given by Doctor Barber, subsequently, to wit: that, 'in the end of this *declaration*, the governor did protest, as in the presence of Almighty God, that he came not in a hostile way, to do them any hurt, but sought all *meanes* possible to *reclaime* them by *faire meanes*, and *to my knowledge*, at the sending out of parties, he gave strict command that, if they met any of the *Ann Arundel* men, *they should not fire the first gun*, nor upon paine of death, plunder any.'

The 'declaration,' however, does not appear to have had any salutary effect; for, although they were permitted to read the 'declaration,' yet, having no other treaty to offer, they were quietly dismissed to their own company, to whom they might have gone, if they would. But it seems that they did not return to governor Stone or his army.

It is possible, that the rapid advance of the party to the harbour of Providence, might have precluded the necessity of it; for, on the evening of the day after, governor Stone and his followers appeared in the river of *Severn*, at Providence, with eleven or twelve vessels, greater and lesser, in which their whole array was transported.

On the appearance of this fleet, captain Fuller called a council of war, at which Mr. William Durand, the secretary of the puritan government at Providence, was appointed to go on board a merchant ship, called the *Golden Lyon*, then lying at anchor in the river, of which one *Heamans* was master. Mr. Durand was directed to affix a proclamation on the mainmast of the said ship, directed to captain *Heamans*, commander thereof; in which proclamation, 'he (*the said Heamans*) was *required*, in the name of the lord protector and commonwealth of England, and for the maintenance of the just *libertyes*, lives, and estates of the free subjects thereof, against an unjust power, to be aiding and assisting in this service.' It appears, that 'the said captain *Heamans*, at first, was unwilling, but afterwards, seeing the equity of the cause, and the groundless proceedings of the enemy, he offered himself, ship and men, for that service, to be directed by the said William Durand.'

Governor Stone, with his little fleet and army, had,

by this time, about 'the shutting in of the evening,' as it is said, on the 24th of March, (O. S.) arrived within the outer harbour of Providence. He was now also within the range of the shot of the Golden Lyon, from whence a gun was fired at him, in order, as is said, to bring him or some messenger on board. Governor Stone did not think it proper to pay any attention to this signal of war, as it appeared; but, having arrived within the mouth of the creek, which forms the southern boundary of the peninsula on which the city of Annapolis now stands, proceeded to land his men on a point of land which lies on the southern side of both the river Severn and the before mentioned creek, nearly opposite to and in an eastern direction from what is called the *dock* or inner harbour of Annapolis, and on which point or peninsula a small fortress, called Fort Horn, was afterwards built during the American revolutionary war. While governor Stone was landing his men on this point of land or peninsula, the commander Heamans, or Mr. Durand, thought it proper to repeat their fire upon the boats of governor Stone as they were rowing to the shore. The shot thereof lighting somewhat near to them, the governor deemed it most prudent to send a messenger on board the Golden Lyon to know the reason of their conduct, with directions to the messenger to inform the captain of the ship that he (governor Stone) thought 'the captain of the ship *had been satisfied.*' To which the captain answered, (in a very blustering tone, as it appears,) 'satisfied with what?—I never saw any power governor Stone had, to do as he hath done, but the superscription of a letter. I must and will appear for these in a good cause.' It would appear that governor Stone and the captain had some explanation previous to the firing of this last gun—at least it is fair so to presume, from the nature of the captain's reply to his message.

Governor Stone having moved his vessels further up the creek during the night, captain Heamans, or the puritans on shore, contrived early the next morning to place a vessel or vessels, 'with two pieces of ordinance' at the mouth of the creek, and by that means blockaded governor Stone's little fleet within the same, so as to prevent them from coming out. The governor soon after, however, on the same day, (*Sunday*, the 25th of March, 1654–'5, O. S.) appeared with his small army, in military parade, on a narrow neck of land, (most probably that on which the remains of the before mentioned *fort* now are,) near where he had landed. The captain of the ship (Heamans) observing this, brought his guns to bear upon them, and firing at them, *killed one man*, and by that means forced them to march further off into the neck. In the meantime captain Fuller, the puritan commander, with his company, consisting of a hundred and twenty men, embarked in their boats, most probably from the peninsula whereon Annapolis now stands, and went up the river some distance, where they landed and marched round the head of the creek to where governor Stone and his people were waiting to receive them, a distance of six miles.

' On the approach of the puritans, the sentry of the people of St. Mary's, or Marylanders, fired his alarm gun, when the men of governor Stone immediately appeared in order. Captain *Fuller* still expecting that governor Stone might possibly give a reason for their coming, commanded his men upon pain of death not to shoot a gun, or give the first onset. Setting up the standard of the commonwealth of England, against which the enemy shot five or six guns, and killed one man in the front, before a shot was made by the other.

'Then the word was given, *in the name of God fall on; God is our strength,*—that was the word for Providence: the Marylander's word was,—*Hey for Saint Maries.*

'The charge was fierce and sharp for the time; but through the glorious presence of the Lord of Hosts, manifested in and towards his poor oppressed people, the enemy could not endure, but gave back, and were so effectually charged home, that they were all routed, turned their backs, threw down their arms, and begged mercy. After the first volley of shot, a small company of the enemy from behind a great tree fallen, galled us and wounded divers of our men, but were soon beaten off. Of the whole company of the *Marylanders,* there escaped only four or five, who run away out of the army to carry news to their confederates. Governor *Stone,* colonel Price, captain Gerrard, captain Lewis, captain Kendall, captain Guither, major Chandler, and all the rest of the councellors, officers and souldiers of the Lord Baltimore, among whom, both commanders and souldiers, a great number being *papists,* were taken, and so were all their vessels, arms, ammunition and provision; *about fifty men slain and wounded.* We lost only two in the field; but two died since of their wounds. God did appear wonderful in the field, and in the hearts of the people, all confessing him to be the only worker of this victory and deliverance.'

In giving the above account of the battle, the words of Mr. Leonard Strong have been used, who, it is probable, was an eye-witness, and in the battle, he being one of captain Fuller's council, at Providence.

It is alleged, that the puritans of Providence, several days after the fight, put to death four of governor Stone's party. We wish it was in our power to contradict and disprove this cold-blooded outrage, even at this late period, for the sake of humanity and the character of the first settlers of our native city; but the evidence seems to be too strong to admit a doubt of its truth.

Doctor Barber says, (and he appears to be entitled to full credit,) that, 'after the skirmish, the governor, upon quarter given him and all his company in the field, yielded to be taken prisoners; but, two or three days after, the victors condemned ten to death, *and executed foure*, and had executed all, had not the incessant petitioning and begging of some good women saved some, and the souldiers others; the governor himselfe being condemned by them, and since beg'd by the souldiers; some being saved just as they were leading out to execution.'

Mrs. Stone, also, in a letter to Lord Baltimore, states that, 'after quarter given, they tried all your councellors by a councell of warre, and sentence was passed upon my husband to be shot to death, but was after saved by the enemy's owne souldiers, and so the rest of the councellors were saved by the petitions of the women, with some other friends which they found there.'

The four who were shot to death after trial by court-martial, were Mr. William Eltonhead, lieutenant William Lewis, Mr. Leggat, and a *German*, whose name is not mentioned, but who is stated to have lived with Mr. Eltonhead. The principle is universally acknowledged, that the captor in war, even in the case of civil commotions, has no right to put his captive to death, after surrender and quarter given. This most sanguinary transaction must, therefore, strike every enlightened individual at this day, as one of those atrocities which the vindictive passions incident to a civil war in any community are too apt to produce.

The puritans of Providence having thus, by the defeat of governor Stone, secured to themselves the government of the province, not only detained him and his followers for some time as prisoners of war, but proceeded to the sequestration of their property, whom they termed delinquents.

Our documents do not mention the length of time that governor Stone and his companions were detained at Providence, but it is supposed they were not liberated until captain Fuller and his council had despatched their messengers to England to prepossess the mind of the government there in their favor; and then not until they had the mortification of being witnesses to the execution of the order for a sequestration of their property.

In this year, Lord Baltimore's right and authority over the province was admitted by the Lord Protector, and captain Josias Fendall was appointed governor by his lordship. What motives Lord Baltimore had for substituting Fendall as governor of his province, instead of governor Stone, does not appear.

1657. It was not until this year, that the puritans, who had settled at Providence, acknowledged themselves as being within Lord Baltimore's province of Maryland—having considered themselves as being a part of Virginia, or a distinct colony. However, on the 24th of March, 1657, negotiations were entered into between the proprietary and the puritan government, for a surrender of the province to Lord Baltimore.

Thus, after a lapse of six years, his lordship was again restored to the full enjoyment of his province, 'to the content and peace of all parties.'

In tracing the early history of Providence, occasion is now taken, to acknowledge the entire indebtedness of the compiler of these Annals to Bozman's able and interesting History of Maryland, for all the incidents and facts having a bearing upon it; and to say, that a full and free use of that work has been made—being sensible that nothing better could have been said on the occasion, than has been, by that admirable historian.

Our records do not afford us any further information relating to the settlement at Providence until the year 1683. This, with several other omissions, unavoidably occur in these Annals, and is to be mainly attributed to the removal of the records and public documents of the province from St. Mary's to Annapolis, some of which were greatly damaged.* To this cause, is to be added, also, the loss of some by the fire which destroyed the state-house in the year 1704, where they were chiefly deposited.

* *Proceeding of the Upper House of Assembly, St. Mary's,* 10th *May,* 1682. *MSS. Journal, page* 418.
'Taking into consideration the ruinous condition of the state-house, (which hath been so chargeable to the country,) occassioned for want of some good, carefull and skillfull overseer at first appointed to supervise the managing and carrying on the building thereof, insomuch

CHAPTER III.

Contempt of Assembly—Trial of Edward Erbery—Condemned and Whipped—Witchcraft—Condemnation of John Cowman—And pardoned—The Quakers remonstrate against taking Oaths—Proceedings of the Assembly thereon—Indian Affairs—Protection of the Indians by the Colonists—Hostility of the Susquehanocks—Causes of—Treaty with them—Murders committed by the Indians—Expedition against them—Five Chiefs of the Susquehanocks murdered—Impeachment of Major Thomas Truman—His Trial and Conviction—Proceedings of the Assembly thereon—Controversy between the Lord Proprietary and the Lower House of Assembly upon the Act for calling Assemblies—Extracts from the Rules of the Lower House of Assembly—Annapolis erected into a Town, &c.—Commissioners appointed to survey and lay out Annapolis—Annapolis becomes the Seat of Government—Governor Nicholson causes the Records to be removed from St. Mary's—Public Ferry—First Corporation of Annapolis—Mr. Richard Beard makes a map of the Town—A Market and Fair—Proposition for a Bridewell—Improvement of Annapolis—A Church proposed to be erected—King William's School established—*William Pinkney* a Student of it—Governor Nicholson projects a Library for Annapolis—A State-House built—Roman Catholics—Persecution of.

1666. IN the absence of other matter connected with the immediate history of Annapolis from the year 1657 to to 1683, the reader will doubtless be gratified at the perusal of such extracts from the MSS. journals of the province, between these dates, of an interesting and amusing character, not before made public.

that the same, in a short time, (if not speedily repaired,) must inevitably fall to the ground, being already so leaky and decayed, as will hardly *secure the records of the province* (there kept) from the weather, this House desire the Lower House to consider thereof, and to concur with this House, in new covering, and making such necessary repairs thereof, as may render the same useful and serviceable for the country, and in making a partition at the stair foot, that both Houses of Assembly may there meet, without which repairs and partition, the *records of the province must inevitably suffer next winter.*'

'Upper House, Saturday, 28*th April*, 1666.

'Then came a member from the lower house, and desired the governor, from the whole lower house, not to discharge Edward Erbery, merchant, from the *sare* of Bristol; in regard, they had something to object against him, as well for abusing the lower house of assembly, as his lordship, last night.'

'Then came a member from the lower house, with this paper following:

'Tuesday, 1*st May*, 1666.

'William Calvert, Esq. motions the house,

'That, whereas there was an abuse committed last night by Edward Erbery, to the disturbance of the whole house, in their quiet and rest, and the clerk of this house informs that the said Erbery did call the whole house papists, rogues, **** rogues, &c. which the speaker is desired to take notice of, and proceed therein, either by presentment or otherwise, as to him shall seem best, and that it be the first thing this house takes into their consideration or debate.'

'Mr. Nicholas Piccard and Mr. Richard Blunt informed the house of certain vulgar and indecent expressions of Erbery concerning the lower house, and that they were ashamed of the place from whence they came.'

'Mr. Richard Hall says, that amongst a great many other extravagant words, Erbery said that Charles Calvert was a rogue.'

'William Calvert, Esq. saith, how that Erbery, in his hearing, said, we, viz. the assembly, were a company of pitiful rogues and puppys, and there is not one in the country deserves to keep me company but

Charles Calvert, who owes me ten thousand pounds of tobacco.'

'Mr. Richard Smith informs that this morning, when Erbery awaked, the said Erbery complained that he was bound; that he remembered all that he had said last night, and that he was not drunk; and in a threatning manner, said he would remember those that bound him.'

'The abuse that Edward Erbery gave to the lieutenant-general and this assembly last night, being taken into consideration, and upon a full debate thereon, had in this house, they do judge the same to be a scandal to the Lord Proprietor, to his lieutenant-general, and to both houses of assembly, and a great reflection upon the whole province in general; and, therefore, unanimously voted by this house, that the said Erbery be brought before this house, to give answer to the abovesaid charge, in relation to those informations now given in against him.'

'Ordered by the speaker that Mr. Edward Erbery be brought into the house by the sheriff, &c.'

'And taxed by the speaker of all those words spoken, who making his appearance after the charge being read unto him, he answered that he remembered none of these words that is alledged, only he confesseth that he was in drink, and being further taxed about the words spoken this morning, (which were averred by a member of this house) he says that he remembers not that ever he spoke such words.

'Which answer being taken into consideration, the house do judge the same altogether unsatisfactory, and that no person of full age shall take advantage by drunkeness in such case.

'Whereupon this house do humbly present the consideration hereof to the upper house, that they would please to signify to this house their resentment of the same, and what they shall judge further necessary to be done with the said Erbery as touching the punishment or otherwise for this house's concurrence therewith.'

'The upper house do order that the said Edward Erbery be tyed to the apple tree before the house of assembly, and be there publickly whipped upon the bare back with thirty-nine lashes, and that the sherriff of St. Mary's county be commanded to apprehend the said Erbery and see this order put in execution, and that the said Erbery do pay the sherriff his fees before he depart out of his custody; and further ordered, that the said Erbery be, after he is whipped, brought into both houses of assembly publickly to ask them forgiveness.'

(Signed)   JOHN GITTINGS, *Clerk*.

The following 'new and unheard of thing in this province,' is extracted from the journals of the upper house in 1674, and it is hoped and believed to be the only judicial transaction of its kind to be found upon its pages, to stain the fair fame of the noble founder, and usually enlightened legislators of this provice.

If it be a matter of surprise that it should be found at all recorded there—is it not also one of wonder and satisfaction that it should be the only one case—when we reflect that the '*witch mania*' had not yet passed from enlightened Europe, and still hung as a dark cloud over other provinces on this continent, and whose advantages, flowing from education and science, were so much greater than that of this more recently settled colony, and will, in this instance, be satisfactorily accounted for, from the 'natural embarrassments incident to the planting of a new colony, and the consequent want of means for a more enlarged education.'

'UPPER HOUSE, *February* 17*th*, 1674.

'Came into this house, a petition of the lower house, as followeth, viz:

'To the honourable Charles Calvert, esquire, Lieutenant General and Chief Judge of the Provincial Court of the Right Honourable the Lord Proprietary,

'The humble petition of the Deputies and Delegates of the Lower House of Assembly,

'Humbly sheweth to your excellency,

'That, whereas John Cowman being arraigned, convicted and condemned upon the statute of the first of King James of England, &c. for witchcraft, conjuration, socery or enchantment used upon the body of Elizabeth Goodall, and now lying under that condemnation, and hath humbly implored and beseeched us, your lordship's petitioners, to mediate and intercede in his behalf with your excellency for a reprieve and stay of execution.

'Your excellencie's petitioners do, therefore, accordingly, in all humble manner, beseech your excellency that the rigour and severity of the law to which the said condemned malefactor hath miserably exposed himself, may be remitted and relaxed by the exercise of your excellency's mercy and clemencie upon so wretched and miserable an object.

'And your petitioners, as in duty bound, will ever pray, &c.'

'UPPER HOUSE, *February 17th.*

'The lieutenant-general hath considered of the petition here above, and is willing, upon the request of the lower house, that the condemned malefactor be reprieved, and execution stayed, provided that the sheriff of St. Maries' county carry him to the gallows, and that the rope being about his neck, it be there made known to him how much he is beholding to the lower house of assemblie for mediating and interceeding in his behalf with the lieutenant-general, and that he remain at the city of St. Maries, to be employed in such service as the governor and council shall think fitt, during the pleasure of the governor.'

The quakers, or friends, who had settled in Maryland at an early period of its establishment, suffering under that system of intolerance and persecution which prevailed against all dissenters at that, and down to a later day, remonstrated against the unjust laws of the province which debarred their testimony on 'affirmation,' and subjected them to heavy penalties for refusing to take the prescribed 'oaths;' although contrary to their conscience, and, in their opinion, the Saviour's positive injunction, declared in his sermon on the mount—*'swear not at all.'* This remonstrance or petition appears upon the journals of the upper house in 1674, and is as follows:

'SATURDAY, 23d *May*, 1674.

'Read in the house, a petition exhibited by certain quakers, as follows, viz:

'This we do lay before the governour and council and assembly, in the wisdom of God, to consider of, from us who are in scorn called quakers.

'What we can say and do instead of an oath, it is in

obedience to Christ's command, that we cannot swear and take an oath, and Christ our Lord and Saviour's command is, 'I say unto you swear not at all.' Though in the old time, they were not to forswear themselves, but perform their oaths to the Lord; and the Lord Jesus Christ's command is, but let your communication be yea, yea, and nay, nay; for whatsoever is more than these cometh of evil: and St. James saith, in his general epistle to the Church of Christ, above all things, my bretheren, swear not; neither by heaven, nor by the earth, nor by any other oath; mark, but let your yea, be yea, and your nay, be nay, least you fall into condemnation. Now, here ye may see, that Christ and apostles *setts* us yea, yea, and nay, nay, over and above an oath and swearing, and in lieu of an oath. See, in obedience to Christ and the apostles' command, it is, that we do not, and *dare* not swear, least we should go into the evil, and so fall into condemnation, as Christ and the apostles saith before. But, according to Christ Jesus and the apostles' command, *doe* keep to yea, yea, and nay, nay, wherein they do double their words to make them of more force. Christ Jesus to the disciples and the apostles to the church; and now, if, that we are called to testifie the truth, or to serve in any office or place or *jurie*, if that we do break our yea, yea, or nay, nay, then let us suffer the same penalty, as they, that do break an oath, or are *foresworne*. And this not repugnant to the laws of England, having the same penalty on the same transgression; for, in Jamaica, their law is so, that our bretheren's testimony upon yea, yea, and nay, nay, as Christ and as the apostles commanded, is taken, and the same in the acts and province laws at Carolina, and the same in the patent and acts at *Road*

Island, and the same in the new country of Jersey, is taken instead of an oath; which the governour and his council and assembly may, by an act of assembly, let us have the same liberty here, as our bretheren have in other places, colonies or provinces, that we may not be put to inconveniences, for you do know what trouble often many of us are put to, because we cannot swear and take an oath, and do lose our rights and that which is due to us from others, and how we have been made a prey upon by many, because we cannot swear, and have lost much in our estates, and cannot be so serviceable in our generation to the country, as we might be, and also what trouble we have had, who have been overseers or executors, or the like, that have been intrusted with orphans, fatherless, and *widdows'* estates or wills, for want of an oath. And, therefore, you having power to *remedie* these things by making an act, we do lay them before you, and that if we do *breake* our yea, yea, or nay, nay, or what we testifie, then let us suffer the same punishment as they do that break their oaths or swear falsly; and this we are willing to suffer, who profess faith in Christ, and would have all that profess the same, to exercise a conscience void of offence towards God and men. So you may remove this oppression if you please, and let us have the same liberty that our friends and bretheren have in other countrys and islands, as we are credibly informed; whose hands are hereunto subscribed in the behalfs of our bretheren.

'WENLOCK CHRISTERSON, JO. HOMEARD,
'WILLIAM PERRIE,   RI. BEARD, &c.'

'Ordered by the house, that the petition here above be sent to the lower house, and offered to their consideration.'

This petition was accordingly sent to the lower house, who returned it with a message requesting to be informed by his excellency and the upper house, whether, in their opinion, the assembly had the power to alter the form of the oath prescribed by the laws of England, in point of evidence between the king and his people, &c. in matters depending within this province or not. To which message, the upper house replied, that they had resolved, that the petition should remain upon the journal till further advice from the Lord Proprietary, who declared that he 'formerly had intentions of gratifying the desire of the said people, called quakers, in that kind;' but, for some reason not mentioned, his lordship desired 'that all proceedings therein be, for the present, suspended.'

This highly respectable and long misunderstood society of christians, were not restored to the rights and privileges, so moderately, but firmly, insisted upon in the foregoing petition, until the year 1702*—when the legislature struck from the statute books this relict of intolerance.

1675.   For several years previous to 1675, the inhabitants of the province of Maryland, and the Indians within, and upon her border county, lived upon terms of peace and amity. Indeed, it could not well be otherwise, such being the nature and benevolent character of the laws and resolutions of the province for the protection of the friendly Indians. From the proceedings of the assembly, the strongest disposition was manifested to cherish and protect them; and in no instance did the government take from the

---

* See act of 1702, chap. 1, sec. 21.

Aborigines one acre of land without a remuneration perfectly satisfactory to them.* The cause of the frequent removals by the Indians grew out of the wars carried on between the different tribes. The Piscattoway and Patuxent Indians, who were uniformly friendly to the colonists, were protected from the more fierce and warlike tribes of Senecas and Susquehanocks, by the forces of the province.

At least in one instance (in 1673) the province rented land 'of the orphans of a Mr. Billingsley,' for the space of five years, for the use of the Mattapanie and Patuxent Indians, until 'some other place might be found for further settlement,' and the expense ordered to be paid out of the public treasury. The Piscattoways were located at the head of the Potomac, and were presented with many implements of husbandry—and every possible inducement held out to encourage them to make a permanent residence there. Three years provision was supplied them, that they might not want, and until they could by the cultivation of their land support themselves. Arbitrators were appointed throughout the province to determine all difficulties which might arise between the English and the Indians:

* '*Resolved*, That if there be any pretence of *conquest*, it can be only supposed against the NATIVE INDIAN INFIDELS; which supposition cannot be admitted, because the *christian inhabitants* purchased great part of the land they at first took up from the Indians, as well as from the Lord Proprietary, and have ever since continued in an amicable course of trade with them, except some partial outrages and skirmishes which never amounted to a general war, much less to a general conquest, the *Indians* yet enjoying their rights and priviledges of treaties and trade with the *English*, of whom we yet frequently purchase their rights of such lands as we take up, as well as of the Lord Proprietary.' *See journal of the house of delegates*, 1722—page 2.

and where even-handed justice was not awarded to the Indian, the offending arbitrator met with the censure of the assembly, and with suitable punishment.

The Susquehanocks commenced hostilities against the colonists in 1639, and committed many murders and depredations on them. This warfare appears to have been brought on by the endeavors of the colonists to stay their incursions against the peaceable and friendly tribes of Piscattoway and Patuxent, and probably the Yoamacoes, with whom the Susquehanocks never ceased to wage hostilities since the first settlement of the Maryland colony at St. Mary's.

In 1652, at the earnest desire of the Susquehanocks, a treaty of peace and amity was concluded between them, the colonists and the friendly Indians. This treaty took place 'at the river Severn, in the province of Maryland,'* on the fifth day of July, in that year. The terms of the treaty then made, appear to have been inviolably observed until this year, (1675) when a circumstance occurred to disturb the harmony which had so long endured between the respective parties; the particulars of which will be presently given from the journals of assembly, under the head of 'the impeachment of major Thomas Truman.'

The Susquehanocks, who had been till about this period, (1675) one of the most powerful of the Indian tribes in Maryland—had in their turn to fly before the more formidable and warlike tribe of Senecas, and were driven by them from the head of the Susquehannah. They took refuge in the neighbourhood of the Piscattoways, at the head of the Potomac. Soon after their reaching this place, Maryland and Virginia

* Now the City of Annapolis.

were induced in consequence of recent murders having been committed on several of the inhabitants, to send out an expedition in that direction. The united forces of Maryland and Virginia invested a fort, then occupied by the Susquehanocks, but belonging to the Piscattoways.

It appears from the journals of assembly that five of the chiefs of the Susquehanocks were enticed from this fort under pretences of friendship, and then treacherously murdered—for which major Truman, who commanded the Maryland forces, was impeached and tried for murder. As another evidence of the justice of the province, even to a 'cunning—skulking, and dangerous enemy,' proof will be adduced from the journals, on the impeachment of major Truman.[*]

'Impeachment of major Thomas Truman.'

'UPPER HOUSE.

1676. 'On Tuesday, May 16th, (1676,) at 8 in the morning, the house met.

'Present: The Right Honourable the Lord Proprietary, the Honourable Secretary, Jesse Wharton, Esq., Thomas Taylor, Esq., Baker Brooke, Esq.

'The Honorable Chancellor enters the house.

'The lower house requested by colonel Burgess and Mr. Weekes, that the commission and instructions from his lordship to major Thomas Truman, touching the late warr with the Indians, may be sent to them by this house. In pursuance whereof the Honourable Secretary and lieut. col. Tailor were by this house

---

[*] This major Truman was at one time a distinguished member of the assembly, and chancellor of the province.

sent with a true copy of the said commission and instructions, who delivered the same to the lower house.'

'LOWER HOUSE, 16*th May*, 1676.

'Voted that a message be sent to the right honourable the Lord Proprietary and upper house, to desire to know in what articles of major Truman's commission and instructions he hath been faulty, and who are the persons that accuse him, and can prove it; that so the said persons may attend this house to give them satisfaction in the crimes and offences of the said Truman.'

'In answer to which message this house returned to the lower house, that it is conceived by this house, that the lower house are the general inquisitors of this province, and ought to become impeachers of the above mentioned Truman, touching his guiltiness of the breach of any of the articles above, as the same shall appear to them upon examination of witnesses. Some of the most considerable of the said witnesses now sitting in their house, and that this house is ready to receive the said impeachment.

'Signed by order,   RICHARD BROUGHTON,
Clerk of the Assembly.'

'Ordered, that Cornet Courtney and William Cole do appear before the lower house, to make report of some matters to them, touching the impeachment of major Thomas Truman.'

'Ordered by the upper house, that captain Henry Darnell do forthwith secure the person of major Thomas Truman in safe custody, till the said major shall clear himself of such crimes and offences whereof he shall stand impeached by the lower house of assembly.'

'Ordered, that captain John Allen and doctor Charles Gregory do, with all expedition, make their appearance before the right honourable the Lord Proprietary and his honourable council, sitting in assembly, to testifie the truth of their knowledge touching the late barbarous and inhumane murder of five Susquehannah Indians, and that the said captain Allen give strict command to his lieutenant to continue ranging the woods in his absence. 'Signed, &c.'

'*To captain John Allen and*
  '*Dr. Charles Gregory, of Charles county.*'

A similar order to the foregoing was issued to Ninian Beale.

'Interrogatories for John Shanks, to be examined touching the late expedition against the Susquehannah Indians.

1st. 'Whether major Truman, with the forces under his command, was at the north side of Piscattoway creek, and did there expect and meet the Virginians.

2d. 'Whether the said major consulted with his officers and those of Virginia afore he held any discourse or treaty with the Susquehannah Indians which came out of the fort; also, whether it was with the knowledge of any of his officers, that he treated and endeavoured to make the Susquehannahs believe he intended no harm or disturbance to them, and what officers or others he knowes were present when orders were given by the major for the putting those great men to death.'

3d. 'Whether he knows that, at any time, the officers of Virginia did desire or put major Truman upon any design pressing him to employ his soldiers about or upon any service during the seige, and if major Truman did, at any time, execute any thing at their request by receiving instructions or directions from them.

4th. 'Whether did major Truman bid the Susquehannahs not to fear him, or tell them that he came only to seek the Seneca's, and that he would lodge that night hard by them, and use that as an argument for them, their wives and children, not to be afraid, or that or any other expression to that effect.

5th. 'What writings, articles of peace or amity did the said Susquehannahs ever produce to major Truman.

6th. 'Did the said Susquehannahs ever shew a *meddall* of silver, with a black and yellow ribbond.

7th. 'Did they shew the said ribbond and meddall as a pledge of amity given them by the former governors of this province, and was the said meddall given to major Truman or any other Englishman, or was it carried back again into the fort.

8th. 'Did major Truman stay at the north side of Pisscattoway creek till the Virginians came thither to him, or did he there treat with them concerning the management of the warr against the Susquehannahs.

9th. 'Did the Susquehannahs ever after offer any treaty of peace, or desire to continue friendship, and whether did major Truman ever demand satisfaction from them for any injuries done, or tell them they were the persons which we suspected had injured us.'

'The answer of John Shanks to several interrogatories put to him by the upper house.

'This deponent saith that he, with the Maryland forces, being at the fort of the Susquehannahs on the Sabboth day, he was sent up to the fort to desire one of the great men, by name Harignera, to come and speak with major Truman, and the said Harignera being dead, this deponent desired some other great men to come and speak with the said major, upon which message of his, there came out three or four of them, and this deponent was commanded by the major to tell them of the great injuries that had been done to the country, and that he came to know who they were that had done them, and the great men replyed, it was the Senecas; and this deponent saith, that there being present other Indians from other towns, the major desired some of their young men to assist as *pilotes*, as well as the neighbouring Indians had done, to join in pursuite of the Senecas, and the said Indians replyed, the Senecas had been gone four days, and that, by that time, they might be at the head of Patapsico river; to which major Truman returned, that he had good horses, and they were good footmen, and might soon overtake them, and the Indians replyed, that they would. And the deponent further saith, that, in the morning following, the Susquehannahs' great men being at the place of meeting before the Marylanders and Virginians, the said great men were taxed again by the Virginians more highly of the injuries done by them in Maryland and Virginia, and they utterly denyed the same. And thereupon, this deponent was commanded to declare to them that they should be bound; and this deponent saith, further, that there was an old paper and a meddall shewed by the said Indians, with a black and yellow ribbond thereto, and that the said Indians did say, the first day, in the evening thereof, that the same was a pledge given and left with them by the former governors as a token of amity and friendship as long as the sun and moon should last. And this deponent saith, to the best of his remembrance, all the Virginia officers were present when the Indians were bound; and this deponent saith, that the first night of meeting with the Susquehannahs, he was ordered to declare to them that major Truman did believe the Senecas had done the mischief, and not they, and that he was well satisfied therein.'

'SATTURDAY, *May the 20th*, 1676.

'The house met.

'Touching the murder of the Susquehannah Indians, captain John Allen being sworn and examined, saith, that about the 25th or 26th day of September, on Sunday morning, the Maryland forces appeared before the fort, under the command of major Truman, who, sending Hugh French and another to the fort, there came out two or three of the Indians, and more afterwards to the number of thirty or forty, and the major examined them concerning the mischief that was done to Mr. Hanson and others, and if they knew what Indians they were, and they told them it was the Senecas. During which discourse between the major and them, came over colonel Washington, colonel Mason, and major Adderton, and they likewise taxed them with the murders done on their side by them, but they made the same reply as to major Truman, that it was none of them; so, when they saw they could get nothing out of them, then they made it appear that three of the said Susquehannah Indians were they that did the murders on the other side. On Munday morning early, the major commanded Mr. Coad and two or three ranks of men, whereof himself was one, to go to the house of Mr. Randolph Hanson, to see if the Indians had plundered it, and, if they found any ammunition, to bring it away; which, accordingly, they did; and after return back to the fort, the deponent saw six Indians guarded with the Marylanders and Virginians, and the major, with the Virginia officers, sitting upon a tree some distance from them; and, after some while, they all rose and came towards the Indians, and caused them to be bound; and after some time, they talked again, and the Virginia officers would have knocked them on the head in the place presently, and particularly, colonel Washington said, what should we keep them any longer—let us knock them on the head—we shall gett the fort to-day. But the deponent saith, the major would not admit of it, but was overswayed by Virginia officers. And, after further discourse, the said Indians were carried forth from the place where they were bound, and they knocked them on the head.

'Colonel Samuel Chew and colonel Jesse Wharton sent to desire the lower house to acquaint this house whether they have drawn up any thing by way of impeachment of major Thomas Truman, and that they would please to signifie the same to this house by a member of their own house.'

'MONDAY MORNING, *May the 22d.*

'The house met.
'Colonel William Burgess, Mr. Robert Carville, Mr. Kenelm Chiseledine, Mr. William Stephens, &c. brought in an impeachment against major Thomas Truman, with several depositions relating thereto, which impeachment is as follows:

'To the Right Honourable the Lord Proprietary of the Province of Maryland, and Avalon, Lord Baron of Baltimore, &c.

'Articles against major Thomas Truman, exhibited by the lower house of assembly to the right honourable the Lord Proprietary, and upper house of assembly.

'We, your lordship's most humble, true, faithfull and obedient people, the burgesses and delegates in your lower house of assembly, being constrained, by necessity of our fidelity and conscience, in vindication of the honour of God, and the honour and welfare of your lordship and this province, do complain and shew that the said major Thomas Truman, late commander-in-chief upon an expedition against the Indians at the Susquehannah forte, hath, by many and sundry ways and means, committed divers and sundry enormous crimes and offences, to the dishonour of Almighty God, against the laws of nations, contrary to your lordship's commission and instructions, and to the great endangering of your lordship's peace, and the good and safety of your lordship's province, according to the articles hereafter mentioned, that is to say :

'We find, upon reading your lordship's commission and instructions, and the affidavits which we herewith send to your lordship and upper house of assembly, and which we humbly submitt to your lordship's examination and serious consideration.

'The first. That the said major Truman hath broken his commission and instructions thus : that the said major Thomas Truman having received six Indians sent out by the Susquehannahs as embassadors to treat with him on the Sunday after the arrival of the Maryland forces, and received their paper and meddall, by which we find they were received as friends, and in amity with us, and had liberty of going back to the fort, and were assured that no intention of force was to be used against them, and that no damage should be done to them, their wives, or children, and that they did, that night, go into the forte, and the next morning did return again with the like number, only one Indian changed, and supposed to come on purpose to treat, and not in any hostile manner, yet the said major Thomas Truman, without calling any council of warr of your lordship's officers under his command, as he ought to have done, did, in a barbarous and cruel manner, cause five of the said Indians to be killed and murdered, contrary to the law of God and nations, and contrary to your lordship's commission and instructions.

'Secondly. That he, the said major Thomas Truman, ought, according to your lordship's instructions, to have acquainted your lordship before he caused the said Indians to be executed, for your lordship's advice and directions in that case, which we do not find he did.

'Lastly. That he hath broken your lordship's instructions in this also, that *that*, if the Virginia officers did advise and consent to the killing of the said Indians, that he did not, in an open council of warr, cause the same to be *judiciously* entered in writing by his clerk or secretary, and such the Virginians consent and desire for the doing thereof, to be signed under their hands, to be kept for justification of himself and the people of this province.

'Therefore, for that, by the said articles, it appears that the said major Thomas Truman hath broken his commission and instructions in murdering the said Indians, to the dishonour of God, and your lordship and this province. They humbly pray that your lordship and upper house of assembly will take such order with the said major Thomas Truman as may be just and reasonable, in terror of others to beware of such offences against your lordship for the future. And your lordship's most humble and obedient servants, as in all duty bound, shall daily pray for your lordship's long and happy dominion over us,' &c.

'LOWER HOUSE, *May the* 22*d*, 1676.

'The committee, having drawn up the above impeachment against major Thomas Truman, and presenting to this house for their further consideration, put to the vote, whether the said impeachment shall be transmitted to the upper house as the committee have drawn it, yea or noe.

'Voted, that it be transmitted to his lordship and upper house, as it is drawn by the committee, together with all the depositions relating thereto annexed to it.

'Signed by order of the lower house,

'ROBERT RIDGELY, *Clerk.*'

'UPPER HOUSE, 26*th May*, 1676.

'Ordered, that the honourable secretary be requested to acquaint major Thomas Truman that his witnesses cannot be sworn by this house to-night.

'To-morrow morning being the day appointed for the tryall of major Thomas Truman, impeached by the lower house, this house desire to know of the lower house how they intend to proceed against the said Truman, and that they will send their vote to this house this night, with the names of the persons who they intend shall manage that affair.'

'LOWER HOUSE, 26*th May.*

'Ordered, that the attorney-general, Mr. Robert Carvile, colonel William Burgess, and Mr. William Stephens manage the impeachment against major Thomas Truman, at his tryall.

'The lower house desiring that the original impeachment against major Thomas Truman, with the original depositions, may be put in the hands of such persons as the lower house have voted to manage the said impeachment.

'The honorable secretary, by order of this house, did go down with the said impeachment and depositions.'

'On Saturday, May 27th, the house met in the afternoon.

'Present, The Right Honourable the Lord Proprietary, the honourable Chancellor and Secretary, colonel Samuel Chew, colonel Jesse Wharton, and colonel Thomas Taillor.

'Major Thomas Truman having due notice given him on Thursday last to prepare for his tryall, this afternoon being called, did make his appearance, and the articles of impeachment against the said major Thomas Truman being read, and after this, the several depositions annexed thereto, which, also, were sworn to by the several and respective deponents in the presence and the hearing of the said major Thomas Truman, Mr. Kenelm Chisledine, his lordship's attorney-general, Mr. Robert Carvile, colonel William Burgess, and Mr. William Stephens, according to a preceding order of the lower house, did manage the said impeachment, and urge the several evidences against the said major Truman, and the said major, by Mr. Benjamin Rozier, his council assigned him, did confess the same, and declared that the said major did no way intend to stand upon his justification; after which confession and declaration, the said major, by his said council, did humbly pray that this house would admit the reading of a certain paper which the said major said he hoped would somewhat extenuate and mitigate the crimes before by him confessed, so that they should not appear so grievous and enormous as in the said impeachment they were held forth to be; and the said major Thomas Truman, by his said council, was admitted to make his defence.

'Whereupon, and upon full hearing on both sides, and after reading of the said major's commission and instructions from his lordship and council, was put the question, whether major Thomas Truman be guilty of the impeachment exhibited against him by the lower house, and voted, *nemine contradicente*, that the said major Thomas Truman is guilty of the first article of the impeachment for commanding five of the said Susquehannahs that came out to treat with them, to be put to death, contrary to the laws of nations, and the second article of his instructions, by which he was ordered to entertain any treaty with the said Susquehannahs.

'Upon which vote, it was ordered that a messenger be sent from this house to the lower house, to desire them to draw up a bill of attainder against the said major Thomas Truman.

'Ordered, that Philip Saunders be sent for, to attend this house in pursuance to a petition exhibited by major Truman for that purpose.'

'UPPER HOUSE OF ASSEMBLY, *June 1st*, 1676.

'Then was taken into consideration the bill of attainder of major Thomas Truman, sent up from the lower house yesterday, and upon serious consideration thereof and debate thereupon, this house do judge that the act drawn up against major Thomas Truman does, in no ways, answer or justifie the impeachment upon which it was grounded, for that, in the said impeachment, the said Truman stands charged of crimes committed against the laws of God, nations, this province, as also against the commission and instructions given him, viz: 'for the barbarous cruelty in causing to be put to death and murdering the five Indians, of which he being found guilty, the punishment prescribed and assigned in the said act of attainder, does no ways agree with, or answer the nature of that defence, it being greatly dishonourable, as well as unsafe and dangerous to lay any fine in such cases, and where such horrid crimes have been committed.'

'That the lower house of assembly having laid the impeachment soe high, (thought, as it is conceived,) no higher then the nature of the crime well deserved; it will be much wondered by those who shall hear and view our proceedings thereon, what shall be the cause why the same hath been past over with so slender and slight a punishment, being no more than what crimes of a more inferior nature might have deserved. That, by this act of attainder, the government will not sufficiently be cleared, nor have it made appear to the world, how much the wickedness of that action is detested and disowned by us; nor in any sort will the lower house of assembly make out that great sense which, in their impeachment, they have expressed to have of that action.

'And which very much concerns the interest and safety of the government, it will not give any satisfaction to the heathens, with whom the publick faith hath been broke, and untill such actions are in a more public manner disowned, that the Indians may take notice thereof. It is not to be expected that any faith or credit will be given to any treaties we shall have with them which, in this dangerous juncture of affairs, the country will stand in need of, and on which we must, in some measure, depend on, as the lower house of assembly were of opinion when they sent the paper in answer to captain John Allen's longer ranging.

'That, if crimes of so high a nature shall deserve no greater punishment than what is inflicted by that act, offences of a lower nature will not require any, and by this means, and through such proceedings as these, no commissions, instructions, powers and directions for the future, will ever be observed, and to no purpose will it be to think to tye up an officer by such hereafter, and so all authority will become ridiculous and contemptible. In fine, by this act the lower house of assembly will have owned the actions of the said Truman more then (as they thought to have done) detested and abhorred them, and so render the government odious to all people that shall become acquainted with the proceedings.'

'LOWER HOUSE, 2d *June*, 1676.

'This paper being read in the lower house, and the debate re-assumed in this house, touching the said bill of attainder, and voted, *nemine contradicente*, that the said major Truman, for his crime, does not deserve death, in regard that several circumstances that appeared at his tryall, extenuate his crime very much, as the unanimous consent of the Virginians and the eager impetuosity of the whole field, as well Marylanders as Virginians, upon the sight of the christians murdered at Mr. Hinson's, and them very Indians that were there killed, being proved to be murderers, both of them and several other christians; and in regard, also, that it appears to this house, that the said crime was not maliciously perpetrated, or out of any design to prejudice the province, but meerely out of ignorance, and to prevent a mutiny of the whole army, as well Virginians as Marylanders; wherefore, this house do not think fitt to recede from their former vote.'

'UPPER HOUSE, *June 2d,* 1676.

'In pursuance to the paper from the lower house, read the 2d of June, touching the bill entituled an act of attainder, his lordship and this house do conceive it not safe for them to vote the killing of the five Susquehannah embassadors no murther, for to them and all the world, it would and will certainly appear the greatest that ever hath been committed.

'That the unanimous consent of the Virginians (if true) does no ways alter the nature of the crime, nor since the said Truman had instructions plain enough to have made him abhorred and abominated so black an action, can as little serve for an extenuation thereof; and whereas, in the said paper, for a further extenuation, it is signified that the said major, to prevent a mutiny of the whole army, was compelled and drawn to that action, this house are of another opinion; for, at the said Truman's tryall, did too plainly appear that his first commands for the killing of those Indians were not obeyed, and that he had some difficulty to get his men to obey him therein, and that after they were putt to death, not a man would own to have had a hand in it, but rather seemed to abhorr the act, which, untill now, hath been termed by all persons, those that were executioners only excepted, the most execrable of murthers.

'That the crime was not maliciously perpetrated as to authority, this house doth believe. But that it was done treacherously, and that in it a great and unheard-of wickedness was committed, by the lower house, cannot be denyed. And whether, by that action, the province will not be prejudiced, and many English murdered, his lordship and this house leaves to the further consideration of the lower house, no way pressing them to recede from their so positive vote, only desiring them that they will take notice that what is now undone lyes at their doors, and not with us who are positive in this, that his lordship and upper house dare not, and therefore resolved, not to proceed upon an act which only bears the title of an act of attainder.'

'UPPER HOUSE, *June* 10*th*, 1676.

'This house, upon perusall of their own journal, do find that this house did not referr it to the consideration of the lower house, what punishment major Truman deserved, but ordered that a message should be sent to the lower house to desire them to draw up a bill of attainder against the said Truman, (which, when the lower house shall think fitt to draw up,) this house, as in the last paper they promised, will proceed upon.'

'LOWER HOUSE, *June* 12*th*, 1676.

'Touching that message received from the upper house on Saturday, in relation to major Thomas Truman, this house do say, that in desiring them to draw up a bill of attainder against major Truman, implies they were to consider not only of his crime, but his punishment also; and, therefore, desire that his lordship would be pleased to send an answer of this house's petition* to his lordship, in behalf of the said Truman, and to pass this bill of attainder as it is drawn in this house.

'This house conceiving it is their undoubted privilege not only to consider of his crime, but punishment.'

'UPPER HOUSE, *June 12th*, 1676.

'In answer to the paper received from the lower house, dated the 12th instant, relating to major Thomas Truman, this house do say, that the bill is only an attainder in the title, not in the body of the act. That this house cannot consent to inflict a pecuniary punishment upon a person who hath been accused by the lower house of murder, and by this house found guilty of the same; and do further say that it is against the priviledges of this house to press this bill upon them any further.'

Here end the proceedings of the assembly in regard to this subject. On reference to an order a few pages back, it will be found that Philip Saunders was summoned to attend the assembly, on the petition of major Truman. What new light Mr. Saunders was able to throw on the matter, favorable to major Truman, our records do not inform us; but we may safely infer that it was of a nature calculated to produce the 'unanimous decision of the lower house,' that major Truman, though guilty of the charge alleged against him, was not deserving of capital punishment, from the facts brought before them, of an extenuating character.

1681. At the meeting of the assembly in August of this year, on calling the lower house, there ap-

---

* This petition is not entered on the journals of the upper house, or it would have appeared in its proper place among these extracts. The journals of the lower house, for this period, are *lost*.

peared twelve vacancies. The lower house immediately presented an address to the Lord Proprietary, stating this fact, and requested that his lordship would appoint some officer to whom the speaker of their house might direct his warrants to cause the said vacancies to be filled; until which, 'they humbly conceived themselves greatly incapacitated to act and do proportionable to the great trust reposed in them, and sufficiently to consult the grand and weighty affairs of the province.' They also remonstrated against his lordship having called but two members from each county, at the present session, when four should have been called from each, according to law and custom in the premises.

His lordship sent a message to the lower house, desiring their presence. On entering the upper house, the Lord Proprietary said, 'that by his proclamation by which they were now called, the law for four delegates is sufficiently disassented to, and that, otherwise, he would gratify their request in issuing out writts for filling up vacancies:' and the lower house was requested to unite with the upper house, with the members then present, and to proceed to the transaction of the business of the province.

The lower house still hesitating to enter upon the 'great and weighty affairs' for which they were convened, his lordship consented that writs might be issued for supplying the vacancies for the present, provided the lower house would acknowledge it as a favor from his lordship, and so enter it upon their journals.

The lower house consented to make such an entry upon their journals, and to agree to two members being elected from each county, instead of four, provided his lordship would consent that the speaker of their house should, in all future vacancies, have the authority to send his warrant to the secretary of the province, to issue out writs to fill all vacancies which might occur by death or otherwise, and stated their unanimous resolution 'to stand to and not to recede from the substance of their address,' and the right of their speaker to issue his warrants in case of vacancies; and that they had 'made all the condesentions they can, without apparent violating their priviledges,' and hoped that the upper house would concur therein.

The upper house objected to grant the authority desired, for the speaker to send out his warrants of election, which they conceived, 'aimed at things wholly new and unheard of in this province.'

The lower house responded to the last message, viewing it as a 'denyal of the just and reasonable proposalls of this house for the future election of deputies,' &c. and passed a unanimous vote, 'that it was the undoubted priviledge of this house, that the speaker of this house issue his warrants,' &c. and considered it 'a very unsafe, ill precedent to proceed any further in the business of the session, and requested his lordship to appoint some person to whom said warrants should be directed.'

The chancellor is thereon sent by his lordship to the lower house, to acquaint them 'that he cannot but wonder how the lower house of assembly assume to themselves a power here that is not only new to us, and unheard of before in this province, but not practiced in Virginia, Barbadoes, or any other of his majesties plantations,' &c.

'His majesty hath the sole power to dispose of his

conquests upon terms he pleases, &c.' and desired to know their positive answer, whether they would join them in the dispatch of business, promising if they would, he would immediately issue writs to fill up the house with four delegates from each county.

The lower house resolved, that if his lordship caused writs to issue as promised, that they would 'proceed upon such matters as shall be recommended to them from his lordship.' But at the same time, they asserted 'their rights and privileges, rather from the rules of England than the imperfect proceedings of the nominated colonies, the first being our inherent right—yea, and birthright, though born in this province.'

'To liken us to a conquered people, we take very heavily, and wish we had not heard, and do wonder it should pass the upper house. But, if the word conquest intends that we are subjects to arbitrary laws and impositions, then we humbly take leave to believe that they are not his lordship's words, but the result of strange, if not evill council.'

'That his majesty has reserved for us the rights and privileges of Englishmen, is that we insist upon.'*

---

* At a later period, the house of delegates passed the following resolution.—See *Journal of the house*, 1722, page 2.

'*Resolved*, That this province is not under the circumstances of a *conquer'd country*; that, if it were, the present christian inhabitants thereof would be in the circumstances, not of the *conquer'd*, but of the conquerors, it being a colony of the *English nation*, encouraged by the crown to transplant themselves hither for the sake of improving and enlarging its dominions, which, by the blessing of God upon their endeavours, at their own expense and labour, has been, in great measure, obtained. And 'tis unanimously *resolved*, That whoever shall advance that his majestie's subjects, by their endeavors and success, have *forfeited* any part of their *English liberties*, are ill-wishers to the country, and mistake its happy constitution.'

The Lord Proprietary, in reply to the last message from the lower house, disclaims any intention to liken the freemen of Maryland to a conquered people, or subject to arbitrary laws or impositions, and hopes that they may no way deserve that severe reflection, and assures them that he had always 'been ready to oblige and shew his kindness to the good people of this province;' and, as a further testimony of it, states his willingness to issue writs as desired, if the lower house will ask it of him 'as a thing that will oblige (at this time) the inhabitants of this province, of whom they are the representatives,' &c.

The lower house accordingly made the request, stating their willingness 'to leave off all disputations about words,' saying, it 'will be matter of great content and rejoyceing to the good people of this province,' &c.

Thus ended this controversy between his lordship and the freemen* of the province, who shewed themselves the worthy ancestors of the Maryland patriots of 1776. Throughout the whole legislative proceedings of this province, the representatives of the people are found to be the firm and unyielding supporters of civil liberty, and no one instance is found upon their records, of their having ever been guilty of timidity or treachery in regard to their own rights and privileges, or the interests of their constituents.

1683. The following extracts are taken from the rules and regulations for the government of the lower house of assembly of this year.

* 'The freemen of Maryland, as they were called, were emphatically so from their origin. They never permitted the Proprietary to entrench upon what they conceived to be their rights; and the records of this period furnish many instances in which they opposed and defeated the designs of the Proprietaries.'—*McMahon's History of Maryland, vol.* 1, *page* 222.

'That *noe* one shall come into the house of assembly whilst the house is sitting, with a sword or other weapon, but shall put the same into the hands of the doorkeeper or other person appoynted thereto, upon penalty of a fine,' &c.

'That noe deputy, burgess, delegate or clerk, during this session of assembly, will be suffered to smoke tobacco in the house, whilst the house is sitting, upon penalty of being fined or censured,' &c.

In 1683 Annapolis was erected into a town, port, and place of trade, under the name of the 'Town Land at Proctors.'

1694. In 1694 it was constituted a town, port, and place of trade, under the name of 'Anne Arundel Town,' and made the place of residence of the collector of the district, the naval-officer, and their deputies, 'for the dispatch of shipping.'

In the same year major John Hammond, major Dorsey, Mr. John Bennett, Mr. John Dorsey, Mr. Andrew Norwood, Mr. Philip Howard, Mr. James Saunders, and Nicholas Greenberry, Esquire, were appointed commissioners to survey and lay out the said town into lots, streets and lanes; also a town-common or pasture, to be fenced in at the public charge within *Leavy-Neck Cove*, and *Acton's Cove*; and which are the coves or heads of the two creeks, now known as *Brewer's* and *Spa* Coves.

In this year, 1694, the seat of government, which had been at the city of St. Mary's from the earliest formation of the province, was by an act of assembly removed. And the place selected as the new site of the government, was a point of land at the mouth of the Severn river, as above stated, *called 'Proctors,'* or

'*The Town land at Severn*,' afterwards known as the '*Town at Proctors*.' At the period of its selection as the future seat of government, it was described as '*The Town land at Severn, where the town was formerly;* and as preliminary to the removal, it was erected into a port of entry and discharge, for the commerce of the province, under the name of '*Anne Arundel Town*,' and for the holding of the meetings of the general assembly and provincial courts.

In February of this year, (1694) Francis Nicholson, Esquire, governor, met in council at the *court-house* at Anne Arundel Town, and issued an order for the 'removal of the records from the city of St. Mary's to Anne Arundel Town, to be conveyed in good strong bags, and to be secured with cordage and hides, and well packed—with guards to attend them night and day, to be protected from all accidents, and to be delivered to the sherriff of Anne Arundel county, at Anne Arundel Town.'

The final removal of these from St. Mary's, took place in the winter of 1694—1695. And the first assembly was held at Anne Arundel Town, on the 28th of February, 1694, (old style.) At the next session, it acquired the name of the '*Port of Annapolis*,' and became the place of sessions for the courts of Anne Arundel county.

1695. In this year it was enacted by the general assembly that there be one or more places laid out and reserved for ship yards. That the naval-officer reside there; and that Anne Arundel Town for the future, should be called, known and distinguished by the name of '*Annapolis*.'

At the session of assembly held in this same year,

(1695) it was voted, 'that a publique ferry be kept upon Severn river at Annapolis, for the accommodation of the publique.' Allen Robinett was appointed the keeper of the ferry, was required to reside in Annapolis, and for his services received nine thousand pounds of tobacco per annum, out of the *publique* revenue.

1696. In 1696, an act of assembly was passed for 'keeping good rules and orders' in the town of Annapolis; and his excellency Francis Nicholson, the honourable Sir Thomas Lawrence, the honourable Nicholas Greenberry, the honourable Thomas Tench, major John Hammond, major Edward Dorsey, Mr. James Saunders and captain Richard Hill, or any five of them, were made the *body corporate* for the said town.

By the same act governor Nicholson was presented with a lot of land within the town common, 'for planting or making a garden, vineyard and summer house.'*

It also appears from the same act, that a 'Mr. Richard Beard, gentleman,' had made a map or plot of the town.

The above named commissioners were authorized to erect and constitute a market, to be held once a week, and a fair once every year; and a new state-house directed to be built. At the same session it was proposed to have a 'Bridewell, if any person would under-

---

* The land surveyed for and presented to governor Nicholson by this act, comprised all that portion of the town, beginning on the north-east side of the present dock (then called Nicholson's Cove,) running with a straight line to East street, with said street to the public circle, with said circle to Francis street and Church street, to the south-east side of the dock.

8*

take to build and keep it; that all idle and vagrant per-
pers may be taken up and put to work there.'

The house determined 'that such Bridewell or house
of correction was very necessary and convenient, but
that the present ill circumstances of this province will
not admit the beginning or carrying on of any new
building then already undertaken.'

For the improvement of Annapolis, it was proposed
and adopted by the house 'that ye townes people be
empowered to purchase a common, and for the commissioners of the said town to make bye-laws, with
power to *ffyne* any persons, inhabitants committing
breach thereof in such *summe* to be ascertained.' 'To
assess ye conduit made at the *publique* charge. That
the common be well cleaned with ye points of land,
and ye place dividing the common to be well ditched.'
'That an handsome pair of gates be made at ye coming in of the *towne*, and two triangular houses built
for ye rangers.' 'To have the way from the gate to go
directly to the top of ye hill without the towne, and to
be ditched on each side and sett with *quick setts* or
some such thing.'

'That part of the land which lye on y^e *creeke*,* by
major Dorsey's house,† whereby his excellency at present lives,‡ be sett aside for publique buildings, and
if in case the same happen to come within any of

---

* This creek made up the ravine just above the governor's pond,
and passed through the lower part of the garden where chancellor
Bland now resides.

† This house is not standing, nor is the precise location of it now
known.

‡ Governor Nicholson then resided in the house now owned and
occupied by G. G. Brewer, Esq.

ye said major's lotts,—propose that land be given him elsewhere for it.

'To have in the said towne two *ffairs* a year, and persons coming thither not to be arrested for one day before the said *ffair* and one day after.'

'That forty foot space be left along the water side within the port of Annapolis, for any person to build warehouses upon, if the owners of such lotts that front upon the same do not build thereon in such a *tyme* to be sett.' 'That the holes made by grubbing up stumps and cutting off tops of stones in the said port of Annapolis be filled up.'

It was also proposed this year to build a church in Annapolis, and a committee was appointed to 'inspect into the proposals for building the same.'

Major Edward Dorsey from the committee, reported 'that there was in *Banck* for building the church at Annapolis, £458 sterling. That they had *discoursed* workmen, and the carpenter demands for his work £250—the bricklayer, having all *stuff* upon the place, £220—the brickmaker £90—that they find no other means to raise money therefor without the assistance of some charitable disposed persons. That the charge of building the said church will amount to £1200 sterling.'

An act passed the same day imposing a tax of 'three pence per hundred on tobacco, to continue and be in force untill the 12th day of May, which shall be in the year of our Lord God, 1698, and to be applied to the building of ye church at Annapolis.' The architect of this church was named Thomas *Ffielder*.

This year a Mr. Gaddes arrived at Annapolis, 'being sent out by his Lordship the Bishop of London'—the house appointed him to read prayers in some vacant parish, and made a provision for his maintenance, of 10,000 pounds of tobacco.

The legislature at its May session, in 1696, passed an act, establishing at Annapolis an academy by the name of 'King William's School,' 'for the propagation of the gospel, and education of youth in good letters and manners.' Of this school the distinguished William Pinkney was a student. Mr. Pinkney who has been justly styled 'the wonder of his age,' was a native of Annapolis, and well may the city boast, as she, with a commendable pride, does, of having sent forth into the world a son whose memory she fondly cherishes, and whose commanding talents and gigantic mind called forth the admiration both of Europe and America.

1697. In 1697, governor Nicholson proposed to the house of burgesses, 'that his Majesty, William III., be addressed that some part of the revenue given towards furnishing arms and ammunition for the use of the province, be laid out for the purchase of books to be added to the books which had been presented by the king, to form a library in the porte of Annapolis; and that a portion of the public revenue be applied to the enlargement thereof; and that the library should be placed in the office, and under the care of the commissary of the province, permitting all persons desirous to study or read the books, to have access thereto under proper restrictions.'

Many of the volumes which were thus presented by the king to Annapolis, are now in the library of St. John's College—to which they were removed on the burning of the state-house in 1704. They are rare and curious works.

In this year (1697) the new state-house which had been ordered to be built on the removal of the seat of government to Annapolis in 1694, being nearly completed, the rooms therein were by an act of assembly, particularly designated and appropriated to the use of the several offices of the government. This house was built of brick, and was a capacious and convenient edifice. This was the state-house destroyed by fire in the year 1704.

The following extracts are made from the journals of assembly of this year—but not unaccompanied by profound regret, that an act of religious bigotry should have ever stained the proceedings of a people whose colony was founded on the holy principles of toleration, and freedom of conscience:

'LOWER HOUSE, *March*, 1697.

'A letter to his excellency the governor, written by a minister of the church of England, giving an account of the presumptions of popish priests in Charles county, in visiting dying and phrantick persons, and endeavoring to make *proselytes* of them, and also administering the sacraments to them in such dying and phrantick condition, was read.

'Whereupon put to the question, if a bill shall be drawn up to restraine such their presumption or not, and carryed by the majority of voices in the negative.

'But *resolved, nemine contradicente*, that his excellency be addressed to issue his proclamation to restraine such their extravagances and presumptions.

'*Resolved*, that the following address be sent to his excellency the governor.

'By the house of delegates, March ye 21st, 1697.

'Uppon reading a certain letter from a reverend minister of the church of England, which your excellency was pleased to communicate to us, complaining to your excellency, how that the popish priests in Charles county do of their own accord in this violent and raging mortality in that county, make it their business to go up and down the country to persons houses when dying and *phranticke*, and endeavour to seduce and make *proselytes* of them, and in such condition boldly presume to administer the sacraments to them. We have put it to the vote in this house, if a law should be made to restraine such their presumption, and have concluded not to make such law at present—but humbly to entreat your excellency that you would be pleased to issue your proclamation to restraine and prohibit such their extravagante and presumptious behaviour. Signed by order.

'W. BLADEN, *Clerk House of Delegates.*'

By several acts of subsequent legislation, the Roman catholics were rendered incapable of voting, unless they qualified themselves by taking the several test-oaths, and making the declaration prescribed by the act of 1716; and all judges of elections were empowered to tender these oaths and declaration to 'any person suspected to be a papist, or popishly inclined;' and, upon his refusal thus to qualify, they might reject his vote. These were the mere *legal* disqualifications of the catholics; but they fell short of the *actual* oppressions practised upon them during many periods of this era. 'When laws degrade, individuals learn to practice wanton outrage; the former stigmatize, the latter catch its spirit, and make its example an excuse for oppression.' Hence the personal animosity of the protestants against the catholics of Maryland was, at one period, carried to such an extent, that, as we are informed, the latter were even excluded from social intercourse with the former—were not permitted to walk in front of the state-house, and were actually obliged to wear swords for their personal protection.*

In 1758, during the time governor Sharpe presided over the province of Maryland, information was given, and complaints were made to Lord Baltimore, that too much countenance was given to the Roman catholics; that, in consequence thereof, their numbers greatly increased; and that many of them behaved in such a manner, as to give the protestants in the province great offence and uneasiness.

Governor Sharpe, in a letter to the Lord Proprietary, dated December 16th, 1758, says: 'I think it my duty, and in justice to myself, I can do no less than to assure your lordship, that since I have had the honour to bear your commission, nothing has been farther from my inclination than to countenance, or give encouragement to persons of that persuasion, nor has there, to my knowledge, been any given them by any persons in authority under me, but, on the contrary, extraordinary burthens have been lately laid on them, particularly by an act of assembly that was made in May, 1756, whereby all landholders of the Romish faith are obliged to pay, by way of land tax, twice as much as the rest of your lordship's tenants, who are protestants.

'It might, perhaps, be unknown, if not to the authors, at least to some of the propagators of the above mentioned report, that the people who first settled in this province were, for the most part, Roman catholics, and

---

* *McMahon's History of Maryland.*

that, altho' every other sect was tolerated, a majority of the inhabitants continued papists till the revolution, soon after which event, an act was made here for the support of a clergyman of the church of England in every parish, which is still in force; and the papists as well as protestants, are thereby obliged to pay annually very considerable sums for that purpose. Other acts of assembly were made afterwards, in the reign of her majesty Queen Ann, subjecting all popish priests that should be discovered here, to all the penalties to which such priests would be lyable in England, but her majesty was pleased to disapprove thereof, and to order that no popish bishop, priest or jesuit should be prosecuted or indicted for exercising his function in any private family within this province. But, notwithstanding her majesty thought fit to allow the papists in Maryland the free exercise of their religion, they were not permitted to sit in either house of assembly, to vote at the election of representatives, to act as magistrates, or to enjoy any place of publick trust or profit, nor have they been since suffered; and to this, I presume, it must be principally attributed, that, altho' half the province were Roman catholicks about sixty years ago, the people of that religion do not, at present, make a thirteenth part of the inhabitants, as I find by the return of the sherriffs and constables who have, in obedience to my orders, made the most strict inquiry in their respective districts, and the rolls returned by the collectors of the land tax shew that they are not possessed of a twelfth part of the land which is held under your lordship as proprietary of Maryland.

'That your lordship may not be at a loss to account for their having many enemies ready to propagate stories to their disadvantage, I must intreat your patience while I inform you, that some time before your lordship was pleased to appoint me your lieutenant-governor, one Mr. *Carrol*, a Roman catholic, died here, and left a considerable estate to his two sons, having appointed two of his relations their guardians and executors of his last will and testament. Both these gentlemen were, at that time, of the same religion as the testator; but, after a while, one of them declared himself a protestant, and, having qualified himself according to law, was chosen by the people of this county to represent them in the lower house of assembly. A difference or quarrell arising between the executors, concerning the administration, he that had not renounced his religion published a peice by way of advertisement, which reflected much on the conduct and character of the other, who had address enough to persuade the house of assembly, which was then sitting, to take notice thereof, and to punish the author for violating their priviledges by libelling, as they said, one of their members. Some Roman catholicks, friends of the gentleman who was thus treated, having taken the liberty to speak disrespectfully of the assembly for such their proceedings, the lower house immediately resented it by resolving that the papists were bad members of the community, and unworthy of the protection and indulgence which had been given them.

After this, their enemies, and many were made such by envy or the hopes of reaping some advantage from a persecution of the papists, were continually representing them as a very dangerous people, enemies to his majesty and their country, nor had this spirit of enmity subsided, when I arrived in the province. Immediately after the defeat of general Braddock it was given out that several Roman catholicks had showed signs of satisfaction and joy at that unhappy event, and that one of their priests had been seen on the frontiers in the dress of an officer. To alarm the people the more, it was, at the same time, rumoured that the negroes had been caballing in many parts of the country—nay, Mr. Chase, rector of St. Paul's parish, in Baltimore county, scrupled not to intimate from the pulpit to his congregation, that the state or situation of the protestants in this province was, at that time, very little different from that of the protestants in Ireland, at the eve of the Irish massacre. In order to learn whether the behaviour of the papists, or of any negroes, had given reason or afforded room for such reports, I convened the gentlemen of the council, and, by their advice, circular letters were sent to the justices of the peace in the several parts of the province, whereby they were directed to enquire whether the Roman catholicks, in their respective counties, had misbehaved, or whether there was any foundation for the reports which had been spread concerning them, and which had made many of his majesty's good subjects in the province very uneasy.

The letters which I shall herewith transmit to your lordship in a packett marked No. 1, will shew that none of the county courts could, upon the strictest enquiry, find that any of the papists had behaved or expressed themselves in an unbecoming manner, tho', indeed, the justices of Prince George's county (who, it seems, had taken extraordinary pains to make discoveries, but in vain,) were too much prejudiced to acquit them, or, at least, to acquit their priests of having ill designs against the government. When the assembly met in April following, the lower house, incited by two or three gentlemen whose interest and popularity were thereby promoted, presented an address to me which was calculated to inflame the people still more against the papists, and to make 'em believe that they, or a few of them, at least, had received extraordinary favours from myself. I cannot help thinking that your lordship was thoroughly satisfied, by the answer I gave the gentlemen the 24th of April, 1656, which is printed in their journal, that the allegations or insinuations contained in their address were false and groundless, and, indeed, I am persuaded that, if they had not been convinced thereof, and been sensible that they had been imposed on, they would not have failed to make a reply. During the same session, the gentlemen of the upper house thought proper to frame a bill for preventing the growth of popery within this province, by which the priests were to be rendered incapable of holding any lands, to be obliged to register their names, and give large security for their good behaviour, forbid to make a proselyte under pain of the penalty for high treason, and it was to have been enacted by the said bill, that no person who should hereafter be educated at any foreign popish seminary, could be qualified to inherit any estate or to hold lands within this province. There were many other restraints to be laid on them by this bill, as your lordship may see, if you shall be pleased to peruse the copy of it which you will herewith receive; but the gentlemen of the lower house refused to pass it without many amendments, and these the upper house would not agree to, being of opinion that the bill, as it was first drawn, was severe enough, and sufficient to answer every good end that could be desired by any protestants who delighted not in persecution.

The step which the gentlemen of the upper house had taken in proposing such a bill, added to the report which the justices had made, had this effect, however, that it quieted the minds of the people, and silenced those who had endeavoured to inflame and terrify them.

I have since ordered another circular letter to be wrote and sent to the justices, desiring them to enquire again, and inform me how the Roman catholicks in the several counties had behaved, since they, the justices, made their last report, in a packett marked No. 2. I shall transmit your lordship copies of all their answers, which will, I am apt to think, incline your lordship to believe that the Roman catholicks who are among us continue to behave as behooves good subjects ; and, upon the whole, my lord, I must say, that, if I was asked whether the conduct of the protestants or papists in this province hath been most unexceptionable since I have had the honour to serve your lordship, I should not hesitate to give an answer in favour of the latter.'*

* Governor Sharpe's MS. Letter-book, in the Maryland state library.

CHAPTER IV.

Dispute between Governor Nicholson and the Lower House of Assembly—They become reconciled—Governor Nicholson leaves this Province to preside over Virginia—Petition of Mr. John Perry—James Crawford, a Delegate, killed by lightning—First public Jail—State-House burnt down—A new one erected—Described—Improvement of the town—A plot for burning of Annapolis, discovered—Bounds of Annapolis—Annapolis chartered—Description of Annapolis—Delegates from Annapolis to receive only *half wages*—Improvements—Mr. James Stoddart appointed to lay off anew the city—Mr. Wm. Parks appointed to compile the Laws of the Province—Improvements—Appropriation to build a Government-House—Mr. Jonas Green appointed Printer to the Province—His character—Editor of the Maryland Gazette—The first public horseracing—Aurora Borealis—South River Club—Military movements at Annapolis—Anniversary of George the Second—Trade and Commerce of Annapolis—The first Ship-Yard—Brig Lovely Nancy—Notices of some of the oldest houses of the town—The old Episcopal Church—Indians—King Abraham and Queen Sarah—*A Hiccory Switch*—A Jockey Club formed—Races—The first Theatre built—The first Lottery drawn in the Province—Governor Sharp arrives at Annapolis—The military march from Annapolis against the French on the Ohio—General Braddock and other distinguished persons arrive at Annapolis—Doctor Charles Carroll, his death—Annapolis entrenched—Hostilities of the French and Indians—Small-pox.

1698. At the close of March session of the assembly in 1698—which had been one of contentious disputation between the lower house and governor Nicholson; the governor closed his address as follows :

'A letter from your house supposed to be for my Lord Bishop of London, has been here read, and his excellency says that he scorns to have his reputation and honour supported and vindicated by some of you, but shall rather look upon it as a scandall to have it so,

9*

for that he can prove one your house to be a villian upon record, if not worse, and of several others, your lives and conversations to be so well known, both in this country and England, that they are not agreeable to truth and justice.'

It appears, however, that before the conclusion of the October session of the same year, a better state of feeling prevailed, between the members of the lower house and governor Nicholson. At this period he was appointed governor of the province of Virginia, and was succeeded in Maryland by governor Blackstone. Before taking his departure, in addressing the two houses of assembly, he embraced the occasion to say— that notwithstanding the public business had been 'interrupted by heats and animosities amongst them— he hoped they were now burried in the depth of oblivion, and that he was not willing to revive them.

'And for as much as he hoped all differences are composed or forgot, he will not make any distinction or separation amongst the gentlemen of the house of delegates, and for what hath happened, he doth believe was through inadvertency, and as he has an esteem for all persons that had shewed themselves truly loyall to his majesty, whensoever, that occasion may require it, he will signalize it by the best services he may doe them,' &c. In reply to which the following address was made, viz :

'The honourable colonel Henry Jowles, chancellor, on behalf of the honourable, his majesty's council— the honourable, the justice of the provincial court— some of the members of the house of delegate,· and the grand jury—presented the following address :

'To his excellency Francis Nicholson, Esq., captain-general and governor of this his majesty's province and territory of Maryland;

'Sir, having lately received information from yourself and others, that his majesty has thought fit to remove you unto another government, that of our neighbour colony of Virginia—and reflecting with ourselves how becoming a thing it is to have always a grateful remembrance of benefits received, we cannot forbear to leave this testimony and acknowledgment under our hands, as it proceeds from our hearts.

'That in your conduct over us in this place, your great care and study has been to promote the practice of piety and worship of Almighty God, by erecting churches, schools, and nurserys of learning, both for reforming of manners and education of youth, wherein you have not only been a large benefactor, but an indefaticable promoter, together with your integrity of maintaining his majesty's honour and authority in this province—your care in providing arms and military instruments for the defence of it. Your regulating and happy settlement of the civil constitution, both as to the courts of justice; and in bringing us out of debt which the public was in, into a condition clear of debt and money in bank, by your promotion of good laws to such purposes; your great care to cause speedy justice to be administered to all persons; your pious and just, your noble and benevolent carriage in all things, deserves better pens, and would take up more paper than this to recount.

'Be pleased, therefore, honoured sir, to accept our humble acknowlegments for the same, as the just though slender tribute of an obliged people, to a generous and good governor, praying to God to bless you and all your pious and noble undertakings, with happiness and success.' So prays your humble and obliged servants. HENRY JOWLES.'

This admirable address is signed by the members of council—provincial court—by thirty-four members of the house of delegates, and by the grand jury.

Governor Nicholson expressed his pleasure, and thanked 'the gentlemen for the character they have been pleased to give him, which is greater than he was able to perform, but that he has endeavoured as much as in him lay, to discharge his duty to God—the King, and the county; and prays God, that they may never find cause of complaint more than he has given.'

In this year, a Mr. John Perry, petitioned to the assembly, complaining that he had been at great expense in building a brick house in the *porte* of Annapolis, and that a certain small market-house had since been so incommodiously erected, that it deprived him of his '*sight and prospect.*'

Upon considering his petition, the house consented that the said market-house should be removed 'at the charge of the petitioner.'

1699. The following memorandum is recorded on the journals of the house of burgesses in the year 1699.

'Memorandum, that on Thursday, July 13th, about four or five of the clock in the afternoon, a violent fflash of lightening broke into the state-house at Annapolis; the house of delegates being there sitting, which instantly killed Mr. James Crauford, one of the members of Calvert county, and hurt and wounded several other members, and shattered and broke most part of the doors and window cases belonging to the said house, and sett ye said state-house on fire in one of the *vpper* chambers, and several other damages; but the fire was presently quenched by the dilligence and industry of his excellency, Nathaniel Blackistone, his majesty's governor.'

The first public prison was built at Annapolis this year, and the manner in which it was to be made, is minutely described on the journals of the house.

This jail was erected on the corner of the lot belonging to the Episcopal parsonage, and was made of wood.

In this year Annapolis was made by an act of assembly—the 'chief place and seat of justice,' within the province, for holding assemblies and provincial courts, and where all writs were made returnable.

1704. In 1704 the general assembly passed an act for building the state-house, to supply the place of the one burned down this year.

At the first session of assembly held in Annapolis after the burning of the state-house, his excellency governor Seymour, in his message says on that subject, 'the late melancholy accident might have been prevented had my often admonitions took place; for I never saw any public building left solely to Providence *but in Maryland.* I hope this sad experiment will awaken your care for time to come, and in the interim your best considerations to secure the laws and records of your country for the advantage and quiet of future generations. What is proper to be done in rebuilding your stadt-house, so very necessary for the accommodation of the public, I leave entirely to your own serious debates and decision, for I have no other aim than the true interest and service of your country.'

At this time the provincial legislature sat in a house belonging to a colonel Edward Dorsey, for which they contracted to pay a rent of twenty pounds sterling per annum.

Immediately after reading the governor's message, the house of delegates appointed a committee to inspect the ruins of the state-house, and to 'make report if the walls now standing are fit and sufficient to rebuild upon.'

This committee reported in favor of rebuilding upon the old walls, and in the same 'form and manner as before.'

The new state or court-house, as it is often termed in the journal of proceedings, was accordingly rebuilt, under contract, by a Mr. W. Bladen, (who had erected all the other public buildings,) the cost of the building not to exceed one thousand pounds sterling, Mr. Bladen to have the benefit of all 'the materials saved out of the fire which appertained to the old court-house.'

This house was finished in 1706,* and is recollected by some few of the present inhabitants of this city—and stood where the present state-house now stands. It is described as having been a neat brick building. It was in form an oblong square, entered by a hall—opposite to the door of which was the judges' seat, and on each side there were rooms for

---

* During the building of this house, the house of delegates met at and held their sessions 'at the house of colonel Edward Dorsey, in Annapolis'—the house met twice a day—to wit: from 8 o'clock to 12 A. M., and from 2 to 4 P. M., and were 'called by beat of drum.'

the jurys to retire. Over the judges' seat was a full length likeness of Queen Anne, presenting a printed charter of the city of Annapolis. In this house the general assembly held its sessions. A handsome cupola surmounted the building, surrounded by balustrades, and furnished with seats for those who desired to enjoy the beautiful scenery around. The portrait of Queen Anne, just mentioned, is said to have been destroyed during the revolutionary war—'when every thing bearing the semblance of royalty was in bad odour with our republican sires.'

About the same period, an armory was built near the court-house, on the north side of it. It is represented to have been a large hall with seats around it, above which the walls were covered with arms, tastefully arranged. It was often used as a ballroom—from the vaulted roof was suspended a wooden gilt chandelier, which when lighted up, produced a brilliant effect by the reflection of the light from the arms. The walls of the hall were also decorated with full length portraits of Queen Anne and Lord Baltimore. The governor and council held their sessions in one of the apartments of this building.

On the south side of the court-house, stood the memorable academy of 'King William,' which is said to have been a plain building, containing school-rooms and apartments for the teacher and his family.

1706. In this year the lower house of assembly directed that three lots be laid out within the city—one for the benefit and advantage of the rector of the parish—one for the sexton, and the third for the clerk of the vestry and commissary's clerk—a house was shortly after built upon one of them for the accommodation of the vestry, which house and lot were annexed to the parson's lot, for the reception and accommodation of a minister forever.

1707. In the proceedings of the house of delegates for this year, a certain Richard Clarke is charged with the design of burning the port of Annapolis—destroying the public records—sacking, and then blowing up the public magazine within the limits of the town—with making and passing base coin, of dollars and pieces of eight—and with the intention of pirating, after he had succeeded in carrying into execution his diabolical and villainous designs. And from the testimony taken before the committee appointed to investigate the truth of these charges, (which testimony is set forth at large in the manuscript journal of this year,) no doubt can remain that such were his intentions. This testimony is highly curious and interesting, but too long to be given here.

In 1705, this same man (Clarke) was outlawed for treasonable designs, and after the above investigation had been finished, an act for his attainder was passed, setting forth that the said Clarke had obstinately refused to surrender himself to justice, and charges him with various treasonable intentions. He was convicted and attainted of high treason, and doomed to suffer death. But whether this worthy was ever *promoted* or *suspended*, our records do not furnish us with any evidence.

In 1707, all the towns in Baltimore and Anne Arundel counties, together with the rivers and creeks, except such as were situated on the Patuxent, were appended to Annapolis.

1708. In the year 1708 Annapolis was erected into a city. From the time of its establishment, the new government spared no efforts to increase its population, and improve its accommodations, so as to give it a permanent hold upon the province; yet, with all these aids, it at first increased but slowly.

A person writing from Maryland, within four or five years after the removal of the legislature to this place, remarks—'there are indeed several places for towns, but hitherto they are only titular ones, except Annapolis, where the governor resides. Colonel Nicholson has done his endeavours to make a town of that place. There are about forty dwelling-houses in it, seven or eight of which can afford a good lodging and accommodations for strangers. There are also a state-house and a free-school, built of brick, which make a great show among a parcel of wooden houses; and the foundation of a church is laid, the only brick church in Maryland. They have two market-days in a week, and had governor Nicholson continued there a few months longer, he had brought it to perfection.'

A later account of it, represents it as in nearly the same condition during governor Seymour's administration in 1708. It yet wanted the rank and privileges of a city until this year; and it received these just as they were departing from the ancient city of St. Mary's. That place, once so venerable in the eyes of the colonists, and yet memorable in its connexion, 'with the foundation of a free and happy State, after ceasing to be the capital, did not long retain its rank. It lost its privilege of sending delegates in 1708. One by one, all its relics have disappeared, and in the very State to which it gave birth, and the land it redeemed from the wilderness, it now stands a solitary spot,' dedicated to heaven, and a fit memento of all perishable things.

Annapolis, its successor, received its charter on the 16th day of August, 1708, which was granted by the honourable John Seymour, then the royal governor of the province. 'It appears to have been one of his favourite designs, and was proposed by him to the assembly, as early as 1704. No measures being adopted by the latter to carry his wishes into effect, he at length conferred the charter by virtue of the prerogative of his office. Under this charter, besides the powers and privileges relative to the organization and exercise of its municipal government, *the city of Annapolis* obtained the privilege of electing two delegates to the general assembly,' and which she has ever since enjoyed—until the adoption of the new constitution of the State, by the general assembly at its December session in 1836. Under it, she is entitled to but one representative, and that privilege will cease after the promulgation of the census of the year 1840, when she will be deemed and taken as a part of Anne Arundel county, in all future elections for the delegates to the general assembly.

The same act declares that the city of Annapolis shall continue to be the seat of government, and the place of holding the sessions of the court of appeals for the western shore, and the high court of chancery. It is also made the residence of the governor by an act of the legislature in 1837.

From the period of the grant of its charter by governor Seymour, Annapolis was continually on the advance. 'It never acquired a large population, nor any great degree of commercial consequence; but long before the American revolution, it was conspicuous as the seat of wealth and fashion; the luxurious habits, elegant accomplishments and profuse hospitality of its inhabitants, were proverbially known throughout the colonies. It was the seat of a wealthy government, and of its principal institutions; and as such, congregated around it many, whose liberal attainments eminently qualified them for society.'

A French writer in speaking of this city as he found it during the American revolution, thus describes it: 'in that very inconsiderable town, standing at the mouth of the Severn, where it falls into the bay, of the few buildings it contains, at least three-fourths may be styled elegant and grand. Female luxury here exceeds what is known in the provinces of France. A French hair dresser is a man of importance amongst them; and it is said, a certain dame here hires one of that craft at one thousand crowns a year. The statehouse is a very beautiful building, I think the most so of any I have seen in America.'

This forms a striking contrast to the account given of it at a much earlier date, and which is to be found in a satire, called 'the Sot-weed Factor, or a Voyage to Maryland; in which is described the laws, government, courts, and constitutions of the country; and also the buildings, feasts, frolics, entertainments, and drunken humours of the inhabitants of that part of America.' In burlesque verse, by Eden Cook, gent., published at London in 1708.

Annapolis is thus mentioned in one part of this curious work:

'To try the cause, then fully bent,
Up to Annapolis I went;
A city situate on a plain,
Where scarce a house will keep out rain;
The buildings framed with cypress rare,
Resemble much our Southwick fair;
But strangers there will scarcely meet
With market place, exchange or street;
And, if the truth I may report,
It's not so large as Tottenham court,—
St. Mary's once was in repute,
Now here the judges try the suit;
And lawyers twice a year dispute—
As oft the bench most gravely meet,
Some to get drunk, and some to eat
A swinging share of country treat;
But as for justice, right or wrong,
Not one amongst the numerous throng,
Knows what it means, or has the heart
To vindicate a stranger's part.'

This poem, with another upon Bacon's Rebellion in Virginia, were re-printed at Annapolis, in 1731; but Mr. Green, by whom it was printed, reminds the reader that it was a description written twenty years before, which did not agree with the condition of Annapolis at the time of its publication. Both of these poems are still in the possession of Mr. Jonas Green, of this city.

By the act granting delegates to Annapolis, it is provided that they be allowed and receive only '*half wages*,' as was allowed to the delegates from the several counties. The reason alleged is—that the burgesses of the several boroughs in England were only allowed half wages, in respect to the salary of the knights of the shires.

Wornell Hunt, Esquire, was appointed and continued the recorder of the city, under the new charter—he having acted as such under the old city regime.

1718. In 1718, commissioners were appointed to survey and lay out ten acres of the public pasture, lying on the north side of the city, and to the 'eastward of the hill, known as the powder-house hill'—into twenty half acre lots, for the enlargement and improvement of the town, and for the 'better encouragement of the poor tradesmen to dwell in the town, and carry on their respective trades.'

These lots were to be taken up by any person who would build a dwelling-house on the same—except persons owning lots within the city—who were prohibited from taking any of them up, until two years had expired.

This addition to the town, was called 'New Town.' The hill mentioned above, still retains the name of 'Powder-house hill,' although no vestage of the house remains.

The ferry-landing then, was within the mouth of the creek, and laid to the west of the pond, known as the Swimming pond.

The general assembly in this year, appointed James Stoddart, Esquire, to survey and lay off anew the city of Annapolis;* the original plat of the town which had been made by Mr. Richard Beard, having

* Mr. Stoddart in his survey, lays out the town as containing 'six million two hundred and twenty-seven thousand three hundred and eighty-four square feet more or less, which makes one hundred and forty-two acres, and one hundred and fifty-three square perches, and two hundred nine and three quarter square feet.' And the public circle about the state-house to be in 'diameter, 528 feet—and the circumference 1159 feet; and contains within it two hundred and eighteen thousand nine hundred and eighty-eight square feet more or less.' And the church circle, in 'diameter to be 346 feet, and the circumference 1087 feet—containing ninety-four thousand twenty-five and a half square feet more or less.'

10*

been destroyed at the burning of the state-house in 1704.

1720. In 1720 a grant of one hundred and twenty feet of ground for a *'sawyer's yard,'* was made to a Mr. Edward Smith.

1727. In this year (1727) Mr. William Parks of this city, was appointed to print a compilation of the laws of the province; there had been no printer it seems until the assembly passed an act this year for his encouragement. This collection of the laws of Maryland is now nearly out of print—but few copies remaining—and is held by the few that own a copy of it, as a rare and curious body of laws as passed by our early legislators.

1728. In 1728, Henry Ridgely, Mordecai Hammond, and John Welsch, or any two of them, were appointed by an act of assembly, and empowered to survey, lay out and mark, 'sixty feet in breadth on the water, three hundred and sixty feet in length, and twenty-five feet at the head of the land formerly allotted to build a custom-house on, and which was to be vested in fee simple in the corporation of Annapolis—provided a market-house was built thereon, within two years after such survey.'

This land thus ordered to be laid off, is the public square at the head of the dock, and is still held by the corporate authorities of our city.

1733. In this year (1733) the sum of £3000 was appropriated for purchasing convenient ground in the city, for the use of the public, and for building a government-house, designed for the governor's residence.

1736. In 1736, 'Charles Hammond, Philip Hammond, Vachel Denton, Daniel Dulany, Esquires, and Richard Warfield,' were empowered to purchase a piece of ground within the town, for a new public jail, to contract for the material, and employ workmen to complete it.

1740. In this year (1740) Mr. Jonas Green was appointed printer to the province, a situation he held to the time of his death, which occurred in March, 1768, being a period of twenty-eight years, that he enjoyed the patronage and confidence of the province; he was a man of ready wit, and great benevolence.

1745. On the 27th of January, 1745, he issued the first number of the 'Maryland Gazette,' and which he edited for twenty-one years. After his death, it was conducted by his widow, Mrs. Anne Catharine Green, aided by her son William; and has ever since been published, down to the present time, by some one of his descendants. Its late editor, Mr. Jonas Green,* is the grand-son of the first editor. The Gazette was the oldest newspaper† published in the United States, and is invaluable as a chronicle of the olden times, for the great amount of interesting matter contained in its files. The passing events of importance, civil, political, religious, in Europe and America, appear to have been faithfully recorded in it.

The first public horse-racing at or near Annapolis,

---

* It is a fact worthy of notice, that the late editor has an unbroken series of this valuable paper, from its first issue, down to the present period, (1839.)

† The Gazette ceased to be published in the latter part of 1839.

is advertised in the Maryland Gazette, 'to take place on the 30th and 31st days of May, 1745—to be run at John Conners,* in Anne Arundel county. The first day's purse £10—the second £5—to be run for by any horse, mare or gelding, ('*Old Ranter*' and 'Limber-Sides' excepted,) to carry 115 pounds, *three heats*, the course two miles, entrance money fifteen shillings the first day, and ten shillings the second day.'

How this race came off, we are not informed. From the exclusion of 'Old Ranter' and 'Limber-Sides,' we may infer that they were somewhat celebrated in their day. Can any of our racers trace the pedigree of their horses to those old sires of the Maryland turf?

1746. The same paper states, that on the first of March, of this year—'from 10 'till near 12 o'clock, P. M., we had a remarkable appearance of the *aurora borealis*, or northern twilight. It extended a full quarter of the compass, and in some places resembled a red hot oven. The coruscations or streams of light, which were numerous, and continually changing shape and situation, reached near fifty degrees towards the zenith.'

The two following extracts are taken from the Gazette:

'March 24th, 1746. The exit of the rebellion was celebrated here by firing off guns, drinking loyal healths, and other demonstrations of joy. There was a ball in the evening—the whole city was illuminated, and a great quantity of punch given amongst the populace at the bond-fire.'

---

* He kept a public house about seven miles from London Town, towards West river—most probably at the place so well known as 'Redmiles's Tavern.'

'July 15. The gentlemen belonging to the '*Ancient South River Club*,' to express their loyalty to his majesty, on the success of the inimitable Duke of Cumberland's obtaining a complete victory over the pretender, and delivering us from persecution at home, and popery and invasion from abroad, have appointed a grand entertainment to be given at their club-house, on Thursday next.'

This extract is made out of respect to that very respectable and ancient club, which is still in existence, and is in all probability the oldest club in the United States of America. The worthy descendants of the *old clubbers*, still meet on their appointed day, (*Thursday*) around the festive board, and drink to the memory of by-gone days.

Three companies raised in this province by captains Campbell, Crofts, and Jordan, sailed from Annapolis, to join other forces destined for the reduction of Canada. It is said, the men 'embarked with cheerful hearts and in high spirits, all well clothed and accoutred.'

The editor, (Mr. Green,) from whose paper many extracts have been and will be made—says, 'October 29th, (Thursday) being the anniversary of the birth of his most sacred majesty, our only rightful sovereign king, George the Second, (whom God long preserve) when his majesty completed his 63rd (a grand climacterical) year, the same was observed here with firing of cannon, drinking loyal healths,' &c., and in his paper of the 11th of November—says, 'Wednesday last, being the fifth of November, that never to be forgotten day of thanksgiving—the reverend Mr. *Whitefield* preached here a very good sermon suitable

to the occasion, from these words in Prov. xiv. 28:
'Righteousness exalteth a nation.' Just as divine service ended, and the congregation were coming out of the church, the ornament on the back of the speaker's pew, gave way, and fell forward on several of the gentlemen of the assembly, which hurt two of them very much, but they are happily now recovered.'

At this period and for many years later, Annapolis had considerable trade and commerce, the arrival and clearances of ships and other sea vessels were frequent and numerous; there were all kinds of mechanics and artificers residing in the place; and from the number and character of the advertisements—many merchants of capital and enterprize abode here.

It was no unusual thing to see from ten to twenty ships and other vessels leaving the harbour, bound for Europe and coastwise; and the port was frequently visited by the king's ships of war.

1747. In 1747, a ship arrived here with rebels, who were termed the 'king's passengers'—and who were said to have been 'favoured with transportation.'

During this year a large ship belonging to Mr. Williams Roberts, of this place, was launched here, called the '*Rumney and Long*,' after the names of the builders. The first ship-yard in Annapolis, that we learn of, was established about this period, and located a few feet below the stone bridge, leading to the grave-yard, the creek then, made up beyond the present jail. The name of this creek is now lost; the water has receded since that time, nearly a quarter of a mile below where the ship-yard was then situated.

This Mr. Roberts built and occupied the house in which colonel Henry Maynadier now resides. He had a blacksmiths shop to the north of his dwelling, on which was a steeple, and in which hung the only bell then in the city, and by which the time of the inhabitants was regulated, until the large bell—now in St. Anne's church—was received. Below this shop his sailmakers and other shops necessary for carrying on ship building were erected. A Mr. Kirkwell and Blackwell, ship builders, were also in his employment.

Tradition tells us, that they built the 'brig Lovely Nancy'—at the launch of which the following incident occurred. She was on the stocks, and the day appointed to place her on her destined element, a large concourse of persons assembled to witness the launch, among whom was an old white woman named Sarah McDaniel, who professed fortune-telling, and was called 'a *witch.*' She was heard to remark—'the Lovely Nancy will not see water to-day.' The brig moved finely at first, and when expectation was at its height to see her glide into the water, she suddenly stopped, and could not be again moved on that day. This occurrence created much excitement amongst the spectators; and captain Slade and the sailors were so fully persuaded that she had been '*bewitched*,' that they resolved to duck the old woman. In the meantime she had disappeared from the crowd; they kept up the search for two or three days, during which time she lay concealed in a house that stood on the lot opposite to the present dwelling of Robert Welch, of Ben. Esquire. The 'Lovely Nancy,' did afterwards leave the stocks, and is said to have made several prosperous voyages.

There was at a later period, another ship-yard on the south-west side of the city, at the termination of Charles street, where the 'Matilda,' and the 'Lady

Lee' were launched—the first was owned by Samuel Chase, Esquire, and the latter by governor Lee.

There was a merchant at this period residing on the banks of the Severn, below Mr. Selby's present dwelling—named Woolstenholm, he had a long range of warehouses, no vestige of which now remains. A wooden platform supported by posts constituted his wharf.

A large blockmaker's establishment stood where Mr. Goodman's store and dwelling now is. There were several large frame buildings on each side of Hanover street, as also opposite to the present ball-room. These were said to have belonged to the neutral French, and was occupied by them during the war between the French and English colonies; they were also used as hospitals during our revolution—soon after that period they were pulled down in consequence of their dilapidated condition.

On the site of Mrs. Bowie's residence, in Church street, formerly stood the 'Three Blue Ball' tavern, which was kept by a Mr. John Ball. This was then the property of Mr. Stephen West, who remitted bills in his own name, called 'Stephen West's money.' Mr. West resided at the wood-yard in Prince George's county, and owned considerable property in this city. This property was purchased by colonel Thomas Hyde, who added the present corner building, and also built the houses in which Doctor Dennis Claude and Mr. George Mackubins now reside. The house of Doctor Claude was formerly the 'Annapolis coffee-house.'

The building occupied by Mrs. Anne Harwood, in Charles street, is said to be the most ancient house now standing in the city. It was used as the printing office of the 'Maryland Gazette,' at its establishment. The house in which the cashier of the Farmers' Bank of Maryland resides, was formerly a tavern, and kept by a Mr. William Reynolds. The small brick house on Doctor's street, now used as the office of the Annapolis and Elkrige Railroad Company, was a stocking manufactory, and conducted by John Bail and Benjamin Beall; it was regarded as a great curiosity, but did not succeed.

West street, then called *Cowpen lane*, had at this period but three houses built on it. The most considerable one was a tavern kept by a Mrs. McCloud; it was afterwards used for a circulating library—the projector and proprietor of which was a Mr. William Rind. It subsequently came into the possession of Mr. Allen Quynn. Not many years since it was purchased by the late Mr. Thomas Harris, and by him modified and improved, and is now an elegant residence, and owned and occupied by John Johnson, Esquire. The house in which Mr. McParlin lives, and that known as 'Hunter's Tavern,' were both erected about this time. The next house built on that street was the Hallam Theatre.

The old market-house stood just below the present gun-house, and was about half the size of the present one. This was the first regular market-house built in Annapolis, and was erected after the year 1717, as will appear by the following extracts from the MS. proceedings of the corporation.

In 1716, the corporation took into consideration 'whether a market-house was requisite or not, and resolved, *nemine contradicente*, that it is very requisite,' and determined it should be built on or near the state-house hill.

In 1717, they resolved that 'none of the inhabitants of this city shall buy any fflesh or ffish, living or dead, eggs, butter, or cheese, (oysters excepted) at their own houses, but shall repair to and buy the same at the *fflagg staffe*, on the state-house hill, untill such a time as there shall be a market-house built—on penalty of 16s. 8d. current money, &c. And that the market be opened at 8 or 9 o'clock in the forenoon, and that the drum beats half quarter of an hour to give notice thereof, and that no person presumes to buy any thing untill the drum be done beating, and that the market days be on Wednesday and Saturday every week.'

There was a large range of buildings near the post-office, called 'Calvert's row'—they were used by Mr. Peale as exhibition rooms, within the recollection of some of the present inhabitants of this place; and in the only remaining one of which, Mr. Jonas Green now resides. The building now owned and occupied by Mrs. Lloyd, was built by governor Ogle, as a family residence; additions and improvements were made to it by his son.

The house formerly occupied by Charles Carroll, of Carrollton, Esquire, is of a more modern date; it was built for a family residence. An upper room of this house was used as a catholic chapel during Mr. Carroll's residence there, and until the present chapel was built. There was for some time a resident priest in the family, but not for a few years previous to Mr. Carroll's removal from this city.

Coeval with these, was the old church, which stood on the site of the present Episcopal church, it was built of brick, and was the only one in the place. It was originally built in the form of the letter T,—neatly finished inside. The principal entrance was towards the east. It was in a ruinous condition previous to the revolution. Its minister often remonstrated with his congregation, and urged them to repair or rebuild it, but did not succeed until the following poem appeared in the Maryland Gazette, descriptive of the old church, pleading its own cause:

'To the very worthy and respectable inhabitants of Annapolis, the humble petition of their old church, sheweth,

> 'That, late in century the last,
> By private bounty, here were placed,
> My sacred walls, and tho', in truth,
> Their stile and manner be uncouth;
> Yet, whilst no structure met mine eye,
> That even with myself could vie,
> A goodly edifice I seemed,
> And pride of all *Saint Anne's* was deemed.
> How changed the times! for now, all round,
> Unnumbered stately piles abound,
> All better built, and looking down
> On me quite antequated grown.
> Left unrepaired, to time a prey,
> I feel my vitals fast decay;
> And often have I heard it said,
> That some good people are afraid,
> Least I should tumble on their head.
> Of which, indeed, this seems a proof—
> They seldom come beneath my roof.
> The stadt-house, that, for public good,
> With me co-eval long had stood;
> With me full many a storm had dared,
> Is now at length to be repaired:
> Or, rather, to be built anew,
> An honour to the land and you.
> Whilst I, alone, not worth your care,
> Am left your sad neglect to bear.

With grief, in yonder field, hard by,
A sister-ruin I espy;
Old *Bladen's* palace, once so famed,
And now too well, the *folly* named.
Her roof all tottering to decay,
Her walls a mouldering all away;
She says, or seems to say, to me,
'Such too, ere long, thy fate shall be.'
Tho', now forever gone and lost,
I blush to say, how little cost,
The handsome pile would have preserved,
Till some new prefect had deserved
A mansion here, from us, to have
As good as *Carolina* gave.
But party, faction (friends that still
Have been the foes of public weal)
The dogs of war against her slipped,
And all her rising honours nipped,
Of sunshine oft a casual ray,
Breaks in upon a cloudy day,
O'erwhelm'd with woe; methinks, I see
A ray of hope thus dart on me.
Close at my door, on my own land,
Placed there, it seems, by your command,
I've seen, I own, with some surprise,
A novel structure sudden rise.
There let the stranger stay, for me,
If virtue's friend, indeed she be.
I would not, if I could, restrain,
A moral stage; yet, would I fain
Of your indulgence and esteem,
At least, an equal portion claim.
And, decency, without my prayers,
Will surely whisper in your ears,
'To pleasure, if such care you shew,
A mite to duty, pray bestow.'
Say, does my rival boast the art
One solid comfort to impart,
Or heal, like me, the broken heart?
Does she, like me, pour forth the strain
Of peace on earth, good will to men?
Merit she has; but, let me say,
The highest merit of a play,

Tho', *Shakespeare* wrote it, but to name
With mine, were want of sense or shame.
Why should I point to distant times,
To kindred and congenial climes,
Where, spite of many a host of foes,
To God a mighty temple rose?
Why point to every land beside
Whose honest aim it is, a pride,
However poor it be, yet still,
At least, to make God's house genteel?
Here, in *Annapolis* alone,
God has the meanest house in town.
The premises considered, I
With humble confidence rely,
That, Phenix-like, I soon shall rise,
From my own ashes to the skies;
Your mite, at least, that you will pay,
And your petitioner shall pray.'

The publication of this poem, had a better effect than all the minister's previous expostulations, and his congregation at last resolved to put up a new building. Accordingly, the old church was razed to the ground, but the erection of a new one was prevented for a time, by the revolution which soon after took place. The theatre was used as church and forum, until the erection of the present church.

A palisade and white railing enclosed the old churchyard, which was at that time the city grave-yard.

The last Indian tribe which was known to frequent Annapolis, is said to have lived on the Potomac. This tribe, the name of which is now lost even in tradition, (sometimes more enduring than musty records)—exchanged their lands with the Calvert family for lands in Baltimore county, where game was more plenty; and, as the white population increased, they retired to the Susquehanna.

11*

The Eastern Shore tribes visited Annapolis occasionally, previous to the revolution; and the visits of old King Abraham and his Queen Sarah are still recollected by some few of the inhabitants of our town.

At a county court held here on Tuesday, the 9th of July of this year, a 'Mrs. S. C. of *Patapsco*, was fined the sum of one penny, for whipping the R——d Mr. N——l W——r with a *hiccory* switch; it being imagined by the court that he well deserved it.'

About this period, a jockey-club was instituted here, 'consisting of many principal gentlemen in this, and in the adjacent provinces, many of whom in order to encourage the breed of this noble animal, imported from England, at a very great expense, horses of high reputation.' This club existed for many years. 'The races at Annapolis were generally attended by a great concourse of spectators, many coming from the adjoining colonies. Considerable sums were bet on these occasions. Subscription purses of a hundred guineas were for a long time the highest amount run for, but subsequently were greatly increased. The day of the races usually closed with balls, or theatrical amusements.' The race course at this time and for many years after, was located on that part of the city just beyond Mr. Severe's blacksmith shop, embracing a circle of one mile, taking in all that portion of the town now built up.

On the 29th of September, in this year, a race was run on this course between governor Ogle's *Bay Gelding*, and col. Plater's *Grey Stallion*, and won by the former—the next day six horses started, Mr. Waters' *horse Parrott*, winning, distancing several of the runing horses. On the same ground some years after, Dr. Hamilton's '*horse Figure,*' won a purse of fifty pistoles—beating two, and distancing three others. '*Figure*' was a horse of great reputation—it is stated of him that, 'he had won many *fifties*—and in the year 1763, to have received premiums at *Preston* and *Carlisle,* in *Old England,* where no horse would enter against him—he never lost a race.' Subsequently, the race course was removed to a field some short distance beyond the city, on which course some of the most celebrated horses ever known in America have run. It was on this latter course that Mr. Bevans' bay horse '*Oscar,*' so renowned in the annals of the turf, first ran. Oscar was bred on Mr. Ogle's farm near this city—he won many races, and in the fall of 1808, it is well remembered, he beat Mr. Bond's '*First Consul*' on the Baltimore course, who had challenged the continent—running the second heat in 7 m. 40 s., which speed had never been excelled.

'*Old Ranter*' was '*Oscar's*' great, great, grand sire.

1752. In the Maryland Gazette of the 18th June, 1752, appeared the following advertisement:

'By permission of his honour the president,* at the *new theatre,* in *Annapolis,* by the company of commedians *from Virginia,* on Monday next, being the 22d of this instant, (*June*) will be performed, 'The Beggars Opera:' likewise, a farce, called the 'Lying Valet'—to begin precisely at 7 o'clock. Tickets to be had at the printing office. Box 10*s.*, pit 7*s.* 6*d.* No persons to be admitted behind the scenes.'

---

* Benjamin Tasker, Esquire, was then the president or governor of the province.

The principal performers belonging to this company, appear to have been Messrs. Wynell, Herbert, Eyanson, Kean, and Miss Osborne—they performed while here, 'The Busy Body,' 'Beaux Stratagem,' 'Recruiting Officer,' 'London Merchant,' 'Cato,' 'Richard III,' with many others. After leaving Annapolis, they performed at 'Upper Marlborough,' 'Piscattaway,' on the Western Shore, and at 'Chester Town,' in Kent county, on the Eastern Shore of Maryland.

During the time they performed here, a Mr. Richard Bricknell and company, exhibited some *curious* wax-figures, representing the 'Queen of Hungary sitting on her throne, and the Duke, her son,' and courtiers in attendance.

1753. The first lottery drawn in this province, was at Annapolis, on the 21st September, 1753, for the purchase of a 'town clock, and clearing the dock.' The highest prize 100 pistoles—tickets half a pistole. The managers were Benj. Tasker, junior, George Stewart, Walter Dulany, and ten other gentlemen of this place.

On the 11th of August, of this year, Horatio Sharpe, Esq., governor of the province, arrived here, in the ship Molly, captain Nicholas Coxen, from London.

In September, (1753) several companies under the command of captain Dagworthy, lieutenants Forty, and Bacon, marched from Annapolis against the French on the Ohio.

1755. On the 3d of April, 1755, general Braddock, governor Dinwiddie and commodore Keppel arrived here, on their way to Virginia. And on the 11th and 12th of the same month, arrived governor Sherley, of Boston, governor De Lancy, of New York, and governor Morris, of Philadelphia, with a number of distinguished gentlemen—they left here accompanied by governor Sharpe, for Alexandria, and on the 17th they returned to Annapolis on their way to their respective governments. A few days after, governor Sharpe set out for Frederick Town.

This period, which just preceded the defeat of general Braddock, near Fort Du Quesne, appears to have been a busy time with their excellencies.

On the 29th of September, of this year, doctor Charles Carroll departed this life, aged sixty-four years—he had resided in Annapolis about forty years. For some years after his coming to this city, he 'practised physic with good success; but laying that aside, he commenced trade and merchandise, by which he amassed a very considerable fortune.' In 1737, he was chosen a member to the lower house of assembly, in which station he is said to have spared no pains or application to render himself serviceable to the county, and his constituents, to the time of his death. He is represented to have been 'a gentleman of good sense and breeding, courteous and affable,' and was held in high esteem by his fellow-citizens. Dr. Carroll owned all of the ground on the lower part of Church street, on the south side, extending back to the Duke of Gloster street; and in 1749 opened *Green street*,—advertising to sell or lease lots on either side of the same.

Mr. Green says in his Gazette of the 6th of Nov., of this year, 'we are now about entrenching the town. If the gentlemen in the neighbourhood of Annapolis, were to send their forces to assist in it, a few days would complete the work.'

This measure it would seem, was taken by the citizens, in consequence of the 'dreadful murders and massacres' committed by the French and Indians upon the border country, and serious apprehensions were entertained by the inhabitants, that Annapolis would fall into the hands of their 'politic, cruel and cunning enemies.' It was asserted by a writer for the Gazette, that the Indians 'were but a little way from the city, and that so entire was their defenceless situation, that even a small party of twenty or thirty Indians, by marching in the night and skulking in the day time, might come upon them unawares in the dead of night, burn their houses, and cut their throats, before they could put themselves in a posture of defence.' Other writers of the day, seemed to think that there was no more danger of 'Annapolis being attacked by the Indians, than London.' The fears of the inhabitants were soon quieted, by the return of several gentlemen who had gone as volunteers to the westward, and who reported they had seen no Indians, except one, and he was '*very quiet,*' for they found him *dead.*

1757. On the 29th of March, of this year, (1757) governor Sharpe arrived here from the northward, accompanied by governor Dobbs, of North Carolina, and governor Dinwiddie, of Virginia.

In this year, the small-pox made its appearance in Annapolis, and continued to afflict and alarm the inhabitants for nine months. Scarcely one of them escaped the disease. Of about one hundred persons who were inoculated, not one died, while those who had it in the natural way, at least one in every six died. On this occasion the physicians of the town inoculated every person who desired it, without fee or reward.

In consequence of the disease being here, the general assembly was prorogued to meet in Baltimore, where it held its sesion for this year.

In the winter of this year, (1757,) five companies of *Royal Americans*, were quartered upon the town.

CHAPTER V.

Forts on the Border Country—Fort Frederick—Reduction of Quebec—A Company of Comedians at Annapolis—Stone Wind-mill erected—Collection for the sufferers by fire at Boston—Ball-room—Cold winter—Stamp Act—Proceeding at Annapolis on—Maryland Gazette—Sons of Liberty—Repeal of the Stamp Act—A new Theatre opened—Gov. Eden arrives at Annapolis—His character—Death and burial—Articles of Non-importation, &c.—Arrival of Brig Good Intent—Resolute course pursued by the Association—Its results—Mr. Wm. Eddis—Annapolis described—Whitehall—Governor Sharpe—His character—Appropriation to build the present State-House—Commissioners appointed—The Foundation laid—Incident—Dimensions of the building—The Architect—Anniversary of the Proprietary's birth—Rejoicings at Annapolis—Ladies of Annapolis—Saint Tamina Society—Their Proceedings—Theatre opened—Trustees appointed by the Legislature, to the Theatre—Theatre pulled down—Causes which led to it—Mr. Dunlap—Trustees appointed to build a new Church—Meeting of the Citizens of Annapolis—Their proceedings on the Act of Parliament for blockading the Harbour of Boston—Some portion of their Resolves dissented from by many Citizens—Proceedings of the Dissentients—Burning of the Brig Peggy Stewart—And the tea on board—The Proceedings had thereon.

BELIEVING the following statement of distances between the several forts which were erected for the defence of the border country, will be interesting to many, it is here subjoined.

'Fort *Frederick* and Fort *Cumberland* stood on the north bank of Potomac river, about fifty miles distant from each other, the first twelve miles beyond Conococheague, the then most western settlement. *Fort Loudoun* was about twenty-five miles north from Fort Frederick; *Rays Town* fifty-three miles west from Fort Loudoun, and thirty-five miles northward from Fort Cumberland; the distance from Rays Town to the *Loylhanning*, is said to have been fifty-eight miles, and thence to *Fort Du Quesne*, was computed to be about thirty-five miles.'

Fort Frederick being 'the only monument of the ante-revolutionary times,' now remaining in the western parts of our State, deserves to have handed down to posterity all that can be now collected relative to its origin and present ruins. It is stated by Mr. McMahon, in his history of Maryland, to have been situated on an elevated and rather commanding position in the plains along the Potomac, distant about one-fourth of a mile from that river, and about ten or eleven miles above the mouth of Conococheague creek. It was constructed of the most durable materials, and in the most approved manner, at an expense of upwards of £6000. When Mr. McMahon saw its ruins in 1828, the greater part of it was still standing, and in a high state of preservation, in the midst of cultivated fields. According to a description given of it at its construction, its exterior lines were each one hundred and twenty yards in length, (the fort being quadrangular,) its curtains and bastions were faced by a thick stone wall, and it contained barracks sufficient for the accommodation of several hundred men. This garrison was built under the personal supervision of governor Sharpe, and by a plan of his own; he appears to have taken great interest in its construction. Its first commander was captain Dagworthy, who on being removed to the command of Fort Cumberland, was succeeded by captain Alexander Beall, who continued in the command of this fort until after the capture of Fort Du Quesne, and the close of the border troubles.

Governor Sharpe, in a letter to Mr. Calvert, dated Annapolis, the 21st of August, 1756, speaking of Fort Frederick, says—'I thought proper to build Fort Frederick of stone, which step I believe even our assembly will now approve of, though I hear some of them sometime since, intimated to their constituents that a stoccado would have been sufficient, and that to build a fort with stone would put the country to a great and unnecessary expense; but whatever their sentiments may be with respect to that matter, I am convinced that I have done for the best, and that my conduct therein will be approved of by any soldier, and by every impartial person. The fort is not finished, but the garrison are well covered, and will, with a little assistance, complete it at their leisure. Our barracks are made for the reception and accommodation of 200 men, but on occasion there will be room for twice that number. It is situated on the North Mountain, near Potomack river, about fourteen miles beyond Conegochiegh, and four on this side Licking-creek. I have made a purchase in the governor's name for the use of the country, of one hundred and fifty acres of land that is contiguous to it, which will be of great service to the garrison, and as well as the fort, be found of great use in case of future expeditions to the westward, for it is so situated that Potomack will be always navigable thence almost to Fort Cumberland, the flats or shallows of that river lying between Fort Frederick and Conegochiegh.'

The general assembly of Maryland in 1790, appointed an agent to sell and convey the right of this State to one hundred acres of land at Fort Frederick, in Washington county.—(See resolution No. 4.)

1759. On the 30th of October, in this year, there was great rejoicing here, in consequence of the reduction of Quebec, by the troops under general Wolfe. The guns at the 'Point Battery' were fired early in the day. The military paraded through the streets, and at 12 o'clock, the cannon from the 'Half-moon Battery' were discharged. 'At night the city was illuminated, and the governor gave a public ball in the council chamber, at which there was a brilliant assemblage of ladies.'

1760. Mr. Green, in his Gazette of the 7th February, in this year, says—'by permission of his excellency, the governor, a theatre is erecting in this city, which will be opened soon by a company of comedians, who are now at Chester Town.'

The company here alluded to, arrived at Annapolis on the 3d of March, and on the same evening opened the theatre. They continued to perform here until the 12th of May following, as will be seen by the annexed list of performances, which is given for the amusement of the curious in these matters, as well as for the gratification of the lovers of the drama.

	Plays.	Farces.
March 3.	Orphans,	Lethe, or Esop in the Shades.
6.	Recruiting Officer,	Miss in her Teens.
8.	Venice Preserved,	Mock-Doctor.
10.	Richard III.	King and the Miller.
13.	Provoked Husband,	Stage Coach.

	Plays.	Farces.
Mar. 15.	Fair Penitent,	Anatomist.
20.	Stratagem,	Lethe.
22.	George Barnwell,	Lying Valet.
24.	Busy-Body,	Mock-Doctor.
27.	Revenge,	Lying Valet.
29.	Bold Stroke for a Wife,	Damon and Phillida.
	(In Passion-week the theatre was closed.)	
April 7.	*Romeo and Juliet,	Stage Coach.
8.	Provoked Husband,	Honest Yorkshireman.
9.	Othello,	Devil to Pay.
10.	Constant Couple,	King and the Miller.
11.	†Romeo and Juliet,	Miss in her Teens.
12.	Suspicious Husband,	Mock-Doctor.
14.	Richard III. *(Ben. of Mr. Douglass,)* Hob.	
15.	Fair Penitent, *(Mr. Palmer,)*	Lying Valet.
16.	Venice Preserved, *(Mr. Murray,)* Devil to Pay.	
17.	Provoked Husband, *(Mrs. Douglass,)* Yorkshireman.	
19.	Revenge, *(Mr. Hallam,)*	Lethe.
22.	Stratagem, *(Mrs. and Miss Dowthaitt,)* Lying Valet.	
23.	Orphan, *(Miss Crane and Comp,)* Lethe.	
24.	Constant Couple, *(Mr. Morris,)*	Yorkshireman.
May 5.	Douglass, *(Master A. Hallam,)*	Virgin Unmasked.
8.	Jew of *Venice*, *(Mrs. Morris,)*	Lethe.
12.	Gamester, *(Mr. Scott,)*	Toy Shop.

From this place the company went to 'Upper Marlbro,' and performed there for several weeks.

In September of this year, the *stone wind-mill* was built, on the point where Fort Severn now stands, and was then 'reckoned to be one of the best built mills in the country'—it is said to have 'ground twelve bushels in an hour.' The owner of the mill was a Mr. James Disney. It was destroyed when Fort Severn was built.

1761. In 1761, there was collected in this city and province for the sufferers by the great fire at

---

* '*Romeo*, by a young gentleman, for his diversion.'

† 'With the funeral procession of *Juliet*, to the monument of the Capuletts.'

Boston in *March* of this year, the sum of $5940 62, a collection that speaks well of the liberal and humane disposition of the 'ancient city and province.'

1764. In 1764, the present 'ball-room' was built from the proceeds of a lottery drawn here for that especial purpose.

1765. The winter of this year was one of uncommon severity. The editor of the Gazette says, 'on Monday, the 5th of February, a very merry set of gentlemen had a commodious tent erected on the ice between the town and Greensbury's point, where they had an elegant dinner, &c. &c., and in the afternoon diverted themselves with dancing of reels, on skates, and divers other amusements.'

STAMP ACT.

On the 27th of August, in this year, 'a considerable number of people, '*Assertors of British American privileges,*' met at Annapolis to show their 'detestation of, and abhorrence to, some late tremendous attacks on liberty, and their dislike to a certain late arrived officer, *a native of this province!* They curiously dressed up the figure of a man, which they placed in a one horse cart, malefactor like, with some sheets of paper in his hands before his face.'

'In that manner they paraded through the streets of the town, till noon, the bell at the same time tolling a solemn knell, when they proceeded to the hill, and after giving it the MOSAIC LAW, at the whipping-post, placed it in the pillory, from whence they took it, and hung it on a gibbet there erected for that purpose, and set fire to a tar-barrel underneath, and burnt it till it fell into the barrel. By the many significant nods of the head, while in the cart, it may be said to have gone off very penitently.'

Such was the reception given to the famous stamp act, by the citizens of Annapolis, who have never been known to falter in the cause or defence of American rights and liberty. The stamp-master was a Mr. Hood, he imported a large quantity of goods and offered them at reduced prices, but such was the indignation of the people, that no one would purchase of him. He made his escape to the north, previous to the burning of his effigy, which is said to have resembled him wonderfully—and in his haste left behind him the materials for a suit of tar and feathers, with which the citizens were about to present him, for his zealous support of the stamp act.

The landing of this officer was successfully resisted at first by the citizens, who repaired in a body to the dock where the attempt was made; a scuffle ensued in which the only three citizens now known to have taken a prominent part in this resistance, were Mr. Charles Farris, Mr. Abraham Claude and Mr. Thomas McNier, the last of whom, had his thigh broken on the occasion. Although they prevented the landing of this officer at this time and place, yet he subsequently effected a landing clandestinely, and was rewarded for his perseverance, as above mentioned.

In the *MSS. Letter Book* of governor Sharpe, is found the following letter from him, to *the Earl of Halifax*, dated Annapolis, the 5th September, 1765, giving an account of the stamp-officer's reception and treatment by the citizens of Annapolis, to wit:

'My lord: I am sorry to have such a reason for troubling your lordship, but it is my duty to inform you, that the proceedings of a great number of the people in this province, since the person said to be appointed distributor of the stamps for Maryland arrived here, gives me too much room to apprehend they will endeavour to prevent the stamp act having its intended effect. Your lordship will, I presume, long before this can reach you, have received an account of the late riotous proceedings of the populace of Boston and other places in the northern colonies, on account of that new act of parliament, and will not therefore, I suppose, be surprised at receiving similar accounts from other parts of North America, nor at my telling your lordship that the inhabitants of this province, incited by their example or actuated by the same spirit, were not satisfied with expressing their indignation against their countryman, Mr. Hood, the distributor, by hanging or burning him in *effigie*, but having in the night of the second instant assembled to the number of three or four hundred, in or near this place, pulled down a house which he was repairing for the reception of a cargo of goods that he had it seems imported for sale. Being very uneasy and much terrified at the contemptuous treatment he had since his return from England, met with from his former acquaintance, and the violent proceedings of the populace, who really are not to be restrained on this occasion, without a military force.

'Mr. Hood intimated to me, that if I thought his resigning the office would reconcile his countrymen to him, and would advise him to take that step, he would even do so, but as I could not take upon myself to give him such advice, and both he and his relations doubted whether he could while the ferment continued, be safe in mine or any other house in the province, he has retired for a few weeks to New York. To what length people who have made such a beginning, may go to render the act of parliament ineffectual, I cannot tell, but am very apprehensive that if the *stamp't* paper was to arrive here and be landed at this time, it would not be in my power to preserve it from being burnt, as there is no place of security here wherein it might be lodged, and the militia is composed of such as are by no means proper to be appointed a guard over it, if therefore a vessel should soon arrive here with the stamp't paper, I shall caution the master against landing it, and advise him either to lye off at a distance from the shore, or return to the men-of-war stationed in Virginia, until the people shew a better disposition, or I have the satisfaction to receive from your lordship some instructions about it.'

Captain Brown, commander of his majesty's sloop Hawke, arrived at this port in December, 1765, with some of the stamped paper destined for this province. But no person authorized to receive and distribute it, being here, and the lower house of assembly and the people being still averse to its reception, it was never landed. Governor Sharpe returned three boxes containing the stamped paper, to England, by a merchant ship, the *Brandon,* captain McLachlan, in December, 1766.

A supplement to the Maryland Gazette appeared on the 31st of October, in deep mourning. The editor determined to suspend its publication, rather than submit to the 'intolerable and burthensome terms,' imposed on all newspapers by the stamp act, declaring in this supplement,

'The times are
Dreadfull,
Dismal,
Doleful,
Dolorous, and
Dollar-less.'

On the 10th of December, he issued 'an apparition of the *late* Maryland Gazette,' and resolved to re-establish his paper, 'under the firm belief that the odious stamp act would never be carried into operation.'

1766. In March, 1766, the '*Sons of Liberty*,' from Baltimore, Kent, and Anne Arundel counties, met at this place, and made a written application to the chief justice of the provincial court, the secretary and commissary-general, and judges of the land office, to open their respective offices, and to proceed as usual in the execution of their duties. This demand was complied with, and the stamp act virtually became null and void.

On the 5th of April, of this year, general joy was diffused throughout the city, by the arrival of an express, bringing information of the repeal of the stamp act, and the afternoon was spent by the citizens in congratulations and mirth, and 'all loyal and patriotic toasts were drank.'

The 11th of June following, was by appointment of the mayor, observed here, as a day of rejoicing and festivity, on account of the 'glorious news,' of the total repeal of the stamp act, and in the evening the city was brilliantly illuminated.

1769. On Saturday evening, the 18th of February, of this year, (1769,) the new theatre was again opened, by the American company of comedians, with the tragedy of Romeo and Juliet. The company then consisted of Messrs. Hallam, Jefferson, Verling, Wall, Darby, Morris, Parker, Godwin, Spencer, Malone, Page, Walker, Osborne, and Burdett, and Mrs. Jones, Walker, Osborne, Burdett, Malone, Parker, and Miss Hallam.

This company appear to have been held in high esteem by the citizens of Annapolis, for their performances, especially of the tragedy of Richard III.

On the 5th of June, in this year, Robert Eden, Esquire, with his lady and family, arrived here in the ship Lord Baltimore. On the ship's coming to anchor off the city, she fired seven guns, which were returned by an equal number, but on the governor's landing in the afternoon, he was met by all the members of the council then in town, and a great number of the citizens, under a discharge of all the cannon on the battery. And on Tuesday morning 'about ten o'clock, he went up to to the *council-house*, attended by his lordship's honourable council, where his commission was opened and published.'

Governor Eden succeeded governor Sharpe, immediately on his arrival, and continued to govern the affairs of the province until 1776, when he returned to England in consequence of the revolution, and the formation of the provisional government of Maryland, which was at this period established. Governor Eden is represented to have been a gentleman, 'easy of access, courteous to all, and fascinating by his accomplishments.'

When he had taken his departure, his property was confiscated. In 1784 he returned to Annapolis, to seek the restitution of his property. He died soon after his arrival, in the house now owned and occupied by Richard J. Jones, Esq. He was buried under the pulpit of the Episcopal church on the north side of Severn, within two or three miles of this place. This church was some years since burned down.

In the month of June, this year, (1769,) a numerous meeting of the citizens of Annapolis was held, 'called by the beating of the drum,' at which were many gentlemen from the several counties of the province, who with the citizens formed, and entered into 'articles of non-importation of British superfluities, and for promoting frugality, economy, and the use of American manufactures,' and passed the following resolution:

'*Resolved*, unanimously, that the said articles be most strictly adhered to, and preserved inviolate; and that each and every gentleman present at this meeting, will use his utmost endeavours to those laudable ends.'

Early in February following, the citizens of Annapolis had an opportunity afforded them, to test the sincerity of their patriotism, by the arrival of the '*brig Good Intent*,' in their harbour, with a cargo of British goods.

Immediately on her arrival, a meeting of the citizens was convened, and three gentlemen were appointed a committee to inquire into the matter, who reported 'that the goods were ordered and shipped contrary to the articles of their association, and ought not to be landed.' The brig was accordingly ordered and compelled to return to London, carrying back a cargo consisting of European goods, to the value of £10,000 sterling.

Thus did the association show their determination to 'adhere strictly' to their articles of non-importation, and proved themselves as independent of foreign luxuries, as they subsequently did of British dominion.

The committee of Annapolis and Anne Arundel, consisted on such occasions of Messrs. Thomas Sprigg, John Weems, B. T. B. Worthington and William Paca.

The resolute course pursued by the association, brought the merchants of the British markets to 'a determination not to ship in future, any goods to *Maryland*, but such as would be agreeable to the association.'

In October of 1769, Mr. William Eddis, (the surveyor of the customs at Annapolis,) writing home to his friends, describes Annapolis and its public buildings, thus:

'Annapolis is nearly encompassed by the river Severn, and with every advantage of situation, is built on a very irregular plan. The adjacent country presents a variety of beautiful prospects, agreeably diversified with well-settled plantations, lofty woods, and navigable waters.

'In our little metropolis, the public buildings do not impress the mind with any idea of magnificence, having been chiefly erected during the infancy of the colony, when convenience was the directing principle, without attention to the embellishment of art.

'The court-house, situated on an eminence at the back of the town, commands a variety of views highly interesting; the entrance of the Severn, the majestic Chesapeake, and the eastern shore of Maryland, being all united in one resplendent assemblage, vessels of various sizes and figures are continually floating before the eye; which, while they add to the beauty of the scene, excite ideas of the most pleasing nature.

'In the court-house, the representatives of the people

assemble, for the dispatch of provincial business. The courts of justice are also held here, and here likewise the public offices are established.

'This building has nothing in its appearance expressive of the great purposes to which it is appropriated, and by a strange neglect, is suffered to fall continually into decay, being, both without and within, an emblem of public poverty, and at the same time a severe reflection on the government of this country, which, it seems, is considerably richer than the generality of the American provinces.

'The council-chamber is a detached building, adjacent to the former, on a very humble scale. It contains one tolerable room, for the reception of the governor and council, who meet here during the sitting of the assembly, and whose concurrence is necessary in passing all laws.

'The governor's house is most beautifully situated, and when the necessary alterations are completed, it will be a regular, convenient, and elegant building. The garden is not extensive, but it is disposed to the utmost advantage; the centre walk is terminated by a small green mount, close to which the Severn approaches; this elevation commands an extensive view of the bay, and the adjacent country. The same objects appear to equal advantage from the saloon, and many apartments in the house, and perhaps I may be justified in asserting, that there are but few mansions in the most rich and cultivated parts of England, which are adorned with such splendid and romantic scenery.

'The buildings in Annapolis were formerly of small dimensions, and of an inelegant construction; but there are now several modern edifices which make a good appearance. There are few habitations without gardens, some of which are planted in a decent style, and are well stocked.

'At present the city has more the appearance of an agreeable village, than the metropolis of an opulent province, as it contains within its limits a number of small fields, which are intended for future erections. But in a few years, it will probably be one of the best built cities in America, as a spirit of improvement is predominant, and the situation is allowed to be equally healthy and pleasant with any on this side the Atlantic. Many of the principal families have chosen this place for their residence, and there are few towns of the same size, in any part of the British dominions, than can boast of a more polished society.'

Mr. Eddis describes the villas, at this period, in the vicinity of Annapolis, as being pleasant and beautiful, particularly that which belonged to governor Sharpe, about seven miles from this place, on the north side of Severn. It is a most delightful situation. The mansion-house is large and elegant. *Whitehall*, the name of this estate, is still in the possession of the descendants of the gentleman to whom governor Sharpe bequeathed it. Governor Sharpe resided in this city, and governed the province of Maryland for many years, with honour to himself and satisfaction to the people; and established a reputation which reflected the highest honour on his public capacity and private virtues.

In this year, (1769,) the general assembly appropriated the sum of £7,500 sterling, to be applied to the building of the present state-house. The building of which was superintended by Daniel Dulany, Thomas Johnson, John Hall, William Paca, Charles Carroll

Barrister, Lancelot Jacques, and Charles Wallace, the majority of whom were empowered to contract with workmen, and to purchase materials; and were also authorized to draw on the treasurers of the western and eastern shores, for whatever further sums might be required to complete the building. The old state-house was accordingly demolished, and the present one erected on its site.

The foundation stone of this edifice was laid on the 28th day of March, 1772, by governor Eden. On his striking the stone with a mallet, which was customary on such occasions, tradition informs us, there was a severe clap of thunder, although a cloud was not to be seen, the day being clear and beautifully serene. In 1773, this building was covered in with a copper roof, and in 1775, this roof was blown off, during the equinoctial gale, the market-house was blown down, and the water is said to have risen three feet perpendicular above the common tide, during the storm.

The dome was not added to the main building until after the revolution.

The dimensions of the building are here given, to wit: Feet.
From the platform to the cornice, about   36
" " cornice to top of arc, or roof,   23
" " top of the roof to the cornice
    of the facade of the dome,   30
" " cornice to the band above the
    elliptical windows,   24
This terminates the view internally,   —113
From the band to the balcony,   22
Height of the turret,   17
From the cornice of the turret to the floor
    of the campanelle, or lantern,   6

	Feet.
Height of the campanelle, or lantern,	14
Height of the pedestal and acorn,	10
Height of the spire,	18—87
Entire height,	200
Diameter of the dome, at its base,	40
do. balcony,	30
do. turret,	17
do. campanelle, or lantern,	10
do. acorn,	3 8 in.
Length of the front of the building,	120
Depth, (exclusive of the octagon,)	82

The architect of this building was a Mr. Joseph Clarke. Mr. Thomas Dance, who executed the stucco and fresco work on the interior of the dome, fell from the scaffold just as he had finished the centre piece, and was killed.

1770. Mr. Eddis, in a letter dated Annapolis, February 20th, 1770, says, 'on Saturday last, our little city appeared in all its splendour. It was the anniversary of the proprietary's birth. The governor gave a grand entertainment on the occasion to a numerous party; the company brought with them every disposition to render each other happy, and the festivity concluded with cards and dancing, which engaged the attention of their respective votaries until an early hour.

'I am persuaded there is not a town in England of the same size of Annapolis, which can boast a greater number of fashionable and handsome women, and were I not satisfied to the contrary, I should suppose that the majority of our belles possessed every advantage of a long and familiar intercourse with the manners and habits of your great metropolis.'

Annapolis has always been celebrated for the elegance and beauty of her female population; and the compliment paid to them by Mr. Eddis in 1770, is equally true at the present time.

1771. In this year, and for many years later, there existed in this city, a society called '*The Saint Tamina Society*,' who set apart the first day of May in memory of '*Saint Tamina*,' whose history, like those of other venerable saints, is lost in fable and uncertainty. It was usual on the morning of this day, for the members of the society to erect in some public situation in the city, a '*May-pole*,' and to decorate it in a most tasteful manner, with wild flowers gathered from the adjacent woods, and forming themselves in a ring around it, hand in hand, perform the Indian war dance, with many other customs which they had seen exhibited by the children of the forest. It was also usual on this day for such of the citizens, who chose to enter into the amusement, to wear a piece of bucks-tail in their hats, or in some conspicuous part of their dress. General invitations were given, and a large company usually assembled during the course of the evening, and when engaged in the midst of a dance, the company were interrupted by the sudden intrusion of a number of the members of 'Saint Tamina's Society,' habited like Indians, who rushing violently into the room, singing the war songs, and giving the whoop, commenced dancing in the style of that people. After which ceremony, they made a collection, and retired well satisfied with their reception and entertainment. This custom of celebrating the day was continued down, within the recollection of many of the present inhabitants of this city.

On Monday, the 9th of September, 1771, the editor of the Maryland Gazette says, 'the new theatre in West street was opened with the *Roman Father* and *Mayor of Garret*, to a numerous and brilliant audience, who expressed the greatest satisfaction, not only at the performance, but with the house, which is thought to be as elegant and commodious for its size, as any theatre in *America*.'

The theatre above mentioned, was built of brick, of handsome structure, the boxes were commodious and neatly decorated, the pit and gallery were calculated to hold a number of persons without incommoding each other; the stage was well adapted for dramatic and pantomimical exhibitions, and several of the scenes reflected great credit on the ability of the painter. In 1782, the general assembly appointed Samuel Chase and Allen Quynn, trustees of this property, for the use of John Henry and others, of the American company of comedians. This theatre was built upon ground leased from St. Anne's Parish, and when the lease expired, about 1814, the vestry of the parish took possession of it, and sold it. It was soon after pulled down. A carriage manufactory is now erected on its site.

Mr. Dunlap, in his history of the American theatre, admits that Annapolis has the honour 'of having erected the first theatre, the first temple to the dramatic muse.' Of this fact there can rest no doubt, for as early as the year 1752, a theatre was built here, and in which were performed some of Shakspeare's best plays.

1774. In 1774, John Ridout, Samuel Chase, William Paca, Upton Scott and Thomas Hyde, Esquires, were appointed trustees for building in Annapolis '*an elegant church*,' which is to be adorned with a steeple. The old church to be pulled down, and the new one erected at the same place.

In return for £1500, contributed by the public authorities, there was provided a pew for the 'governor, a large one for the council, one for the speaker, pews for the members of the legislature, judges and strangers, all of which are to be in the most airy, agreeable and commodious part of the church, and to be properly ornamented.'

The old church was accordingly razed to the ground, and the present Episcopal church erected on the site; of which more will be said in another place.

On the 25th of May, of this year, (1774,) in consequence of the 'act of parliament for blocking up the harbour of Boston,' a meeting of the citizens of Annapolis was called, when the following proceedings were had:

'At a meeting of the inhabitants of the city of Annapolis, on Wednesday, the twenty-fifth day of May, 1774, after notice given of the time, place, and occasion of this meeting,—

'*Resolved*, That it is the unanimous opinion of this meeting, that the town of Boston is now suffering in the common cause of America, and that it is incumbent on every colony in America, to unite in effectual measures to obtain a repeal of the late act of parliament, for blocking up the harbour of Boston.

'That it is the opinion of this meeting, that if the colonies come into a joint resolution to stop all importation from, and exportation to Great Britain, till the said act be repealed, the same will preserve North America, and her liberties.

'*Resolved*, Therefore, that the inhabitants of this city will join in an association with the several counties of this province, and the principal provinces of America, to put an immediate stop to all exports to Great Britain, and that after a short day, hereafter to be agreed on, that there shall be no imports from Great Britain, till the said act be repealed, and that such association be on oath.

'That it is the opinion of this meeting, that the gentlemen of the law of this province bring no suit for the recovery of any debt due from any inhabitant of this province, to any inhabitant of Great Britain, until the said act be repealed.

'That the inhabitants of this city will, and it is the opinion of this meeting, that this province ought immediately to break off all trade and dealings with that colony or province, which shall refuse or decline to come into similar resolutions with a majority of the colonies.

'That Messieurs John Hall, Charles Carroll, Thomas Johnson, jun., William Paca, Matthias Hammond, and Samuel Chase, be a committee for this city to join with those who shall be appointed for Baltimore Town, and other parts of this province, to constitute one general committee; and that the gentlemen appointed for this city inmmediately correspond with Baltimore Town, and other parts of this province, to effect such association as will secure American liberty.'

Mr. Eddis, writing from Annapolis to England, on the 28th of May, immediately after the above proceedings were had, begins his letter by saying, 'all America is in a flame! I hear strange language every day. The colonists are ripe for any measures that will tend to the preservation of what they call their natural liberty. I enclose you the resolves of *our* citizens; they have caught the general contagion.

'Expresses are flying from province to province. It is the universal opinion *here*, that the mother country cannot support a contention with these settlements, if they abide strictly to the letter and spirit of their associations.'

After the publication of the resolves entered into on Wednesday, the 25th of May, had appeared, several gentlemen of influence expressed their belief, that if the sentiments of the people had been properly taken, it would not appear that the *whole* of the proceedings received their unanimous support. And to obviate this objection, hand-bills were distributed, and a general attendance was earnestly requested, in consequence of which, on the evening of the 27th, a second meeting of the citizens was held, when the proceedings of the previous meeting of the 25th of May were fully sustained.

But on the ensuing Monday, a protest made its appearance, signed by one hundred and thirty-five persons, amongst whom are to be found the names of many of the first importance at that day in this city, and in the neighbourhood, and is as follows:

'To the Printers: '*May* 30*th*, 1774.

'A publication of the enclosed protest, supported by the names of a considerable number of the inhabitants of the city of Annapolis, will, it is presumed, furnish the most authentic grounds for determining the sense of the majority, on a question of the last importance.

'We whose names are subscribed, inhabitants of the city of Annapolis, conceive it our clear right, and most incumbent duty, to express our cordial and explicit disapprobation of a resolution which was carried by forty-seven against thirty-one, at the meeting held on the 27th instant.

'The resolution against which we protest, in the face of the world, is the following:

'That it is the opinion of this meeting, that the gentlemen of the law of this province, bring no suit for the recovery of any debt due from any inhabitant of this province, to any inhabitant of Great Britain, until the said act be repealed.' *Dissentient.*

First—'Because we are impressed with a full conviction, that this resolution is founded in treachery and rashness, inasmuch as it is big with bankruptcy and ruin, to those inhabitants of Great Britain, who, relying with unlimited security on our good faith and integrity, have made us masters of their fortunes, condemning them *unheard*, for not having interposed their influence with parliament in favour of the town of Boston, without duly weighing the force, with which that influence would probably have operated; or whether, in their conduct, they were actuated by wisdom and policy, or by *corruption* and *avarice*.

Secondly—'Because whilst the inhabitants of Great Britain are partially despoiled of every legal remedy to recover what is justly due to them, no provision is made to prevent us from being harrassed by the prosecution of internal suits, but our fortunes and persons are left at the mercy of domestic creditors, without a possibility of extricating ourselves, unless by a general convulsion, an event in the contemplation of sober reason, replete with horror.

Thirdly—'Because our credit as a commercial people, will expire under the wound; for what confidence can possibly be reposed in those, who shall have exhibited the most avowed, and most striking proof that they are not bound by obligations as sacred as human invention can suggest.

'Lloyd Dulany, William Cooke, James Tilghman, Anthony Stewart, William Steuart, Charles Steuart, David Steuart, Jonathan Pinkney, William Tuck, Thomas Sparrow, John Green, James Brice, George Gordon, John Chalmers, John Anderson, John Unsworth, James Taylor, William Cayton, George Ranken, Robert Moor, Jonathan Parker, Brite Seleven, John Varndel, John Annis, Robert Ridge, Robert Nixon, Thomas Kirby, Williams Edwards, Robert Lambert, William Eddis, John Clapham, Elie Vallette, Robert Buchanan, William Noke, James Brooks, Richard Murrow, John Brown, John Hepburn, Colin Campbell, Nathaniel Ross, William Niven, James Kingsbury, James Barnes, John Sands, James Williams, Joseph Williams, John Howard, William Munroe, John D. Jaquet, John Norris, John Steele, N. Maccubbin, Shoem. Thomas Hammond, Thomas Pipier, Thomas Neal, William Tonry, James McKenzie, Nicholas Minsky, Martin Water, John Warren, William Chambers, James Clarke, Denton Jacques, Joseph Dowson, Thomas Macken, Richard Burland, Dan. Dulany, of Dan., R. Molleson, Robert Couden, William Aikman, George French, John Parker, Archibald Smith, Thomas Bonner, Matthias Mae, Alexander

McDonald, David Crinnig, John Timmis, David Atchison, James Maynard, William Harrison, Robert Kirkland, William Ashton, Robert Morrison, Charles Bryan, John Haragan, Hugh Hendley, Richard Thompson, Reverdy Ghiselin, Charles Marckel, John Randall, William Stiff, James Mitchel, Charles Roberts, Samuel Skingle, Thomas Stiff, Henry Jackson, William Devenith, James Hackman, Charles Barber, John Evitts, James Maw, Jordan Steiger, Joseph Richards, Edward Owens, Thomas Pryse, J. Wilkinson, Robert Key, Lewis Jones, William Willatt, John King, William Prew, Thomas Towson, William Howard, John Donaldson, Dan. Dulany, of Walter, William Worthington, Thomas B. Hodgkin, William Wilkins, Thomas French, Joseph Selby, William Gordon, Thomas Hyde, John Maconochie, Philip Thomas Lee, John Ball, Samuel Owens, Samuel Ball, Thomas Braithwaite, James Murray, Richard Mackubin, Michael Wallace, William Hyde, Nathan Hammond, Peter Psalter, Joseph Browing, Thomas Hincks, Lewis Neth, Edward Dogan, J. H. Anderson, Richard Burt, Henry Horsley, Cornelius Fenton, Richard Addams, George Ranken, senior, Edward Wilmot, Robert Lang, George Nicholson, Benjamin Spriggs, John Horton, Charles Wright, Constantine Bull, Amos Edmons, Henry Sibell, Joshua Cross, John Woolford, Sam. H. Howard, Oliver Weeden, Alexander Finlater, Con. McCarty, Jonathan Simpson.'

Brig Peggy Stewart.—On Saturday the 15th of October, 1774, the brig Peggy Stewart arrived at Annapolis from London, with servants and a quantity of goods, among which were seventeen packages, containing two thousand three hundred and twenty pounds of tea, consigned to Thomas Charles Williams and company, merchants, in Annapolis.

This intended importation was immediately discovered, and the citizens were summoned to a general meeting. On examination, it appeared, that Messrs. Williams had, on this occasion, imported a larger quantity of *that detestable plant*, as it was then termed, than by any former opportunity; and that Mr. Anthony Stewart, the proprietor of the vessel, had paid the duties thereon; though he was not in any manner concerned in the shipment of the tea. This being deemed a submission to the contested claim of the British parliament, very severe censures were passed on the parties concerned, and a general spirit of resentment appeared to have predominated. After several modes of proceeding had been proposed and discussed, it was determined to appoint a committee to attend the vessel, and prevent the landing of the tea, until the sense of the country could be fully ascertained. The ensuing Wednesday was appointed for that purpose, and proper measures were pursued to give the necessary information.

Mr. Stewart, apprehensive of the consequences likely to ensue, solicited a previous meeting of the citizens on the following Monday, trusting that, by timely submission, measures might be taken to prevent the assembling of so numerous a body as were expected to come in from the county, from whom he had much to fear, with respect to his person and property.

At this meeting it was proposed by some, that Messrs. Stewart and Williams, who were desirous to make atonement for the offence they had committed, might be permitted to land and burn the tea, in any place that should be appointed for that purpose.

This motion was, however, strongly opposed by others, who insisted on matters remaining as they were, until the time appointed for the county meeting, in order that a more public acknowledgment and satisfaction might be made.

Mr. Stewart, with a view to moderate the resentment which his conduct had occasioned, distributed the following hand-bill and affidavit, which were also publicly read, but without any apparent effect in his favour.

'To the gentlemen of the committee, the citizens of Annapolis, and the inhabitants of Anne Arundel county.

'Gentlemen: I find by a hand-bill, that you are requested to meet to take into consideration what is proper to be done with the tea, the property of Thomas C. Williams and Co., now on board the brig Peggy Stewart, and finding my conduct censured for having paid the duty on that tea to the collector, I take the liberty to present a plain narrative of the part I have acted therein, and the motives by which I was actuated. Deeply interested as I am in the peace and harmony of this country, no man would be further than myself from taking any steps to disturb them. I am not in the least connected with any thing that relates merely to the importation, indeed so cautious have I been of infringing in the least, any of the resolutions of America, that I did not order a single farthing's worth of goods by that vessel, though I could have done it on such easy terms as to freight and shipping charges, much less should

I have thought of ordering any tea, after the disturbance which the importation of that article had occasioned on the continent. When the brig arrived, the captain informed me she was very leaky, and that the sooner she was unloaded the better.

'I told him to enter his vessel, but not the tea, which I found, on inquiry of the collector, could not be done. Under these circumstances, the brig leaky, and fifty-three souls on board, where they had been near three months, I thought myself bound, both in humanity and prudence, to enter the vessel, and leave the destination of the tea to the committee.

'The impropriety of securing the duty did not then occur to me, neither did I know the tea would be suffered to be lodged as a security for the payment. I had nothing in view but to save the vessel from a seizure, and of having an opportunity of releasing the passengers from a long and disagreeable confinement.

'The duty on tea has been paid hitherto, both in Virginia and Maryland, by every importer of goods, in this case I am not the importer. If I have erred in my part of the transaction, I declare, upon my honour, it is without the least intention; I have infringed no rules prescribed by the general resolutions of this province. It happened, unluckily, that the tea was put on board of captain Jackson's brig, in the manner as will be seen by the annexed affidavit, and it can be incontestably proved, the captain refused taking tea on board.

'Mr. Williams was in London when the tea was shipped, and must have known that many merchants had refused to ship that article. I have only to add, that I am sincerely sorry for my conduct on this occasion, which has been the cause of so much uneasiness, and freely submit it to your candid consideration.

'I am, gentlemen,
'Your most humble servant,
'ANTHONY STEWART.

'*Annapolis, Oct.* 17, 1774.'

'AFFIDAVIT.—Captain Richard Jackson, master of the brig Peggy Stewart, deposeth and saith,

'That immediately after the landing of his cargo in London, he applied for, and obtained a *general* permit from the custom-house, to receive *India and other goods* on board for exportation; and (as is always customary in such cases,) gave security, and took an oath not to re-land the same in any part of Great Britain. But having great reason to believe, any importation of tea would be unfavourably received in America, he was fully determined, and had resolved not to receive any on board; and publickly on the Exchange of London, in the month of July, refused to receive tea, which was offered to be shipped by Kelley, Lott and Co. This deponent further saith, that by the method of shipping goods from London, *tea* may be put on board any ship, without the knowledge of the master. All goods are examined at the custom-house, and sent by the shipper, in lighters, on board the ship, with only a common bill expressing the parcels, and not the quantities contained, or the qualities of them; these are received by the mate of the ship, who gives a receipt on the lighter-bill, which is again returned to the shipper, and the master signs his bills of lading *at London*, by the lighter-bill, specifying the parcels, without knowing the contents, and clears out the ship at the custom-house with merchandize, without knowing or mentioning of what nature.

'The cockets containing the particulars of each parcel, are sent by the officers of the customs at London, to the custom-house at Gravesend, and there lodged to be called for by the captain or master of the ship on his passage to sea. In this manner the goods shipped in the Peggy Stewart, were received on board. And this deponent further saith, that he saw Thomas Charles Williams, to whom the tea is consigned, and Amos Hayton, who shipped the same, frequently in London, neither of whom ever mentioned to him their intention of shipping any; that he did not know of any tea being on board, until after he had received his cockets at Gravesend, and that he would not have received the same had he known thereof. RICH. JACKSON.'

'Sworn before me this 17th Oct., 1774,
PHIL. THOS. LEE.'

On Wednesday, the appearance, agreeably to expectation, was numerous, and the delegated committee were attended by Messrs. A. Stewart and Williams, who acknowledged the impropriety of their proceeding, and signed the paper, of which the following is a copy:

'We James Williams, Joseph Williams, and Anthony Stewart, do severally acknowledge, that we have committed a most daring insult, and act of the most pernicious tendency to the liberties of America; we the said Williams's, *in importing the tea*, and said Stewart, *in paying the duty thereon*, and thereby deservedly incurred the displeasure of the people now convened, and all others interested in the preservation of the constitutional rights and liberties of North America, do ask pardon for the same; and we solemnly declare, for the future, that we never will infringe any resolution formed by the people, for the salvation of their rights, nor will we do any act that may be injurious to the liberties of the people, and to shew our desire of living in amity with the friends of America, we request this meeting, or as many as may choose to attend, to be present at any place where the people shall appoint, and we will there commit to the flames, or otherwise destroy, as the people may choose, the detestable article, which has been the cause of this our misconduct.

ANTHONY STEWART,
JOSEPH WILLIAMS,
JAMES WILLIAMS.'

Mr. Stewart, on account of what was deemed a cheerful and ready compliance with an unconstitutional act of the British legislature, was particularly obnoxious, and though he publicly read his recantation, expressed in the most submissive terms, there were some who were warmly disposed to present him with a suit of tar and feathers. Others were in favour of the destruction of the brig, which had imported the hateful commodity, whilst many others declared, that the paper signed by the offenders, with their unextorted consent to burn the tea, was a sufficient punishment and satisfaction. But to determine this point with certainty, it was proposed and assented to, that a division should take place on the following question; Whether the vessel should or should not be destroyed?

When it was carried in the negative by a considerable majority; the citizens in general, appearing averse to violent measures. But as the minority were chiefly persons who resided at a distance from Annapolis, as some of them had great influence in their neighbourhood, and intimated a determined resolution to proceed to the utmost extremities, the instant they could collect sufficient numbers to support them, Mr. Stewart was induced by the advice of Charles Carroll, of Carrollton, Esquire, and from an anxious desire to preserve the public tranquillity, as well as to secure his own personal safety, to propose setting fire himself to the vessel, which being immediately assented to, he instantly repaired on board, accompanied by several gentlemen who thought it necessary to attend him, and having directed her to be run aground, near the wind-mill point, he made a sacrifice of his valuable property, and in a few hours the brig, with her sails, cordage, and every appurtenance, was effectually burnt.*

Mr. McMahon in his history of Maryland, says, in reference to the affair of the Peggy Stewart—'the tea burning at Boston has acquired renown, as an act of unexampled daring at that day in the defence of American liberties, but *the tea burning at Annapolis*, which occurred in the ensuing fall, far surpasses it in the apparent deliberation and utter carelessness of concealment, attending the bold measures which led to its accomplishment.' 'This instance, in its manifestation of public feeling, is of a character with those which occurred in other parts of the province, and

---

* Eddis' Letters.

they evince the prevalence throughout it, of the most determined and resistless opposition to the measures of the English government.'

CHAPTER VI.

Tea Burning in Frederick County—The Citizens of Annapolis organized into Military Companies—Proceedings of the Baltimore Committee of Observation—The ship Totness, with salt on board, burnt just below Annapolis—General Charles Lee—Massachusetts' Colony—Lord Viscount Barrington—Addresses—Gen. Burgoyne—and Gen. Lee—Council of Safety—Chart of the Harbour of Annapolis—Appropriation to fortify the City—Fortifications—Slaughter Houses—Certain Citizens ordered to leave the City—Colonel John Weems before the Committee of Safety—Their proceedings thereon—Captures in the Chesapeake, by Capt. Nicholson, of the ship Defence—Offers Battle to Otter sloop of War—Balls prohibited throughout the Province—A Declaration of the Delegates of Maryland—Meeting of the Associations of the City of Annapolis—Their Proceedings—Maryland Troops leave Annapolis for Philadelphia—Letters from Philadelphia—Appeal to Maryland—Responded to—Battle on Long Island—Maryland Troops—Major Gist—Maryland Officers made prisoners at Long Island—Thomas Johnson, jr. Esq. Governor of Maryland—British Ships of War pass up the Bay—Gov. Johnson's Proclamation—Mr. Griffith—Baltimore Troops—Battle of Brandywine—General Smallwood—Colonel Smith—Fort Mifflin—Surrender of General Burgoyne—Count Pulaski—Battle of Monmouth—Letter from Commodore Grason to Gov. Johnson—Battle at the Capes—Winter of 1780—Chesapeake crossed by carts and carriages—Baron de Kalb—Battle of Camden—The Baron wounded—His death—Congress voted a Monument to his memory—To be erected in Annapolis—Inscription for the Monument—Extracts of Letters relative to the Battle of Camden—Maryland Troops—Battle of the Cowpens—Col. Howard—Maryland Troops—British Sloops of War off Annapolis—General Lafayette drives them down the Bay—Meeting of the citizens of Annapolis—To consider the Acts of Assembly—For the Emission of Money

Bills—Their Proceedings—Militia Assembled at Annapolis—British Fleet arrives before York—Troops landed—Maryland Regiment marches from Annapolis to join the Southern Army—The Recruiting Service—Gen. Smallwood—The Fourth Maryland Regiment marches from Annapolis to join the Marquis de la Fayette—The French Fleet, &c. at Annapolis—From the Head of Elk—The French Army arrives from the North about the same time, on their way to Virginia—Battle of Eutaw—Extract of a Letter from Camp—Col. Howard—Maryland and Virginia Troops—Officers killed and wounded at Eutaw—Surrender of Lord Cornwallis—Rejoicing at Annapolis.

TEA BURNING *in Frederick county,* (taken from the Maryland Gazette, Dec. 22, 1774.

'The committee for the upper part of Frederick county, Maryland, having met at Elizabeth Town,* on the 26th of November, which was the day appointed for the delivery of John Parks' chest of tea, in consequence of his agreement published in the Maryland Journal of the 16th ult.

'After a demand was made of the same, Mr. Parks offered a chest of tea, found on a certain Andrew Gibson's plantation, Cumberland county, Pennsylvania, by the committee for that place, which tea he declared was the same he promised to deliver.

'The committee are sorry to say that they have great reason to believe, and indeed with almost a certainty, that the said chest of tea was in Cumberland county at the time Parks said upon oath it was at Christen Bridge.

'After mature deliberation, the committee were of opinion, that John Parks should go with his hat off, and lighted torches in his hands, and set fire to the tea, which he accordingly did, and the same was

* Now Hagerstown, in Washington county, Maryland.

consumed to ashes, amongst the acclamations of a numerous body of people. The committee were also of opinion that no further intercourse should be had with the said Parks. Every friend to liberty is requested to pay due attention to the same.

'Voted, the thanks of this committee to that of Cumberland county, for their prudent and spirited behaviour upon this occasion.

'Signed by order of the committee.

'JOHN STULL, *President.*

'N. B. The populace thought the measures adopted by the committee were inadequate to the transgression, and satisfied themselves by breaking his door and windows.'

'ANNAPOLIS, *December* 22, 1774.'

'In compliance with the recommendation of the deputies of the several counties of this province, at their late convention, to such of the gentlemen, freeholders, and other freemen of this province, as are from sixteen to fifty years of age, to form themselves into companies, and to chuse their officers; on Saturday last a number of the citizens met, and chose their officers agreeably to the recommendation; the companies are composed of all ranks of men in this city, gentlemen of the first fortunes are common soldiers; this example, it is not doubted, will be followed by every town and county in this province.

'It is said that there are a sufficient number of citizens to form another company, which it is hoped will be immediately done.'

'BALTIMORE, *April* 19*th*, 1775.'

1775. Extracts from the proceedings of the Baltimore committee of observation.

'*Committee Chamber, April* 3, 1775.

'Information being made to the committee that a few individuals, inhabitants of this town, have of late worn pistols or private arms, alleging in justification of their conduct,

'That a motion had been made in the committee to sacrifice some of the persons in this town, who differed from them, or were averse to the public measures now carrying on in this province; and that they wore arms against any such attempts.'

'The committee, to remove any prejudice that may be taken by the public against them, and to prevent the ill effects of such false and injurious reports, if circulated without contradiction, do solemnly declare, that no such motion was ever made, or any entry relative to the same, minuted in their proceedings. A few members of the committee were of opinion, that the names of such persons, who upon application, had refused to contribute for the purchase of arms and ammunition, should be published, but even this measure was over-ruled in the committee as improper at that time.

'Our meetings have been held in public, nor has any person who thought fit to attend, ever been excluded. Our records are free and open for inspection.

'From the public we receive our authority, not by personal solicitation, but a free and voluntary choice, to that tribunal we submit our actions.

'Although we have uniformly persevered, and are determined to persevere in carrying into execution the association and measures of the congress, yet in no instance have we exceeded the line pointed out by that assembly, and our provincial assembly: and abhorring every idea of proscription, the committee call upon the persons who have circulated the aforesaid report, to disclose the author.

('A true extract from the minutes.)

'R. ALEXANDER, *Sec.*'

'*April* 15*th*, 1775.

'The committee of observation for Baltimore county, reflecting on the many mischiefs and disorders, usually attending the fairs held at Baltimore town, and willing in all things, strictly to observe the regulations of the continental congress, who in their eighth resolution, have advised to discountenance and discourage every species of extravagance and dissipation, especially horse-racing, cock-fighting, &c., have unanimously resolved to recommend it to the good people of this county, and do hereby earnestly request, that they will not themselves nor will suffer any of their families to attend, or in any wise encourage the approaching fair at Baltimore town; and all persons are desired not to erect booths, or in any manner prepare for holding the said fair.

'We are persuaded the inhabitants of the town in particular will see the propriety of this measure, and the necessity of enforcing it, as the fairs have been a nuisance long before complained of by them, as serving no other purpose than debauching the morals of their children and servants, affording an opportunity for perpetrating thefts, encouraging riots, drunkenness, gaming, and the vilest immoralities.

'SAM. PURVIANCE, Jun., *Chairman.*'

'*April* 18*th*, 1775.

'The chairman of the committee for Baltimore county

has this day received from Mr. John Veazey, £306 5s. 0d., being the very generous donation of Cecil county, for the relief of the distressed inhabitants of Boston.'

'ANNAPOLIS, *July 20th*, 1775.

'The ship '*Totness*,' captain Harding, belonging to Mr. Gildard, of Liverpool, having on board a cargo of salt and dry goods, in coming up the bay, ran aground near the three Islands at the mouth of West river; upon this the committee immediately met, and after consideration, determined she should proceed on to Baltimore, her intended port, but before she could get off, highly resenting so daring an infringement of the continental association, a number of people met, went on board, and set her on fire.'

The following handsome compliment to general Charles Lee, by the congress of the Massachusetts colony, is inserted here, in respect to the memory of that accomplished gentleman and distinguished officer. General Lee, up to the 22d of June, 1775, was an officer in the British army, on half pay. On that day he addressed a letter to Lord Viscount Barrington, secretary of war, in which he said,—

'Although I can by no means subscribe to the opinion of divers people in the world, that an officer on half pay is to be considered in service, yet I think it a point of delicacy to pay a deference to this opinion erroneous and absurd as it is. I therefore apprize your lordship in the most public and solemn manner, that I do renounce my half pay from the date hereof. At the same time, I beg to assure your lordship that whenever it shall please his majesty to call me forth to any honourable service against the natural hereditary enemies of our country, or in defence of his just rights and dignity, no man will obey the righteous summons with more zeal and alacrity than myself; but the present measures seem to me so absolutely subversive of the rights and liberties of every individual subject, so destructive to the whole empire at large, and ultimately so ruinous to his majesty's own person, dignity, and family, that I think myself obliged in conscience as a citizen, Englishman, and soldier of a free State, to exert my utmost to defeat them.'

'CAMBRIDGE, *July* 6*th*, 1775.

'To the honourable Charles Lee, Esq., major-general of the continental army.

'Sir: The congress of the Massachusetts colony, possessed of the fullest evidence of your attachment to the rights of mankind, and regard to the distresses which America in general, and this colony in particular, are involved in, by the impolitic, wicked and tyrannic system, adopted by administration, and pursued with relentless and savage fury, do with pleasure embrace this opportunity to express the great satisfaction and gratitude they feel on your appointment as a major-general in the American army.

'We sincerely congratulate you on your safe arrival here, and wish you all possible happiness and success in the execution of so important a trust. We admire and respect the character of a man who, disregarding the allurements of profit and distinction his merit might procure, engages in the cause of mankind, in defence of the injured, and the relief of the oppressed. From your character, from your great abilities and military experience, united with those of the commander-in-chief, under the smiles of Providence, we flatter ourselves with the prospect of discipline and order, success and victory.

'Be assured, sir, that it will give us great pleasure to contribute to your happiness. May the favour and blessings of heaven attend you. May divine Providence guard and protect you, conduct you in the paths of honour and virtue, grant you the reward of the brave and virtuous, the applauses of mankind, and the approbation of your own conscience, and eternal happiness hereafter.'

To which general Lee replied,—

'Gentlemen: Nothing can be so flattering to me as the good opinion and approbation of the delegates of a free and uncorrupt people. I was educated in the highest reverence for the rights of mankind, and have acquired, by a long acquaintance, a most particular regard for the people of America. You may depend, therefore, gentlemen, on my zeal and integrity. I can promise you nothing from my abilities. God Almighty grant us success, equal to the righteousness of the cause. I thank you, gentlemen, for an address which does me so much honour, and shall labour to deserve it.'

On the arrival of general Burgoyne in America, general Lee, who had been on terms of intimacy and friendship with him, addressed him a letter, in which he sets forth in bold relief the 'wickedness and treachery' of the British government, and expresses his deep regret that 'men of such a stamp as Mr. Burgoyne and Mr. Howe, can be seduced into so impious and nefarious a service by the artifice of a wicked and insidious court and cabinet,'—and says, 'not less than 150,000 gentlemen, yeomen, and farmers are now in arms, determined to preserve their liberties or perish.' He defends the Americans against the charge of cowardice, and passes a high encomium on their bravery, and reminds him of some instances of the reverse, 'particularly where the late col. Grant (he who lately pledged himself for the general cowardice of America,) ran away with a large body of his own regiment, and was saved from destruction by the valor of a few Virginians.'

General Burgoyne, in reply to this letter, defends the course he pursued, and justifies that of his government, but expresses great personal regard for general Lee, and desires to have an interview with him, for the purpose of delivering into his own hand some letters, 'as well as to renew the rights of our fellowship.' To this general Lee replied by the following card:

'CAMBRIDGE, *Head Quarters, July* 11*th*, 1775.

'General Lee's compliments to general Burgoyne—would be extremely happy in the interview he so kindly proposed. But as he perceives that general Burgoyne has already made up his mind on this great subject, and that it is impossible that he (general Lee) should ever alter his opinion, he is apprehensive that the interview might create those jealousies and suspicions so natural to a people struggling in the dearest of all causes, that of their liberty, property, wives, children, and their future generations. He must therefore defer the happiness of embracing a man whom he most sincerely loves, until the subversion of the present tyrannical ministry and system, which he is persuaded must be in a few months, as he knows Great Britain cannot stand the contest. He begs general Burgoyne will send the letters which his aid-de-camp has for him. If Gardiner is his aid-de-camp, he desires his love to him.'*

1776. On the 21st of January, of this year, (1776,) we find the following proceedings were had by the council of safety, relative to the harbour of Annapolis:

'*Resolved*, That Messrs. Lancelot Jacques, Charles Wallace, William Hyde, Allen Quynn, James Brice, William Whetcroft, and Beriah Maybury, or any three of them, be requested to make a chart of the land and water at the mouth of this river, specifying the width and depth of the channel between Horn point and Greensbury's point, and some distance without and within the same.'

On the 16th of March following, the gentlemen returned a chart of their survey, but which, like many other of our public documents, is not to be found among the archives of our State.

The convention of Maryland appropriated the sum of five thousand nine hundred pounds to fortify this city. But the council of safety doubting the sufficiency of that appropriation to erect suitable fortifications for the defence of the city, expressed their opinion to the convention that, with an additional sum, batteries might be erected on Greensbury's,

---

* See Appendix, for a letter from general Lee to the president of the council of safety of Maryland, justificatory of the part he took in advising the seizure of the person and papers of governor Robert Edin—a letter replete with the noblest sentiments of patriotism and zeal, in the cause of American liberty.

Horn, and Windmill points, and other places adjacent, between those places and the city, on the south side of the river, which would fully answer the purpose of preventing men-of-war approaching the town. They therefore asked, and obtained from the convention, authority to draw on the treasury for whatever sums they might deem necessary to complete the fortifications, and to build a number of 'row-gallies or gondolas.'

Fortifications were accordingly erected on Horn point, Beamen's hill, and Windmill point, besides several breast-works which were made at various other places. These were all completed, with great vigour and perseverance, under the superintendance of Messrs. James Brice, John Bullen, Charles Wallace, William Wilkins, Beriah Maybury, John Brice, John Campbell, Joshua Fraizer, and Allen Quynn.

The council of safety, apprehending that the great number of slaughter-houses then in the city, would engender disease, adopted on the 22d day of July, the following order:

'*Whereas*, it hath been represented to the council of safety by physicians and others, that the intolerable stench arising from slaughter-houses and spreading green hides to dry in the city of Annapolis, may be productive of pestilential disorders and ill consequences to the troops and others residing in the said city. Therefore, ordered, that no butcher or other person shall, after the 26th day of this instant, presume to slaughter bullocks, mutton, or any kind of meat, or put up green hides to cure within the limits of said city for and during the term of three months, thence next ensuing.'

On the 18th of December, several of the citizens of Annapolis having received letters demanding their immediate departure from the city, and the council of safety being informed thereof, expressed their sense of the illegality of such a measure, by the following proceedings:

'In Council of Safety, Dec. 19, 1776.

'We are called upon by the duty of our station to take notice of the powers assumed by some persons yesterday evening in ordering divers of the inhabitants of the city of Annapolis into banishment, without any cause assigned, by cards transmitted them. We are of opinion such cards are contrary to our association, flying in the face of the resolves of congress and convention, and against the letter and spirit of our declaration of rights. The peace of the State ought and must be preserved, and all offenders brought before the proper judicatures for tryal. Therefore we earnestly recommend to all associators and other well disposed persons to discourage such extra-judicial and disorderly proceedings, tending in their consequences to prejudice the common cause, and to the destruction of order and regular government.'

And on the 23d of the same month, the following further proceedings were had:

'*Whereas*, we have received information that on Wednesday, the 18th day of this instant, (December) in the evening, cards were delivered to sundry persons in the city of Annapolis, to the following effect:

'You are hereby ordered to depart this city to-morrow, 9 o'clock. Signed,   J. WEEMS,
'In behalf of Anne Arundel county.'

'Which cards we are informed were delivered by Stephen Steward, Junior, the council of safety having taken the same into consideration, are of opinion that such cards are contrary to the resolves of congress and convention, and against the 21st section of the declaration of rights, which asserts:

' 'That no freeman ought to be taken or imprisoned, or deprived of his freehold, liberties or privileges, or outlawed, or exiled, or in any manner destroyed, or deprived of his life, liberty or property, but by the judgment of his peers or by the law of the land.'

'Ordered, therefore, that the said John Weems and Stephen Steward, Junior, attend the council of safety on the thirtieth day of December, to shew by what authority the said cards were so made out and delivered.'

On the 30th of December, colonel John Weems and Stephen Steward, Junior, accordingly appeared before the council of safety, and acknowledged that they had been active in making out and delivering the cards mentioned in the order of the board, and having promised that they would not intermeddle in the same manner again, but would leave all persons to be dealt with according to the law of the land. They were dismissed by the council, on condition that they pay the messenger his fees.

On Tuesday, the 5th of March, about seven in the evening, information was received at this place, that a man-of-war and two tenders were coming up the bay, and had taken a New England schooner lying at the mouth of the Patuxent river, the wind blowing hard at S. W. and the general expectation was, that they would be at Annapolis in a few hours, the necessary dispositions were made to receive them in case they thought proper to land, and expresses were despatched to Baltimore and other parts of the province, to communicate the intelligence. Between twelve and one o'clock on Tuesday night the wind shifted, and blew a violent gale at N. W., and so continued all day on Wednesday, during which time there was no certain information of the position of the vessels. On Thursday there was a light breeze up the bay, and about two o'clock the vessels hove in sight, and at half past three came opposite to the city with some prizes, and stood up the bay. Off the mouth of this harbour they burnt a shallop loaded with oats, and in the evening anchored off the mouth of the Patapsco. On Friday night intelligence was received, that the vessels were the *Otter sloop-of-war*, and two tenders, and the general opinion was entertained, that they were going to Baltimore to take or destroy the *ship Defence*. The Defence, however, being got ready on Friday night, towed down the river, manned with a number of brave fellows, all of whom were Americans in their hearts, and most of them by birth, attended by several smaller vessels, crowded with men, to assist in case of an engagement. Captain Nicholson, of the *Defence*, got under way early on Saturday morning, resolved to re-take Hudson's ship, (a large vessel the *Otter* had made a prize of, loaded with wheat and flour,) and to engage the Otter, if she moved to assist the tenders which guarded the prize; the morning was thick and hazy, and the *Defence* got nearer to them than was expected, before they discovered her bearing down upon them, those on board the tenders appeared much alarmed, and pushed off with precipitation, and on a signal given, more hands were sent by the *Otter* to assist in rowing them off, which was effected with difficulty, leaving three or four small prizes, besides Hudson's ship, all of which fell into the hands of captain Nicholson, who having manned the prize ship, and seeing the *Otter* get under way, clued up her courses and prepared for battle, expecting her to come up, but the '*Otter*' having waited about two hours, as if in expectation of captain Nicholson's coming down, at length bore away, and in the afternoon came to anchor off this port. Captain Nicholson continued his station some time, and having performed his duty in the most gallant manner, returned with his prizes to Baltimore.

On Sunday morning the Otter sloop and her tenders made sail and went down the bay. The regulars, militia, and the people in general, behaved on this occasion in the most spirited and patriotic manner.

At this period of gloom and general distress, balls were prohibited in this place, and throughout the province, by a resolve of the convention. The public mind at this period, disinclined as it was to the indulgence of the ordinary pleasures and amusements of life, was devoted to matters of a serious character, and therefore musket and cannon *balls* lost none of the public favour under the interdiction referred to.

'ANNAPOLIS, *July 6th*, 1776.

'*A declaration of the delegates of Maryland.*

'To be exempt from parliamentary taxation, and to regulate their internal government and polity, the people of this colony have ever considered as their inherent and unalienable right: without the former, they can have no property; without the latter, no security for their lives or liberties.

'The parliament of Great Britain has of late claimed an uncontroulable right of binding these colonies in all cases whatsoever, to force an unconditional submission to this claim, the legislative and executive powers of that State have invariably pursued for these ten years past, a studied system of oppression, by passing many impolitic, severe and cruel acts for raising a revenue from the colonists, by depriving them in many cases of the trial by jury, by altering the chartered constitution of one colony, and the entire stoppage of the trade of its capital, by cutting off all intercourse between the colonies, by restraining them from fishing on their own coasts, by extending the limits of and erecting an arbitrary government in the province of Quebec, by confiscating the property of the colonists taken on the seas, and compelling the crews of their vessels, under the pain of death, to act against their native country and dearest friends, by declaring all seizures, detention, or destruction of the persons, or property of the colonists, to be legal and just.

'A war unjustly commenced, hath been prosecuted against the united colonies with cruelty, outrageous violence and perfidy; slaves, savages and foreign mercenaries, have been meanly hired to rob a people of their property, liberty and lives; a people guilty of no other crime than deeming the last of no estimation without the secure enjoyment of the former. Their humble and dutiful petitions for peace, liberty and safety, have been rejected with scorn; secure of and relying on foreign aid, not on his national forces, the unrelenting monarch of Britain hath at length avowed by his answer to the city of London, his determined and inexorable resolution of reducing these colonies to abject slavery.

'Compelled by dire necessity, either to surrender our properties, liberties and lives, into the hands of a British king and parliament, or to use such means as will most probably secure to us and our posterity those invaluable blessings.

'We, the delegates of Maryland, in convention assembled, do declare, that the king of Great Britain has violated his compact with this people, and that they owe no allegiance to him. We have therefore thought it just and necessary to empower our deputies in congress to join with a majority of the united colonies in declaring them free and independent States, in framing such other confederacy between them, in making foreign alliances, and in adopting such other measures as shall be judged necessary for the preservation of their liberties; provided the sole and exclusive rights of regulating the internal polity and government of this colony be reserved to the people thereof. We have also thought proper to call a new convention, for the purpose of establishing a government in this colony. No ambitious views, no desire of independence, induce the people of Maryland to form an union with the other colonies. To procure an exemption from parliamentary taxation, and to continue to the legislatures of these colonies the sole and exclusive right of regulating their internal polity, was our original and only motive.

'To maintain inviolate our liberties, and to transmit them unimpaired to posterity, was our duty and first wish; our next, to continue connected with, and dependent on Great Britain. For the truth of these assertions, we appeal to that Almighty Being who is emphatically styled the searcher of hearts, and from whose omniscience nothing is concealed. Relying on His divine protection and assistance, and trusting to the justice of our cause, we exhort and conjure every virtuous citizen to join cordially in defence of our common rights, and in maintenance of the freedom of this and her sister colonies.'*

'At a meeting of the associators of the city of Annapolis, on Thursday, the 11th of July, 1776.

   'WILLIAM ROBERTS, ESQ., *Chairman.*
   'JOHN DUCKETT, *Clerk.*

'1st. *Resolved*, That it is the duty of every inhabitant of the city of Annapolis, and all persons having property therein, to contribute every assistance in their power for the protection and defence of the city and the inhabitants thereof, and that Mr. James Brice, Mr. John Bullen, Mr. Charles Wallace, Mr. William Wilkins, Mr. Beriah Maybury, Mr. John Brice and Mr. John Campbell, or a majority of them, or of any three or more of them, be a committee to act on behalf of the inhabitants of this city, and that they wait on the 'council of safety,' and inform them that the inhabitants will afford every assistance in their power for putting the city into the best posture of defence; and that the inhabitants will in person, or by others employed at their expense, labour on any intrenchments or works, which the council shall think necessary.

'2d. *Resolved*, That the said committee be empow-

---

* See Appendix, for two letters from John Hancock, Esquire, to the convention of Maryland, one dated June 4th, and the other July 8th, 1776.

ered to call on every inhabitant of the city, and every person having property therein, to labour in person, or to furnish some person to labour in his stead, at such time and place as the committee shall think proper, on the works as may be ordered by the council of safety, to be erected for the defence of the city.

'3d. *Resolved,* That the said committee be authorized to execute all matters which may be recommended by the council of safety, for the defence of the city, or for keeping the peace and good order therein.

'4th. *Resolved,* That no member of this meeting will, and that it is the opinion of the meeting that no inhabitant of the city of Annapolis ought, to buy from or employ, any merchant, tradesman,' or any other person who hath not subscribed the association.

'5th. *Resolved,* That application be made by the committee to the council of safety not to employ in the public service any non-associator, and that they be requested to give a preference to such tradesmen and others as have manifested their attachment and zeal to the liberties of America.

'*Ordered,* That copies of the above resolutions be transmitted by the chairman to the associators of Baltimore town for their opinion and concurrence.

'*Ordered,* That the names of the non-associators in this city be published and distributed among the inhabitants.

'*Resolved,* That this meeting be adjourned to the 10th day of August next, and that the committee have power to call a meeting at any time before, if they shall think proper.

'True copy of the proceedings.

'Test,   JNO. DUCKETT, *Clerk.*'

'ANNAPOLIS, *July* 11*th*, 1776.

'Yesterday evening six companies of the first battalion of Maryland troops stationed in this city, and commanded by Col. William Smallwood, embarked for the head of Elk in high spirits, and three companies of the same battalion stationed in Baltimore town, embarked yesterday morning for the same place, from thence they are to proceed to Philadelphia.'

Extracts of a letter from Philadelphia, dated,

'*July* 6, 1776, *Saturday morning.*

'General Howe has landed a great body of troops on Staten Island: his force cannot be ascertained. General Washington and his troops are in high spirits. The strength of our army at New York cannot be ascertained, the militia pour in so fast that it is impracticable. The Jersey militia, amounting to 3500, have acquired great honour, in forming and marching with such alacrity and expedition. They have for some time past got over to New York. The battalions of our city (every one of them) are marching to Trenton and Brunswick, in the Jerseys. The rifle battalion in the pay of this province, marched yesterday for the same places. The militia in the counties are also ordered to march: out of these bodies they mean to form their quota of the flying camp, to be posted in the Jerseys, and to be at the command of general Washington. It is expected that the lower counties and Maryland will immediately march their quotas of militia, to compose the flying camp, to this city, to defend it in the absence of its own battalions.

'Your hour of trial is come, your plighted faith, your public honour, the love of your country, and its dearest liberties, in this moment of imminent danger, demand that you instantly fly to the assistance of a sister colony.'

'*Saturday, noon.*

'An express is just arrived from general Washington, Howe's army consists of 10,000 men : Admiral Howe is not yet arrived, but hourly expected with 150 sail, having on board 20,000 troops. The enemy's grand army will consist of 30,000. The whole militia of this province are ordered to the Jerseys. We are in anxious expectation to hear from Maryland, nor can we for a moment entertain a doubt that our brethren will not desert us, in the day of our distress. The farmers here have left their harvest, and cast away the scythe for the musket. I should rejoice to hear you have imitated so laudable, so glorious an example.'

How Maryland responded to this appeal to her patriotism and love of country, is well known. The battle-fields of Long Island, White Plains, Camden, the Cowpens, and of Eutaw, tested the valor of her sons, and proved them to be worthy of the freedom they were resolved to achieve, or perish in the attempt.

In council, as well as in the field, they were ever found ready to support the freedom and independence of America.

Extracts of letters from New York.

'NEW YORK, *August* 27*th*, 1776.

'I sit down in the midst of confusion to tell you that our people have been engaged with the enemy on Long Island, all this morning, and are at it yet; we cannot get at particulars.

'P. S. The first battalion of New York, colonel Lasher, and the Pennsylvania and Maryland battalions behaved with the greatest bravery, even to a fault. They were commanded by Lord Sterling. We forced the enemy into their lines.'

'PHILADELPHIA, *August* 31*st*.

'You will no doubt be very anxious to receive a particular account of the late engagement between our troops and the enemy on Long Island.

'Smallwood's battalion of Marylanders were distinguished in the field by the most intrepid courage, the most regular use of the musket, and judicious movements of the body. When our party was overpowered and broken by superior numbers surrounding them on all sides, three companies of the Maryland battalion broke the enemy's lines and fought their way through. Captain Veazey and lieutenant Butler, are among the honourable slain. The Maryland battalion lost 200 men and twelve officers—severe fate. It is said our whole loss is five or six hundred.'

'NEW YORK, *September* 1.

'Last Monday morning we went over to Long Island,* and about midnight we were alarmed.' 'Upon which near three thousand men were ordered out, consisting chiefly of the Pennsylvania and Maryland troops.' 'The Delaware and Maryland battalions made one party.' 'Our orders were not to fire until the enemy came within fifty yards of us, but when they perceived we stood their fire so coolly and resolutely, they declined coming any nearer, although

---

* See Appendix, for an official account of this battle from colonel Smallwood, to the convention of Maryland.

treble our number. In this situation we stood from sunrise to twelve o'clock, the enemy firing upon us the chief part of the time, when the main body of their army, by a rout we never dreamed of, had entirely surrounded us, and drove within the lines, or scattered in the woods, all our men, except the Delaware and Maryland battalions, who were standing at bay with double their number, broke the enemy's lines and forced their way through.'

'Many thought they would surrender in a body, without firing; when they began the attack, general Washington wrung his hands, and cried out, *good God, what brave fellows I must this day lose!* Major Gist commanded the Maryland battalion, the colonel and lieutenant-colonel being both at New York. All our officers behaved extremely well. Captain Smith and lieut. Steret conducted their companies to a charm.'

'Our army was drove to the lines. The enemy came within one hundred and fifty yards of our fort, but were repulsed with great loss.'

'A list of Maryland officers made prisoners at Long Island.

'Capt. Daniel Bowie, wounded; lieutenants William Steret, William Ridgely, Hatch Dent, Walter Muse, Samuel Wright, Joseph Butler, wounded, Edward Praul, Edward de Courcy; ensigns James Fernandes, William Courts.'

1777. On Friday, the 21st of March, 1777, Thomas Johnson, Junior, Esquire, the first republican governor of Maryland, was proclaimed at the state-house, in the presence of a great number of people, all of whom expressed the highest satisfaction on the occasion; after which a procession was formed, consisting of the several branches of the government, mayor and city authorities, military, strangers and citizens.

On a signal of three vollies of small arms from the soldiery, who were paraded in front of the state-house, thirteen cannon were fired.

The procession then repaired to the 'coffee-house' and partook of a sumptuous entertainment, during which many patriotic toasts were drank. The whole concluded with an elegant ball in the evening.

'On Thursday, the 21st of August, between two and three hundred sail of British ships-of-war, transports, &c., passed the mouth of this harbour, (Annapolis,) about 9 o'clock, A. M., and stood up the bay.'

Immediately after this fleet had passed Annapolis, governor Johnson issued his proclamation, calling on all the county lieutenants, field and other officers of the militia of the western shore of this state, to march at least two full companies of each battalion immediately to the neighbourhood of the Susquehanna river, in Cecil and Harford counties, and in concluding the proclamation, says, 'to defend our liberties, requires our exertions; our wives, our children, and our country, implore our assistance: motives amply sufficient to arm every one who can be called a man.' The governor received information by express, that the eastern shore militia 'were collecting in great numbers, determined to make the most obstinate resistance against this invasion of the State.'

Mr. Griffith, in his 'Annals of Baltimore,' says, 'Lord Howe's fleet anchored near the mouth of Patapsco river, but proceeded to Turkey point, on Elk river, near which the British army under sir William

Howe was landed.' That, 'the independent company now under captain John Sterett, trained as infantry, mounted their own horses, proceeded to watch the enemy on the bay side, and arriving before them at the head of it, joined the main army, including the Maryland line, near Newport, but were then ordered back by the commander-in-chief to assist in protecting their homes.'

'On the 11th September, was fought the battle of Brandywine, at which the Maryland line was present and shared the disasters of the day.'

'General Smallwood, with Maryland militia, including captains Sterett, Cox and Bailey's companies from Baltimore, joined general Wayne the 21st September, immediately after Grey's sanguinary night attack on the Americans at the Paoli.

'Those companies in which many citizens who left numerous families dispersed about the country, or exposed to the depredations of the maritime forces of the enemy in the bay, went in the ranks volunteers, shared in the route of Wayne and in the more equal conflict at Germantown, 4th of October, at which place the patriotic Cox, with several of his townsmen, laid down their lives in their country's cause.

'At the same time colonel Smith commanding a small detachment of continental troops at fort Mifflin, with the aid of commodore Hazlewood's flotilla, in which lieutenant Barney then served, was successfully opposing the passage of Howe's fleet, which had returned from the Chesapeake into Delaware, for which congress voted the colonel a sword.'

'The gloom occasioned by the passage of the fleet to Philadelphia was soon reversed, and confidence generally and forever restored, by the news which arrived here on the 21st October, of the success of general Gates at Saratoga, and the surrender of general Burgoyne and his whole army four days before.'

1778. 'Early in 1778, Count Pulaski's legion of cavalry and infantry, raised partly in this State, was organized here. The corps suffered severely in Jersey in the same year, and the next lost their gallant commander in Georgia.*

'On the 28th of June, the British were unsuccessfully attacked, but finally retired from the fields of Monmouth, in Jersey, where the Maryland line shared the danger and the glory of the day.'

'ANNAPOLIS, *July* 9, 1779.

1779. 'Extract of a letter from commodore Grason, on board the Chester galley, to his excellency, our governor.

'On Monday morning (the 28th of June,) we weighed and stood out to sea, at 8 o'clock saw a ship and a schooner standing in for Cape Henry, and immediately gave them chase, till within about two leagues of them, they then tacked and stood towards us, which gave me an opportunity of getting nearer the Cape, and in shoal water, when we were about three leagues from Cape Charles, and four miles from

---

* At the attack on Savannah, 'while penetrating the works at the head of about two hundred horse, in order to charge in the rear, Count Pulaski received a mortal wound.'—*4th vol. Marshall's Life of Washington.* The brave Count Pulaski died of his wound on the 13th of October, and his corpse was carried to Charlestown, and there interred with great military funeral pomp, and with every other mark of respect that a generous and grateful people could show a hero, who had sacrificed his life in defence of their liberties.'—*Maryland Gazette, Nov.* 12, 1779.

the ship, it fell almost calm. I then anchored, hoping she would have done the same, but she still kept under way; finding the tide driving her further from us, as soon as the crew had dined, which was half past two o'clock in the afternoon, we weighed and rowed down to her; at four we fired a shot, which she returned with a broadside; in about ten minutes the action became general, and continued without intermission till after sun-set, when the wind sprung fresh up southerly, she then made all the sail in her power, and stood to sea, we continued the chase till near ten o'clock, at which time she was quite out of gun-shot; we then hauled in for the land. She was quite a clean ship, just out of port, mounted with 18 four and six pounders, and two stern chasers on one deck, four carriage guns and several swivels on the quarter deck and forecastle. I have the greatest pleasure in assuring your excellency, that the officers and men behaved with great conduct and bravery, and that we had not one man killed or wounded, except captain Dashiell, who received a slight wound on his hip-bone by a cannon-ball.'

1780. The winter of 1780, was one of unusual severity, the Chesapeake bay was frozen from its head to the mouth of the Potomac. For many days together persons travelled from Annapolis to Poplar Island, Rock Hall, and Baltimore, on the ice, and crossed to and from Kent Island in carts and carriages, a distance of seven miles across; the ice was six or seven inches thick. It is said to have been one of the coldest winters ever known in our climate.

On the 8th of September, of this year, the tidings of Baron de Kalb's death reached Annapolis, he having died from wounds received at the battle near Camden, South Carolina. His death was much regretted by the citizens, to whom he had greatly endeared himself by his manly virtues, and patriotic bearing, while he sojourned in this city. And such was the esteem in which this veteran, the hero and patriot of the two Hemispheres, was held by the American congress, that soon after his death was known, in the fullness of their gratitude and deep sense of his eminent services in the cause of American liberty, passed the following resolution:

'*In Congress, October*, 1780.'

'*Resolved*, That a monument be erected to the memory of the late major-general, the Baron de Kalb, in the city of Annapolis, in the State of Maryland,' with the following inscription:

'Sacred to the memory of
THE BARON DE KALB,
Knight of the royal order of military merit,
Brigadier of the armies of France,
and
Major-general in the service of the United States
of America.
Having served with honour and reputation for
three years,
He gave a last and glorious proof of his
attachment to the liberties of mankind,
and the cause of America,
In the action near Camden, in the State of
South Carolina,
on the 16th August, 1780;
Where, leading on the troops of the Maryland and
Delaware lines, against superior numbers,
and animating them by his example to deeds
of valour,

He was pierced with many wounds, and
on the 19th following expired, in the 48th year
of his age.
The *Congress* of the United States of America,
in gratitude to his zeal, services and merit,
have erected this monument.'

Thus it seems that congress, impelled by a patriotic and laudable spirit of gratitude and justice to the memory of this great man, passed the above resolve, and doubtless in good faith to have this mark of their sense of De Kalb's merit carried into execution. But why it may be inquired, has this monument to heroic worth never been erected? Has congress determined by this delay to sanction the stigma, which has often been cast upon the *gratitude of republics?* Sixty years have elapsed, and yet the congress of a great and free nation neglects to redeem its plighted faith to the ashes of the departed patriot!!

It is ardently to be hoped that some gallant son of the patriots of '76, will urge, and successfully urge, the speedy execution of this righteous and just resolve of *an American* congress.

Annapolis, of all others, is the place where this monument should be erected, as then wisely determined by congress. The immortal De Kalb commanded the 'glorious old Maryland line,' he was well known and loved here, and to this day his memory is enshrined in the hearts of many of the inhabitants of the 'ancient city,' whose ancestors saw, conversed with, and blessed him.

Extracts from letters, relating to the battle of Camden, South Carolina.

'BALTIMORE, *August 29th,* 1780.

'On the 16th inst., at two o'clock, A. M., a bloody battle was fought between his excellency, general Gates, at the head of about 3000 men, 900 of whom were regulars, and the British forces under the command of earl Cornwallis, consisting of 1800 regulars, and 2400 refugees. The contending armies engaged each other with the greatest fury, and the prospect for some time was extremely favourable to the American troops, who charged bayonets on the enemy, which obliged them to give ground, and leave some of their artillery in the possession of our advancing troop.'

'WILLIAMSBURG, *September* 2.

'Since my last, advice is received from general Gates, very few of Sumpter's party have suffered, our greatest loss is the baggage and stores. Eternal honour is due to the Maryland and Delaware brigades, they killed and wounded upwards of 500 of the enemy, and made their retreat good. De Kalb is mortally wounded.*

* The Baron de Kalb, while making a vigorous charge at the head of a regiment of infantry, fell under eleven wounds. His aid-de-camp, lieutenant-colonel Du Buysson, embraced him, announced his rank and nation to the surrounding foe, and begged that they would spare his life. While he thus generously exposed himself to save his friend, he received several dangerous wounds, and with his general, was taken prisoner. Although he received every attention and assistance it was in the power of the conquerors to bestow, the Baron expired in a few hours. He spent his last breath in dictating a letter expressive of the warmest affection for the officers and men of his division; of the great satisfaction he derived from the testimony given by the British of the bravery of his troops; of his own admiration of the firm opposition they had made to a superior force, after being deserted by the rest of the army; of the infinite pleasure he received from the gallant behaviour of the Delaware regiment,

'The second Maryland brigade, which was on the right, was the last engaged; the efforts of those troops to recover the day was heroically brave.'

1781. On the 17th of January, was fought the battle of the Cowpens, in which the Maryland troops were again distinguished. Chief Justice Marshall in his life of Gen. Washington, in giving the details of this battle—says, 'believing the fate of the day to be decided, the British pressed on with increased ardor, and in some disorder; and when the Americans halted, were within thirty yards of them. The orders, then given by Col. Howard to face the enemy, were executed as soon as they were received; and the whole line poured in upon them a fire as deadly as it was unexpected. Perceiving the confusion occasioned by this sudden fire, Howard seized the critical moment, and ordered his regiment to charge them with the bayonet. These orders were instantly obeyed, and the British line was broken.' 'The British were driven from the ground with considerable slaughter, and were closely pursued. Both Howard and Washington pressed the advantage they had respectively gained, until the artillery and a great part of the infantry had surrendered.'

'This complete and decisive victory cost the Americans in killed and wounded, less than eighty men.'

'Seldom has a battle in which greater numbers were

and the companies of the artillery attached to his brigades, and of the endearing sense he entertained of the merit of the whole division he commanded. Congress afterwards directed a monument to be erected to his memory, with an inscription, testifying their sense of his worth and gratitude for his services.'—*4th vol. Marshall's Life of Washington.*

not engaged, been so important in its consequences as that of the Cowpens. By it, Lord Cornwallis was not only deprived of a fifth of his numbers, but lost, so far as respected infantry, that active part of his army, which, in the species of war about to be entered on, is most useful to those who possess it, and most terrible to an enemy. Had the issue of the engagement been such as was to have been expected from the relative strength of the two detachments, and Morgan's corps, like that of Buford, been cut to pieces, it is impossible to say what consequences would have resulted to the southern States.'*

In March of this year Annapolis was blockaded by two British sloops-of-war, the '*Hope*' and '*Monk*'—which for a time prevented the French troops from proceeding to the Head of Elk. Marquis de Lafayette, who commanded these troops—and who was then at Annapolis, raised the blockade by a manœuvre, which would have done credit to a practical cruiser: and which is mentioned in a letter written immediately after his arrival at the Head of Elk, to general Washington.†

* *Fourth vol. Marshall's Life of Washington.*

'*Head of Elk, April 8, 1781.*

† *Extract.*—'On my arrival at Annapolis, I found that our preparations were far from promising a speedy departure. The difficulty of getting wagons and horses, is immense. There are not boats sufficient to cross over the ferries. The state were very desirous of keeping us as long as possible, as they were scared by the apparition of the *Hope* of twenty guns, and the *Monk* of eighteen guns—which blockaded the harbour, and which as appears from intercepted letters, were determined to oppose our movements. In these circumstances, I thought it better to continue my preparations for a journey by land, which, I am told, would have lasted ten days on account of ferries;

On the 18th of July, 1781—at a meeting of the citizens of Annapolis—Charles Wallace, Esq. in the chair, and George Ranken, clerk, was taken into consideration 'the late law of the general assembly, for the emission of two hundred thousand pounds, to defray the expenses of the present campaign; and the subscription and association recommended by the legislature, to support the credit and value of the said emission'—it was among other things, resolved by the said meeting—'that as sufficient means could not be raised to carry on the war by *taxes*—that the emitting of bills of credit was necessary, and deemed it to be the duty, and real interest of every citizen of the State—who was determined to prosecute the war in defence of his property and liberty, to exert every effort to support the value of the said bills of credit, at par with gold and silver—and that every man ought to associate to receive the said bills at par.

James Brice, Jeremiah T. Chase, Allen Quynn, Frederick Green, Nicholas Maccubbin, jr. Samuel H. Howard, and Thomas Harwood, Esquires, were appointed a committee, to attend to the conduct of associators, and to see that none of them violated their faith and honour, by wilfully depreciating the said bills of credit—and that they should publish the name of any such offender, who should be deemed *infamous*, and

and, in the meantime, I had two eighteen pounders put on board a small sloop, which appeared ridiculous to some, but proved to be of great service.

'On the morning of the 6th, commodore Nicholson went out with the sloop, and another vessel full of men. Whether the sound of eighteen pounders, or the fear of being boarded, operated upon the enemy, I am not able to say; but, after some manœuvres, they retreated so far as to render it prudent for us to sail for this place.'

that to deal or associate thereafter with such an one, should be considered as dishonourable. That the credit of the paper money depended solely on public opinion, and must receive its value from the association of the principal merchants and inhabitants of Baltimore town, and the principal farmers in the several counties—all of whom were earnestly recommended to receive it at par, with specie.

In August, 1781—we are told, that two thousand three hundred militia, were assembled at Annapolis, on one day's notice, from Baltimore town, and its vicinity—when an attack was apprehended from the British fleet which had entered the bay, but which passed up York river, and landed their troops at Gloucester and York.

This fact, which evinces the ardor that prevailed amongst our militia of that day, is deemed too creditable to their patriotic spirit, to be passed, unnoticed.

On the 28th of the same month, the third Maryland regiment, commanded by Lieut. Col. Peter Adams, marched from this city to join the southern army. This regiment was raised here—and is said to have had 'all the appearance of a veteran corps'—they were enlisted for three years, and were well equipped for the field. The mutual good offices which had been exchanged between the citizens, and officers of this regiment while here, rendered their departure a cause of much regret. The ardor that pervaded their ranks, on the prospect of taking the field, and their military appearance, inspired every beholder with a pleasing confidence, that they would render essential services, and be an honour to their country; nor did they disappoint these expectations—as it is well known that the

Maryland troops discharged their duty both in the camp, and on the battle field; and exhibited examples of intrepidity and military perfection, seldom equalled by the oldest troops.

The recruiting service then carried on at this place, was under the direction of major-general Smallwood, whose distinguished services in the field, were only equalled by his unremitted attention to this important branch of the service.

On the 7th of September in the same year, the 4th Maryland regiment, commanded by major Alexander Roxburgh, marched from this city to join the Marquis de La Fayette. This regiment had its full complement, consisting of upwards of six hundred rank and file. When we consider the short time in which the two regiments above mentioned were raised, it affords additional testimony of the zeal and ability with which Maryland aided in prosecuting the war, and establishing our independence.

On the 12th of September, a fleet of transports arrived here, from the Head of Elk, having on board the artillery, grenadiers, and light troops of the allied army, on their route to James' river. And on the 18th, about four thousand French troops, with a train of artillery, marched into the city from the northward, on their way to Virginia.

At this time there were anchored off the mouth of our harbour, the 'Romulus,' 'Gentile,' and several other frigates belonging to America's illustrious ally. This must have been a spirit-stirring scene to our little city—and made all hearts feel confident in the success of the common cause.

On the 8th of September in this year, was fought

the battle of Eutaw—where the troops of Maryland, commanded by the 'hero of the Cowpens,' again distinguished themselves.

Extract of a letter, dated

'CAMP, *at Trout Springs, September 12th,* 1781.

'The battle of Eutaw, which was fought the 8th instant, happened upon the same ground, on which according to the tradition of this country, a memorable battle was fought above a century past, between a body of speculating Europeans, and the natives of the soil. In the first we are told, six hundred men fell, and we find an Indian mound erected as a monument to perpetuate their glory. In the second, double that number were killed and wounded; but whether this christian nation will give such an honourable testimony of the great worth of those who now sleep in the bed of honour, is a matter not to be expected. Our victory was complete, though the fate of the day mingled sorrows in the triumph. I will enclose you a list of the killed and wounded of the Maryland brigade, &c. which will give you a tolerable idea of the importance of the action.

'General Greene, who is one of the bravest and best soldiers himself, is highly satisfied with the behaviour of the troops in general, but particularly with our brigade; he saw them make a charge with trailed arms through the hottest of the enemy's fire, and was so delighted with their firmness and vivacity, that he rode up to me, and complimented them in the field. He has also done it in general orders, and made the Virginians a compliment in the same style. They behaved with equal courage.

'If any former misconduct or accident in war had

left a stain upon the Maryland troops, their exemplary conduct upon this occasion should obliterate it forever. Around the monument which I mentioned, four of our excellent officers and many of our brave brother soldiers fell. Let them rest in that ancient bed of honour. May their virtues only be remembered, and their spirits enjoy eternal glory.'

'Officers killed and wounded in the Maryland brigade.

'Captains Dobson and Edgerly, and lieutenants Duvall and Gold, killed. Lieutenant-colonel Howard, wounded in the shoulder; Captain J. Gibson, in the arm; Lieutenant Hugon, in the groin; Lieutenant Woolford, thigh broke; Lieutenant Ewing, dangerously in the body; Lieutenant Lynn, leg broke; Ensign Moor, thumb shot off.'

General Greene thought himself principally indebted for this victory, to the free use made of the bayonet by the Maryland and Virginia troops.

The first intelligence of the surrender of Lord Cornwallis was communicated by the Count de Grasse, in a letter to the governor of this State—and reached Annapolis, on Saturday evening, the 20th of October, 1781, by express—and which was hailed by the joyful acclamations of the citizens, and firing of the artillery. And on Monday afternoon, a *feu de joie* was fired by the artillery, and select militia, and in the evening the town was brilliantly illuminated.

CHAPTER VII.

General Washington arrives at Annapolis—Public Dinner—Ball—The Citizens address him—His Answer—He leaves the City—The Birth of a Dauphin celebrated at Annapolis—Count Rochambeau arrives at Annapolis—Embarks for France—Cessation of Hostilities—Public Rejoicing—Public Dinner—Toasts on the Occasion—State-House Illuminated—Ball—Peace—General Greene arrives at Annapolis—Corporate Authorities of the City address him—General Greene's Reply—The Society of Cincinnatti for the State of Maryland formed in Annapolis—Officers of the Maryland Line—Congress in Session at Annapolis—General Washington arrives there—Is entertained by the Citizens—Corporate Authorities address him—His Reply—General Washington resigns his Commission into the hands of the Congress—Proceedings of Congress thereon—General Washington again visits Annapolis accompanied by General Lafayette—They are entertained by the General Assembly—General Lafayette—Addressed by the Governor and Council, and by the Legislature—His Answers—The General Assembly naturalizes General Lafayette—St. John's College—The President of the United States arrives at Annapolis—His Reception—Annapolis—Baltimore—Citizens of Annapolis address the President of the United States—The President's Reply—Defence of Annapolis—Tribute to the Memory of Washington—General Tureau, arrives at Annapolis—His Reception—*William Pinkney* arrives at Annapolis—His Reception—Public Dinner—Officers and Crew of the Frigate Philadelphia—Meeting of the Citizens of Annapolis—Frigate Chesapeake—Proceedings of the Citizens—Piracy in the Chesapeake Bay—Pirates Captured—Conclusion.

On Wednesday, the 21st of November, 1781, general Washington arrived in this city, on his way to the northward. 'When the citizens received the pleasing information of his excellency's arrival, all business ceased, and every consideration gave way to their impatience to behold their benefactor, and the deliverer of his country. On his appearance in the streets, people of every rank and every age eagerly pressed forward to feed their eyes with gazing on the man, to whom, under Providence, and the generous aid of our great and good ally, they owed their security, and hopes of future liberty and peace; the courteous affability, with which he returned their salutes, lighted up ineffable joy in every countenance, and diffused the most animated gratitude through every breast.'

'You would have thought the very windows spoke. So many greedy looks of young and old through casements darted their desiring eyes upon his visage; and that all the walls, with painted imagery, had said at once, 'God save thee, Washington.'

'The general's arrival was announced by the discharge of cannon, and he was accompanied to his excellency the governor's, by the honest acclamations of the whigs; a few tories, to expiate their crimes, and shuffle off the opprobium of their characters, feebly joined in applauding the man whose successes had annihilated their hopes, and whose conduct was a satire on their principles. The president of the senate, speaker of the house of delegates, members of the general assembly and council, and many of the citizens, hastened to offer their tribute of affection, which was richly repaid by the engaging frankness and affectionate politeness of the reception. The evening was spent at the governor's elegant and hospitable board with festive joy, enlivened by good-humour, wit, and beauty.'

'On the next day the general partook of a public dinner given by the legislature, as a mark of their respect, and to render the participation of his company as general as possible. In the evening the city was beautifully illuminated, and an assembly prepared for the ladies, to afford them an opportunity of beholding their friend, and thanking their protector with their smiles.'

'His excellency, to gratify the wishes of the fair, crowned the entertainment with his presence, and with graceful dignity and familiar ease so framed his looks, his gestures, and his words, that every heart overflowed with gratitude and love, and every tongue grew eloquent in his praise. When he retired from the assembly—with one united voice, all present exclaimed:

'Unrivalled and unmatched shall be his fame,
And his own laurels shade his envied name.'

The day on which general Washington reached Annapolis, the following address was presented by the citizens:

'*To his Excellency General Washington:*

'The citizens of Annapolis feel themselves happy in having an opportunity, personally, to express their affection for, and gratitude to, your excellency. Your private character forces admiration from the foes of virtue and freedom.

'We derive peculiar pleasure from the contemplation, that the successes at Trenton and Princetown laid the corner stone of our freedom and independence, and that the capture of Earl Cornwallis and his army has completed the edifice, and secured the temple of liberty to us and our posterity. These brilliant and important events are the more agreeable to every American, from the reflection that they were planned by, and executed under, the immediate command of your excellency.

'The love of your country alone, which induced you to accept the command of our armies at the expense of domestic happiness; the persevering fortitude and equanimity of soul you have displayed on every occasion, and the very important services rendered America, justify us in saluting you as the patriot, the hero, and the saviour of your country.

'Our prayers, with those of millions, are daily offered up to the Supreme Ruler of the Universe, for your health, safety and happiness.

   (Signed,)   JOHN BULLEN, *Mayor.*
'ANNAPOLIS, *November* 21, 1781.'

To which address general Washington made the following reply:

'*Sir,*—I am obliged by the polite and affectionate address of the citizens of Annapolis. Nothing can be more flattering to me than to know, that my general conduct has met the approbation of my countrymen: it is the most grateful reward for those services which I have ever, in the course of my command, endeavoured to render them, but which their too great partiality has oftentimes over-rated. That the State in general, and this city in particular, may long enjoy the benefits which they have a right to expect from their very spirited exertions in the prosecution of this just war, is the sincere wish of,

    'Sir, your most obedient and
      'Very humble servant,
        'G. WASHINGTON.
'*The Worshipful* JOHN BULLEN, Esq.,
   '*Mayor of the City of Annapolis.*
'ANNAPOLIS, *November* 21, 1781.'

By this visit Annapolis had an early opportunity of manifesting the gratitude and love which pervaded every American bosom, to the father of his country, and the honour of making one of the first public addresses after the crowning act of all his other successes during the Revolutionary war. For the reader will observe, it was presented but a short time after the capitulation at Yorktown.

On Friday the 23d, general Washington left the city, attended by the prayers of her citizens for his health, safety and happiness.

On Tuesday, the 25th of June, the birth of a *Dauphin*, was celebrated here—a public dinner was given in the state-house, to a numerous and most respectable assembly, where many toasts were drunk, suitable to the occasion. Five hundred discharges of cannon were fired through the day; and at night a splendid ball was given to 'the fairer part of creation.'

1783. On the 4th of January, 1783, his excellency, general count Rochambeau, with his suite, arrived in this city, and the next morning embarked on board his most christian majesty's frigate 'Le Emeraude,' for France.

Official intelligence being received by his excellency the governor, of a general cessation of hostilities—Thursday, the 24th of April, in this year, was appointed as the day of public rejoicing. And on which occasion, a convenient and extensive building was erected on Carroll's Green, sufficient for the accommodation of many hundreds. Thirteen pieces of artillery were planted, and an elegant dinner provided.

The proclamation being read—thirteen cannon were discharged, to announce the glorious and memorable event. The gentlemen then repaired to dinner, at which were present, 'his excellency the governor, the honourable council, members of the senate and delegates of the assembly, and a large number of gentlemen, both of town and country; who with unfeigned satisfaction congratulated each other on the blessings of peace—the rising glory of their country—the prospects of her commerce—her future grandeur, and importance in the scale of nations.'

'After dinner the following truly liberal, generous, and patriotic toasts were drunk, each attended with thirteen cannon:

1. The third of February, 1783—in perpetual memory, on which day a virtuous war was concluded by an honourable peace.
2. The United States—may their confederacy endure forever.
3. Friendship with France—may every nation imitate the depth and moderation of her policy, by which the freedom of navigation has been secured, the liberty of these States confirmed, and the blessings of peace and commerce diffused throughout the globe.
4. His excellency General Washington.
5. The generals, officers and soldiers of our army—may their services be remembered, and generously rewarded by a grateful people.
6. The French generals, officers and troops, who served in America.
7. The Marquis of Fayette—may our posterity ever retain a grateful sense of his strong attachment to this country, and of the important services rendered it in the field and cabinet.
8. The immortal memory of the gallant soldiers and virtuous citizens who gloriously fell in the late war.
9. The patriots of America—honour crowns their

labours; may future ages revere their memory, and emulate their fame.

10. The United Netherlands, and the friendly powers in Europe.

11. May the influence of the present revolution be extended to all the nations of the earth, by introducing among them that spirit of humanity, and religious toleration, which has so peculiarly distinguished this country, and united the efforts of all denominations of christians in the support of freedom.

12. The Commissioners of the United States at Paris.

13. The State of Maryland—may she ever support religion, learning, and virtue; preserve justice, public faith, and honour; give every encouragement and attention to agriculture and commerce; and on all occasions maintain with dignity her national character.'

At night the state-house, a superb building, was beautifully and magnificently illuminated; and an elegant entertainment was given to the ladies at the ball-room, which concluded the evening.

Thus Annapolis, which had ever been energetic in maintaining the war, was among the first in the Union to hail with joy the blessings of an honourable peace.

On the 25th of September, (1783,) major-general Greene, and his suite, arrived in the city, from the south, on his way to the north.

The next day the corporation met, and presented him with the following address:

'To the Hon. *Major-General Greene:*

'*Sir,*—We, the mayor, recorder, aldermen, and common council, of the city of Annapolis, impressed with the most grateful feelings for the eminent services rendered these United States, and the cause of liberty, by the southern army under your command, beg permission to congratulate you on your arrival in this city, and to testify, with the sincerest respect and regard, the lively sense we entertain of the invaluable blessings secured to us, by your conduct and unremitted assiduity, in the noblest cause that ever graced a soldier's sword.

'Justice would wear the aspect of adulation, were we to enumerate the many signal endowments which endear you to the inhabitants of this city, and inspire us with the warmest and most respectful gratitude. They are such as will ever engage our prayers to Divine Providence, that you may long continue to possess the affections of a generous republic; to share the sweets of domestic felicity; and to experience the happy reward of your distinguished virtues.

'This address springs from the heart; and we solicit your acceptance of it, as the genuine sentiments of a grateful people.

'*Signed by order and in behalf of the corporation.*
'JAMES BRICE, *Mayor.*
'ANNAPOLIS, *September* 26*th*, 1783.'

To which his excellency returned the following answer:

'ANNAPOLIS, *September* 27*th*, 1783.

'*Gentlemen*,—It is with the highest satisfaction I receive your affectionate address, and feel my bosom glow with gratitude upon the occasion.

'The happy termination of the war affords the most pleasing field for contemplation, and while it promises the richest harvest to the good citizens of America, it gives the sweetest pleasure, and most desirable repose to the soldier. If the operations of the southern army have answered the expectations of the public, or have had any influence upon this great event, I shall consider it one of the most happy employments of my life. And if to this I may venture to flatter myself, that my conduct either merits, or meets in the smallest degree, the approbation of the public, I shall be still more happy. The honour you have done me, and the troops under my command, are too sensibly felt to be fully expressed, or properly acknowledged.

'I beg leave to return my most sincere thanks to the corporation, for the interest they take in what concerns my future happiness, peace, and prosperity.

'I have the honour to be, gentlemen,
   'Your most obedient, humble servant,
      'NATH. GREENE.
'*To the Corporation of the City of Annapolis.*'

On the 21st of November, 1783, the order of the Society of Cincinnati, for the State of Maryland, was formed in Annapolis, by the officers of the Maryland line—who had here assembled for that purpose. Otho H. Williams in the chair, and John Eccleston, secretary.

The officers of the order elected were, major-general Smallwood, president; brigadier-general Gist, vice-president; brigadier-general Williams, secretary; colonel Ramsey, treasurer; and lieutenant-colonel Eccleston, assistant treasurer. Annapolis was the place appointed for their annual meetings—the proceedings of the order upon the occasion are to be seen at large in the Maryland Gazette, of the 27th of November, 1783.

The congress of the United States being then in

session, at the city of Annapolis, general Washington arrived there with his suite, on Friday, the 17th December, 1783, for the purpose of resigning his commission into their hands. He was met a few miles from the city, by generals Gates and Smallwood, accompanied by several of the principal inhabitants of the place, who escorted him to Mr. Mann's hotel, where apartments were prepared for his reception. His arrival was announced by the discharge of cannon. After receiving visits from many of the citizens, he waited on the president of congress, with whom he and the members of that body, with the principal military and civil officers of the State, dined on Saturday.

On Sunday morning, he returned the visits of the citizens and others who had waited on him.

On Monday, congress gave general Washington a public dinner, at the ball-room, where upwards of two hundred persons of distinction are said to have been present; and where every thing was provided by Mr. Mann, in the most elegant and profuse style.

After dinner many toasts were drunk, accompanied by the discharge of cannon.

At night the state-house was illuminated, where a ball was given by the general assembly, at which a very numerous and brilliant company of ladies was present.*

The following address was made to general Washington, on this occasion, by the corporate authorities of the city.

---

* On this occasion general Washington opened the ball with Mrs. James Maccubbin, of this city, one of the most beautiful women of her day.

'*To his excellency General Washington:*

'The mayor, recorder, aldermen, and common council, of the city of Annapolis, congratulate your excellency on the restoration of peace, and the establishment of the freedom and independence of the United States of America. The citizens feel themselves particularly happy, in this opportunity afforded them, of expressing their sincere approbation of your most distinguished and unexampled conduct through every stage of the war, and the high sense they entertain of your excellent virtues, fortitude, and unremitting perseverance, under the pressure of the greatest difficulties. To you they esteem themselves principally indebted, under the favour and smiles of Providence, for the inestimable blessings of peace and freedom. This acknowledgment flows from hearts filled with gratitude, and the most perfect respect and veneration for your person and character.

'In your retirement to the peaceful and pleasing scenes of domestic tranquillity, may America long experience the benign influence of your example, and benefit by the salutary suggestions of your wisdom; and may you, sir, long enjoy your health, and the heavenly sensations arising from a consciousness of having done every thing for your country, and wrested her from the oppressive hand of unrelenting tyranny, without the hope of any reward, but the approbation of a free people.

'We are, with every sentiment of esteem and respect,
 'Your excellency's most obedient servants.
'*Signed per order and on behalf of the corporation.*
 'J. T. CHASE, *Mayor.*'

To which address he replied:

'*To the worshipful the Mayor, Recorder, Aldermen and Common Council of the city of Annapolis:*

'Permit me, gentlemen, to offer you my sincere thanks for your congratulations on the happy events of peace, and the establishment of our independence.

'If my conduct throughout the war has merited the confidence of my fellow-citizens, and has been instrumental in obtaining for my country the blessings of peace and freedom, I owe it to that Supreme Being, who guides the hearts of all: who has so signally interposed his aid in every stage of the contest, and who has graciously been pleased to bestow on me the greatest of earthly rewards—the approbation and affections of a free people.

'Though I retire from the employments of public life, I shall never cease to entertain the most anxious care for the welfare of my country. May the Almighty dispose the heart of every citizen of the United States to improve the great prospect of happiness before us! And may you, gentlemen, and the inhabitants of this city, long enjoy every felicity this world can afford.

'G. WASHINGTON.

'*December*, 1783.'

'The United States in congress assembled:

'*December* 23, 1783.

'According to order, his excellency, the commander-in-chief, was admitted to a public audience, and being seated, the president,* after a pause, informed him,

---

*General Mifflin.

that the United States in congress assembled, were prepared to receive his communications; whereupon he arose and addressed congress as follows:

'*Mr. President,*—The great events on which my resignation depended having at length taken place, I have now the honour of offering my sincere congratulations to congress, and of presenting myself before them, to surrender into their hands the trust committed to me, and to claim the indulgence of retiring from the service of my country.

'Happy in the confirmation of our independence and sovereignty, and pleased with the opportunity offered the United States of becoming a respectable nation, I resign, with satisfaction, the appointment I accepted with diffidence: a diffidence in my abilities to accomplish so arduous a task; which, however, was superseded by a confidence in the rectitude of our cause, the support of the supreme power of the Union, and the patronage of Heaven.

'The successful termination of the war has verified the most sanguine expectations; and my gratitude for the interposition of Providence, and the assistance I have received from my countrymen, increases with every review of the momentous contest.

'While I repeat my obligations to the army in general, I should do injustice to my own feelings not to acknowledge, in this place, the peculiar services, and distinguished merits of the gentlemen, who have been attached to my person during the war. It was impossible the choice of confidential officers, to compose my family, should have been more fortunate. Permit me, sir, to recommend, in particular, those who have continued in the service to the present moment, as worthy of the favourable notice and patronage of congress.

'I consider it as an indispensable duty to close this last act of my official life, by commending the interests of our dearest country to the protection of Almighty God, and those who have the superintendence of them to his Holy keeping.

'Having now finished the work assigned me, I retire from the theatre of action, and bidding an affectionate farewell to this august body, under whose orders I have so long acted, I here offer my commission, and take my leave of all the employments of public life.'

He then advanced and delivered to the president his commission, with a copy of his address, and having resumed his place, the president returned him the following answer.

'*Sir*,—The United States in congress assembled, receive with emotions too affecting for utterance, the solemn resignation of the authorities under which you have led their troops with success through a perilous and doubtful war. Called by your country to defend its invaded rights, you accepted the sacred charge, before it had formed alliances, and whilst it was without funds or a government to support you. You have conducted the great military contest with wisdom and fortitude, invariably regarding the rights of the civil powers through all disasters and changes. You have, by the love and confidence of your fellow-citizens, enabled them to display their martial genius, and transmit their fame to posterity. You have persevered, till these United States, aided by a magnanimous king and nation, have been enabled, under a just Providence, to close the war in freedom, safety, and independence; on which happy event we sincerely join in your congratulations.

'Having defended the standard of liberty in this new world; having taught a lesson useful to those who inflict and to those who feel oppression, you retire from the great theatre of action, with the blessings of your fellow-citizens—but the glory of your virtues will not terminate with your military command, it will continue to animate remotest ages.

'We feel with you our obligations to the army in general, and will particularly charge ourselves with the interests of those confidential officers, who have attended your person to this affecting moment.

'We join with you in commending the interests of our dearest country to the protection of Almighty God, beseeching him to dispose the hearts and minds of its citizens to improve the opportunity afforded them, of becoming a happy and respectable nation. And for you we address to him our warmest prayers, that a life so beloved may be fostered with all his care; and that your days may be happy as they have been illustrious; and that he will finally give you that reward which this world cannot give.'*

Mr. Green, the editor of the Maryland Gazette, in allusion to the resignation by general Washington, of his commission to congress, says:

'Here we must let fall the scene—few tragedies ever drew more tears from so many beautiful eyes, as were affected by the moving manner in which his excellency took his final leave of congress. After which he immediately set out for Virginia, accompanied to South

---

* Ninth vol. Journal of Congress, pages 12, 13, 14.

river, by his excellency our governor,* with the warmest wishes of the city for his repose, health and happiness. Long, long may he enjoy them.'

1784. On Monday, the 29th of November, 1784, general Washington, arrived at Annapolis, accompanied by the Marquis de la Fayette. On the day following, the general assembly of this State, being then in session, to manifest their gratitude and attachment to those distinguished men, directed an elegant ball to be provided for their entertainment. Mr. Green says, 'the evening was crowned with the utmost joy and festivity, the whole company being made happy by the presence of two most amiable and all-accomplished men, to whom America is so deeply indebted for her preservation from tyranny and oppression.'

The following addresses were presented by the executive and legislative bodies, respectively, to the Marquis, during this visit at Annapolis, with his answers.

'ANNAPOLIS, *November* 30*th*, 1784.
In Council.

'*Sir*,—We, the governor and council of Maryland, beg leave with the most entire respect and heart-felt satisfaction, to embrace this first opportunity of your presence in the metropolis of this State, since the establishment of our peace, to offer you our warmest congratulations, and to express our high and grateful sense of the illustrious share which you bore in the accomplishment of that happy event.

'The early and decided part which you took in the cause of American liberty and glory, your generous services for us in the court of your august monarch,

* William Paca.

our great and good ally, and your wise and magnanimous conduct in the field, upon many of the most arduous occasions of the war, have endeared your name to America, and enrolled it high in the list of patriots and heroes, the supporters of her liberty, and founders of her empire.

'May, sir, your future days be as great and honourable as the past, and may heaven take under its peculiar care and protection, a life so eminently distinguished for its attachment and devotion to the rights and liberties of mankind. With every sentiment of regard and respect, we have the honour to be, sir, your most obedient humble servant,

'WILLIAM PACA.

'*The honourable the Marquis de la Fayette.*'

'*To his excellency the Governor and the honourable Council of the State of Maryland.*

'*Sir,*—In the polite attention of your excellency and council, I find myself equally obliged to your attachment, and honoured by your approbation.

'To have been early adopted among the sons of freedom, to have seen French and American standards united in the cause of mankind, to have so peculiarly shared in the confidence and friendship of the United States, are ideas the more pleasing to me, as I am assured, when I reflect upon the difficulties this country overcame, that she will attend to the means of splendor and happiness, which now, thank God, are in her disposal.

'I beg, sir, your excellency and council will accept the warmest acknowledgments, and sincerest wishes that an affectionate heart can most respectfully bestow.

LA FAYETTE.'

'*November* 30, 1784.

'*Sir*,—The general assembly of Maryland, are happy in having an opportunity of personally testifying the grateful sense they and their constituents entertain of the important services which you rendered these United States during the late war. The strong attachment which you have manifested to its interests in situations the most trying and difficult, still continues to actuate your conduct; to this attachment and predilection we partly attribute the commercial arrangements lately adopted by his Most Christian Majesty, which bid fair to perpetuate and extend the friendly intercourse and connexions between his subjects and the citizens of these United States.

'May the Great Ruler of the Universe long preserve a life which has been so early dedicated to the service of humanity, and engaged in the most useful and brilliant actions.

'GEO. PLATER, *Pres. Sen.*
'THO. C. DEYE, *Sp. Ho. Del.*

'*The Marquis de la Fayette.*'

'*To the Honourable the General Assembly of Maryland:*

'*Gentlemen*,—On this opportunity so pleasingly anticipated, of my respectful congratulations to your general assembly, I meet such precious marks of your partiality, as most happily complete my satisfaction.

'Amidst the enjoyments of allied successes, affection conspires with interest to cherish a mutual intercourse; and in France you will ever find that sympathizing good will, which leaves no great room for private exertions. With the ardor of a most zealous heart, I earnestly hope this State, ever mindful of the public spirit she has conspicuously displayed, will to the fullest extent improve her natural advantages, and in the federal Union so necessary to all, attain the highest degree of particular happiness and prosperity.

'While you are pleased, gentlemen, to consider my life as being devoted to the service of humanity, I feel not less gratified by so flattering an observation than by your friendly wishes for its welfare, and the pleasure I now experience in presenting you with the tribute of my attachment and gratitude.   LA FAYETTE.'

During the sitting of this legislature, the following act was passed:

'An act to naturalize major-general the Marquis de la Fayette and his heirs male forever.

'*Whereas*, the general assembly of Maryland, anxious to perpetuate a name dear to the State, and to recognize the Marquis de la Fayette for one of its citizens, who, at the age of nineteen, left his native country, and risked his life in the late revolution; who, on his joining the American army, after being appointed by congress to the rank of major-general, disinterestedly refused the usual rewards of command, and sought only to deserve, what he attained, the character of patriot and soldier; who, when appointed to conduct an incursion into Canada, called forth by his prudence and extraordinary discretion, the approbation of congress; who, at the head of an army in Virginia, baffled the manœuvres of a distinguished general, and excited the admiration of the oldest commanders; who early attracted the notice and obtained the friendship of the illustrious general Washington; and who laboured and succeeded in raising the honour and name of the United States of America; therefore,

'*Be it enacted, by the General Assembly of Maryland,* That the Marquis de la Fayette, and his heirs male forever, shall be, and they and each of them are hereby deemed, adjudged, and taken to be, natural born citizens of this State, and shall henceforth be entitled to all the immunities, rights and privileges of natural born citizens thereof, they and every of them conforming to the constitution and laws of this State, in the enjoyment and exercise of such immunities, rights and privileges.'

From this period Annapolis rather declined in her commerce and importance as a city. Until about this time, the merchants of Baltimore had here been obliged to register, enter and clear vessels—but a custom-house being now established there, Thomas Sollers, Esquire, naval officer, was authorized to grant registers for vessels at that port. Baltimore, with a thriving and enterprizing people in the interior, attracted the produce of the country, until Annapolis gradually lost all trade of importance. This was done without rivalry, from the force alone of circumstances and location.

Now Baltimore is truly styled the 'emporium of the state;' and her increasing population and greatness is viewed by every well-wisher of the State, with pleasure—for the interests of Baltimore and those of the State at large, are too closely united and identified to permit the indulgence of any other feelings than such as must arise in the bosom of every Marylander gratified at the growing importance of the one, and prosperity and honour of the other.

To the conclusion of this volume from this time, several years will be passed by without notices of any kind in regard to the city of Annapolis; no records or documents are to be found which afford any information deemed sufficiently interesting or amusing to detail.

1789. St. John's College was opened and dedicated on the 11th of November, 1789, with much solemnity, in the presence of a numerous and respectable concourse of people. The members of the general assembly, the chancellor, judges of the general court, together with the gentlemen of the bar, the corporate authorities of the city, and principal inhabitants thereof, preceded by the students, the faculty, and the governors and visiters of the college, walked in procession from the state-house to the college hall. An eloquent sermon, well adapted to the occasion, was preached by the Rev. Dr. W. Smith, who presided for the day. An oration was also delivered by the Rev. Ralph Higinbothom, on the advantages of a classical education.

1791. On the 25th of March, 1791, the president of the United States, accompanied by his private secretary, major Jackson, reached Annapolis. He was received with every mark of respect and affection, by the citizens, and entertained by them during his visit with their usual and known hospitality. Public dinners and balls were given on the occasion, and all seem to have vied with each other to make their distinguished guest sensible of the gratitude of a free and enlightened people. On his leaving the city, a company of gentlemen attended him as far as South river ferry, where they took leave of their illustrious fellow-citizen.

1798. At a meeting of the citizens of Annapolis, convened at the state-house on the 28th of June, 1798, the following address to the president of the United States, was unanimously agreed to:

'*To the President of the United States:*

'The address of the citizens of Annapolis, respectfully sheweth:

'That gratefully sensible of the blessings we enjoy under a government freely adopted, after mature deliberation, by the American people, and desirous of perpetuating these blessings to the latest posterity, we view with no less surprise than indignation, the treatment of our envoys by the French Directory, and the proffered terms of an ignominious and precarious peace, dependent on the caprice of fleeting and corrupt ministers; we remark with contempt, the opinion entertained that these terms ought to be accepted, because our disunion will render opposition to the enterprizes of France against this country unavailing.

'Threatened, as we are, with conditions harder than these, with a dismemberment similar to that of Venice, and with revolutionary systems, which the rulers of France, intoxicated with success, and insatiable of plunder, have produced among several European states within their grasp, we cannot doubt, that all true Americans will unite cordially in defence of their independence, and, by union, avert those calamities with which a timid and temporising policy has overwhelmed those countries, the victims of avarice, ambition and intrigue.

'Believing, as we do, that the executive of the united government has maintained an impartial neutrality, and that it has sedulously and faithfully endeavoured to cultivate the friendship of France, to reconcile subsisting differences, and to remove every just cause of complaint against the United States, (if any there be,) we are determined to support, to the utmost of our abilities, the measures which the government may think proper to adopt for the protection of commerce, the defence of the country, and in vindication of the insulted rights of an independent nation.

'We should lament the necessity of engaging in a war, which the American people and government have anxiously sought to avoid; but war, with all its horrors, would be preferable to base submission. On the removal of the present rulers of France, it may be expected that a milder policy will succeed that spirit of aggrandisement and conquest which has disorganized Europe; that the French nation, whose sagacity equals its courage, will embrace a different conduct towards us; it must reprobate the measures which may force us to be its foe; a speedy reconciliation and reparation of injuries, we confidently hope, would result from such a change. But as this event may be distant, it is prudent to be prepared against the worst; the plans, therefore, now adopted, or about to be adopted, by congress, for putting this country in the best posture of defence, meet our entire approbation. We believe this to be a very general sentiment, and we wish its expression to be as general, that the Directory may cease to project on the supposed disunion of our citizens, the dismemberment and ruin of our country.

'We admire, sir, and applaud, that firmness of temper which, as the chief magistrate of a free people, you have displayed during your administration. Averse from war, and dreading its concomitant evils, you have evinced an earnest disposition to preserve the peace of your country, while it could be preserved without the sacrifice of its honour and its rights. Persevere, sir, in the same line of conduct; we trust you may rely on the hearty support of the American people, whose calm good sense discerns their true interests, and whose firm and deliberate courage, under the protection of Providence, will maintain them.

'Signed by order of the citizens,
'NICHOLAS CARROLL, *Chairman.*'

To which address the president transmitted the following answer:

'*To the Citizens of Annapolis, in the State of Maryland.*

'*Gentlemen,*—I am sensible of the honour done to me, and the service to the public, by your unanimous address.

'The voluntary acknowledgment of freemen of the blessings they enjoy under a government of their own institution and election, may safely be believed to be sincere.

'With you, gentlemen, I wish to perpetuate these blessings to the latest posterity; but the fate of Venice cannot fail to remind us of the frailty of all human institutions, and of the necessity of constant vigilance, fortitude and valour, in defence of them, while it calls to our minds the *esto perpetua* of its great patriot and historian, Father Paul.

'With you I consider, with astonishment and indignation, the repeated and persevering contempt and insolence with which our ambassadors to the French

Directory have been treated; no kind of justification or apology can be made for it.

'You do no more than justice to the executive authorities of the United States, in believing that it has maintained an impartial neutrality, and that it has sedulously and faithfully endeavoured to cultivate the friendship of France.

'Your determination to support the measures which government may adopt for the protection of commerce, the defence of the country, and in vindication of the insulted rights of an independent nation, is consistent with the character of virtuous citizens and zealous patriots.

'I agree with you, that war is preferable to any base submission; nor is it possible that submission itself should avoid war.

'Although the sagacity of the French nation is equal to its courage, we must consider the powers that be, as their representatives, until they shall determine otherwise, nor will prudence permit us to trust the safety of our country to precarious and contingent events.

'The applause of the citizens of Annapolis is very flattering to me. My aversion to war, which to me, personally, could bring in its train neither pleasure, profit nor glory, nor any other effect than an incessant anxiety, and unremitted labour, may easily be believed. Yet I cannot sacrifice the honour or essential rights of my country, even at the shrine of peace, but especially when it is obvious that such sacrifices could produce nothing but war.

'I have the most confident reliance on the support of the American people, their good sense, their discernment of their true interests, their firm and deliberate courage; nor will I entertain a doubt that under the protection of Divine Providence, these virtues and talents will preserve them.   JOHN ADAMS.

'*United States, May* 4, 1798.'

The citizens of Annapolis in the above spirited address, showed that the stern courage and patriotic ardor which they had been taught in the school of the revolution, were not in the least abated. And that they who were amongst the first to hail with joy, an honourable peace with Great Britain, were now among the earliest of the sons of freedom to repel with indignation the insult and oppression of an ambitious and turbulent Directory; and preferred war, with all its train of evils, rather than basely to submit to the dictation of a foreign power.

In August of this year, 1798, the citizens subscribed a liberal and adequate sum for the purpose of erecting a battery and mounting cannon thereon, for the defence of the city and harbour, and appointed the following named gentlemen a committee to carry the same into effect, viz: John Davidson, John Shaw, John Gassaway, James Williams and Samuel Godman, Esquires.

1800. The 22d day of February, 1800, being the day appointed by the proclamations of the president of the United States and of the governor of this State, 'as a day of mourning, humiliation and prayer,' the same was observed in this city in the most public and solemn manner, as a just tribute to the memory of the immortal Washington.

The day was ushered in by a morning gun; and the colours were suspended from the dome of the statehouse, in mourning.

At half past ten o'clock, the procession proceeded from the state-house, in the following order:

      The Governor.
    Ministers of the Gospel.
      Executive.
 Chancellor and Judges of the General Court.
   Officers of Government.
   Professors of the College.
  Mayor and Corporation of the City.
    Officers of Militia.
     Infantry.
     Citizens.

During the procession, minute guns were fired—the bell tolling.

The services of the day were performed in St. Anne's church. The Rev. Mr. Higinbothom delivered a discourse from the following words: '*It is appointed for all men once to die;*' 'in which (it is said by one who was present) the eminent virtues and distinguished services of the deceased, were portrayed in strong and eloquent language.'

In the afternoon, the Rev. Mr. Roberts officiated in the same church, who addressed the congregation in an eloquent and masterly discourse from the following text: '*Know ye not that there is a prince and a great man fallen this day in Israel.*'

1804. On the 15th November, 1804, the French frigate 'Le President,' of 44 guns, captain Le Brosse, arrived and anchored off Annapolis, having on board the celebrated general Tureau, the minister plenipotentiary from the emperor of the French, to the United States. In the afternoon she fired a salute, which was returned by captain Muir's company of artillerists. The next day the general landed under a salute of 17 guns, and was received by the governor; and on the following day he left this city for Washington.

On the 21st of the same month, the honourable William Pinkney arrived here from his embassy in England. The arrival of this distinguished man, was hailed with joy by his fellow-citizens—a large concourse of whom, attended by the members of the state legislature, waited on him. The citizens presented him with a congratulatory address, and invited him to partake of a public dinner. Mr. Pinkney accepted the invitation, and in his reply acknowledged the peculiar sensibility with which he read the kind and flattering testimonial of his fellow-citizens' approbation and esteem, and said—'to meet with such a reception from the inhabitants of my native city, to which in every vicissitude of life and fortune, I have always felt, and shall continue to feel, the most lively attachment, is more grateful to my heart than I am able to express.'

1805. On the 15th of September, 1805, the release of the officers and crew of the frigate Philadelphia, from Tripolitan captivity, was celebrated by our citizens with every demonstration of joy becoming an event which was hailed with a general exultation throughout our country, especially as their deliverance was effected by the valour and bravery of our gallant little navy.

1807. The citizens of Annapolis held a meeting on the 29th of June, 1807, and took into consideration what measures it became them to adopt in relation to the outrage which had been committed upon the frigate Chesapeake, by the British naval force then on our coast.

His excellency governor Wright, was unanimously requested to take the chair, and John Johnson, esq. was appointed secretary.

After the cause of the meeting had been stated in an appropriate address from the chair, several spirited resolutions were adopted, expressive of their sentiments of detestation and resentment, with which they viewed the unprovoked attack upon the Chesapeake—pledged their lives and fortunes to co-operate with the government of the United States in any measure of retaliation which might be adopted. Also, renouncing all intercourse with the British ships-of-war stationed on our coast, until the decision of our government should be known; with other declarations on the same subject, and with arrangements for carrying the design of these resolutions into effect.

On the 26th of August of this year, the startling information was received here of a piracy having been committed in the Chesapeake bay, about thirty miles below Annapolis, by a French pirate, in the capture of the ship Othello, captain Glover, bound to Baltimore.

Spirited preparations were immediately made, and the 'Holy-Hawk' packet, with two brass four-pounders, under command of capt. Muir of the artillery, and capt. Duvall of the infantry, with a detachment of their respective companies, armed with muskets and boarding pikes, accompanied by a boat from the 'L'Eole,' (then lying in our harbour,) with thirty-three volunteers, French and American, under the command of lieut. Mann, of the United States' navy, and an officer of the '*L'Eole*,' sailed in pursuit of the pirate. They proceeded some distance down the bay, but returned without encountering the modern *Kidd*. Detachments from Baltimore, under captains Samuel and John Sterett, in conjunction with captain Porter, of the U. S. navy, were more fortunate. The piratical vessel was taken to that port. Five of the crew, who had passed through this place, were captured by our citizens a short distance from town, and were also taken to Baltimore. A gentleman, then high in authority, assured the captors of these five unarmed French pirates, 'that they deserved well of their country.'

Nothing material transpired from this period until the war of 1812, when the citizens of Annapolis were still the same patriotic and zealous people in the cause of their country, and for which they have ever been distinguished in times of peril and danger: always as resolved to repel an invasion of their soil, as were their ancestors to resist tyranny and oppression.

CHAPTER VIII.

BRIEF DESCRIPTION OF THE CITY OF ANNAPOLIS, AND ITS MORE PROMINENT PUBLIC BUILDINGS.

City of Annapolis—Its Population—Shipping—Its Site—Its Advantages—Naval Academy—The Round Bay—Rail Road—Its proximity to the seat of the National Government—Its Harbour—The Treasury—The Government-house—St. John's College—Episcopal Church—Roman Catholic Chapel—Methodist Church—African House of Worship—The Farmers' Bank of Maryland—Court-house—City Hall—City Hotel—Ball-room—Theatre—The Garrison at Fort Severn.

ANNAPOLIS, the capital of Maryland, received its name in 1708, in honour of Queen Anne, the then reigning monarch of England. It is situated on the south branch of the river Severn, thirty miles south from Baltimore, and forty miles east-north-east from Washington, in latitude 38° 58' north; longitude, Washington city, 0° 31' east.

Its population is about three thousand; shipping, 4006 tons. It stands on a peninsula formed by Acton's creek on the south, and Covey's creek on the north; the heads of these two creeks being within half a mile of each other. Its greatest length is little more than a mile, and in breadth something more than half a mile. It covers an area of about an hundred and forty-three acres. The site of the city is one of great beauty, commanding an extensive view of the Chesapeake and the surrounding country, which exhibits a great diversity of landscape and picturesque scenery. The appellation of the *'beautiful city,'* has often been applied to her, especially when clothed in nature's brightest livery.

Annapolis is the natal place of some of the most distinguished men America can boast of; and has the honour of being the native place of five of the most beautiful and accomplished peeresses of our mother land.

This city is admirably adapted as a location for a *Naval Academy*, an institution which has long been desired by all classes of our citizens. Her central position between the north and the south; her proximity to the seat of our national government; her fine and commodious harbour, which gives her great commercial advantages—all combine to recommend her to the general government as decidedly the best location in the Union for the site of such an institution. There is water bold and extensive enough for all desirable purposes; and only seven miles from the mouth of the Severn is the Round Bay, a beautiful sheet of water, which of itself presents a commodious and secure harbour for ships-of-war, and in every respect is an eligible depot for naval stores. The Annapolis and Elkridge rail road being finished, the distance between Annapolis and Washington can be accomplished in less than three hours, which removes at once all the force of the objection heretofore made on the ground of its difficulty of access during the winter.

It now occupies three hours by steamboat travel between this place and Baltimore; by the rail road, two hours, and perhaps less, will suffice to pass from one to the other. And thus will Annapolis be rendered a suitable and convenient outer or winter harbour for the great emporium of our State, whose harbour is frequently closed by ice, while this is open all the winter, unless it be one of unusual severity.

The public buildings are the state-house, the treasury, the government-house, St. John's college, Episcopal church, Roman Catholic chapel, Methodist church, African house of worship, the Farmers' Bank of Maryland, court-house, city hall, city hotel, ballroom, theatre, the garrison at fort Severn.

THE STATE-HOUSE.

The state-house is situated on a beautiful elevation in the centre of the city. It has elicited alike the admiration of the citizen, the sojourner, and the stranger, for the beauty of its structure.

The main building is of brick, and the superstructure which surmounts it is of wood.

The height from the base to the top of the spire is two hundred feet. From the platform of the dome, which is one hundred and thirty-five feet high, the spectator has one of the most delightful panoramic views to be found within the United States. It commands a view of nature in all the beauty of poetic scenery—the ancient city—its environs—the adjacent country—the noble Chesapeake, and the eastern shore beyond it, for an extent of thirty miles around, breaks upon the view of the delighted eye.

The hill on which stands this noble edifice, is enclosed by a neat and substantial granite wall, surmounted by a handsome iron railing, which is entered by three gates, one situated at the head of Francis street, and in front of the building, the second to the south-west, and the third to the north-east of the circle.

The main entrance to the building is through a portico of but modest pretensions, and opens into a spacious and beautiful hall, in which is had a view of the interior of the dome, the stucco work of which was made from plaster brought from St. Mary's county.

On the right hand of the hall is the senate chamber. This room is judiciously and tastefully fitted up for the use of the senators of our State. It is 34 feet by 40; it has a lobby and gallery for the accommodation of visitors. Persons of distinction are often invited within the bar of the senate, where seats are provided for them. Portraits at full length, of the distinguished Charles Carroll of Carrollton, Samuel Chase, William Paca, and Thomas Stone, ornament the walls. These gentlemen were the four signers of the declaration of independence, on the part of Maryland, and were at that period all citizens of Annapolis; each of them in his day filled various posts of honour and responsibility, and shared largely the confidence and esteem of his fellow-citizens.

The first named gentleman was the last survivor of that illustrious band of patriots who signed the declaration of American independence.

There is also in this room a portrait of the 'hero of the Cowpens,' the virtuous and excellent John Eager Howard, who has with the rest of his compatriots, gone to the land of his fathers, there to reap the rewards of an honourable and well-spent life. In 1788–'89 and '90, Mr. Howard was governor of Maryland. The first and last named portraits were painted by Mr. Sully; the others by Mr. Bordley, both native artists. There is likewise in this room a portrait of the elder Pitt, the friend of America. In this picture lord Chatham is represented at full length, in

20*

the attitude and costume of a Roman orator—with decorations of emblematical figures, expressive of his noble principles. It was painted by Charles Wilson Peale, (who was a native of Annapolis,) while in England, and presented by him in the year 1794, to his native State.

This room is still more memorable as being the spot upon which was consummated the greatest act in the life of the greatest man of any age. It was here that Washington, after having rescued his country from foreign dominion and usurpation, nobly laid down his authority on the altar of liberty—resigning his commission into the hands of congress.

And in this room, too, was ratified by the same congress, the treaty of peace with Great Britain, of 1783, recognizing our independence.

Adjoining the senate chamber is the committee room, neatly fitted up for the purposes to which it is applied.

On the left of the hall, immediately opposite to the senate chamber, is the chamber of the house of delegates, of the same dimensions of the senate chamber, neatly fitted up, and accommodates seventy-nine members, who sit at desks conveniently arranged. It has also a lobby and gallery for the accommodation of spectators, and with it are connected committee rooms. From the walls of this room is suspended a large picture, presenting a full length likeness of general Washington, attended by general La Fayette and colonel Tilghman, his aids-de-camp; the continental army passing in review. In his hand he holds the articles of capitulation at Yorktown.

This picture was painted by Charles Wilson Peale,

in pursuance of a resolution of the general assembly of Maryland.

At the termination of the hall of entrance, the State library is situated, which is appropriately fitted up. There are seven alcoves on the first floor, and ten arches on the gallery. It contains at this time twelve thousand volumes, and is calculated to hold twenty thousand. It is of but recent origin, and has for the short period of its existence, under the fostering care of the legislature, already become valuable as a State institution.

This portion of the hall was formerly occupied by the general court of Maryland, and used as a hall of justice until 1804, when that court was abolished. It remained unoccupied from that period until the year 1834, when it was fitted up and appropriated to its present purpose.

In the public hall are two archways, the one on the right, leads by a flight of stairs to the State department, directly over the senate chamber. This room was occupied under the late constitution of the State, by the governor and council. It has recently undergone repair, and is neatly and appropriately furnished.

The executive business is here transacted by the governor and the secretary of State.

A room north of the State department, formerly occupied as the State library, is now the office of the adjutant-general.

Opposite to the door of the State department, a gallery leads to the armory, and to the dome of the building. The arrangement of the armory is considered by many as one of great beauty, the arms being disposed of upon the ceiling and walls of the room.

The archway on the left of the public hall, leads by a flight of stairs to the court of appeals' chamber, immediately over the hall of the house of delegates, and to the chancery office, which occupies the west angle on the second floor; likewise to one of the committee rooms of the house of delegates.

In the rear of the building are two entrances, the one on the west leads to the land office, and the other to record rooms of the court of appeals.

THE TREASURY.

Within the circle enclosing the state-house, on the eastern margin of the hill, stands the treasury department. This building is venerable as well as memorable, for having been the legislative hall of the provincial government. In the larger room, the lower house, and in the smaller one, the upper house of assembly sat for many years; such accommodations contrast strikingly with those of the present day.

From the state-house and Episcopal church circles, respectively, many of the streets radiate, and intersect each other at convenient points. The plan is a peculiar and an agreeable one, when viewed from some prominent point.

GOVERNMENT–HOUSE.

The main building of the government-house, was erected by Edmund Jennings, Esq., and was purchased from him by governor Eden, when he presided over the province of Maryland; and by whom were built the wings and long room.

This edifice has a handsome court and garden, extending, with the exception of an intervening lot, to the water's edge. From the portico looking to the garden, a fine prospect regales the vision. The building consists of two stories, and presents an extensive front; there are on the lower floor a large room on each side of the hall as you enter, and several smaller ones; the saloon, on the same floor, is nearly the length of the house. On each side of the edifice are commodious kitchens, carriage-houses and stables, with spacious lots. Towards the water, the building rises in the middle in a turreted shape. It stands detached from other structures, and is altogether a delightful and suitable mansion for the residence of the chief magistrate of our State.

ST. JOHN'S COLLEGE.

In 1784, the general assembly of Maryland passed an act for founding a college on the western shore, and incorporated the institution by the name of the 'Visitors and Governors of St. John's College;' and for the purpose of providing a 'permanent fund for the further encouragement and establishment of the said college,' the sum of £1750 was 'annually and forever thereafter given and granted, as a donation by the public, to the use of the said college.'

The legislature also granted for the use of the institution, four acres of land, (now known by the name of the College Green,) and which land had been in the year 1744, conveyed by Stephen Boardley to Mr. Bladen, the then governor of Maryland. Mr. Bladen projected the present college building, as a noble mansion for the residence of the governors of Maryland. A Mr. Duff (the architect) came over from Scotland to superintend the construction of the building. Materials of every kind were provided equal to the spirit of public liberality, and the edifice was nearly completed in a style of superior magnificence, when an unhappy contention took place between the governor and legislature, which increased to such a degree, that at a period when a very trifling sum would have rendered it a noble residence, the further prosecution of the design was discontinued, and it remained for a long time a melancholy and mouldering monument of the consequences resulting from political dissensions. It received the *cognomen* of the 'governor's folly.'

The depredations of time had greatly injured the interior of the building, which in an unfinished state, continued many years exposed to the inclemency of the weather. But the legislature, actuated by sentiments which reflect the highest credit on their patriotism and wisdom, having determined to endow and found a college for the education of youth in every liberal and useful branch of science, wisely resolved to repair the damages sustained, and to apply the building to the purposes of education.

The agents appointed by the legislature for soliciting subscriptions and donations for St. John's college, were the Rev. John Carroll, the Rev. Wm. Smith and Patrick Allison, Doctors of Divinity, and Richard Sprigg, John Steret and George Diggs, Esqs., with power to appoint other agents.

By an act of assembly passed in 1785, the funds of 'King William's school,' which had been founded at Annapolis ever since the year 1696, were conveyed to St. John's college.

In thus establishing a seminary of learning at the seat of government, our patriots and statesmen manifested their sense of the great importance of, and the happy results which would flow from an institution of this character, under the State patronage, and how inseparably it was connected with the interest and happiness of our people. For years the flourishing condition of St. John's fully realized the most sanguine expectations of its noble and enlightened founders. Scholars and statesmen were sent forth from her halls, who have been the pride of her own and the admiration of other States, and who have earned for themselves the highest reputation, and reflected honour on their alma mater. But alas! this noble and efficient monument of the wisdom of our progenitors, was but too soon to meet a sad reverse of fortune. For as early as the year 1805, we find that political discord—that horrible hydra with its hundred heads—reared its crest against this institution, and by an act of the legislature in that year, the funds of the college were withdrawn. This paralyzed its energies, and reduced it to a languishing condition, in which posture it remained until 1811, when the legislature, partially awakened to a sense of duty and justice to the cause of education, granted $1000 annually, and again in 1821, granted to its visitors and governors a scheme of a lottery, by which was added to its permanent funds, twenty thousand dollars.

In 1831, when the efforts of its visitors and governors were crowned with success in obtaining the services of its present able principal, a still brighter prospect dawned upon this old and favoured institution of our State. By the united and unceasing exertions of the faculty, visitors and governors of the institution, it was again placed in a prosperous condition.

The efforts thus made to revive this venerable seminary of learning, could not but attract the further attention of our legislature. In 1833, the State came nobly to the rescue of good old St. John's, and passed an act of compromise, by which $2000 per annum, in addition to former grants, were secured to the college forever, and which the visitors and governors accepted in full of their legal and equitable claims; and a deed of release, enjoined by the provisions of the act, was executed and entered upon the records of the court of appeals.

At a meeting of the board of the visitors and governors of the college, held on the 15th of February, 1834, the principal was authorized and requested to collect subscriptions, to be applied to the erection of suitable buildings for the accommodation of students, and for the improving and extending the library and the philosophical apparatus of the institution.

For the purpose of carrying this object into effect, the principal visited several parts of the State, and succeeded in obtaining a subscription of more than twelve thousand dollars. From the proceeds of which has been erected a beautiful edifice, finished in a style of elegance that reflects great credit upon its projectors.

This building is designed for one of the professors, and the students; there are twenty private rooms in it, intended for separate studies for members of the advanced classes, and two large dormitories for pupils in the preparatory branches. A building like this had long been greatly needed, and will add much to the prosperity of the institution. It will accommodate at least sixty students in all the departments.

There is a library in the institution, but by no means

such an one as it should be; although there is a large collection of books, and some of them of rare and curious editions, yet they are not of the kind most needed in an institution of the highest order of science. And it is ardently hoped that the State, under whose auspices this institution has been so recently revived, will bestow an adequate fund for furnishing its library with all the standard authors in literature, in science and the arts; and especially with all the philosophical and scientific journals published in this country and in Europe.

There have been at all times at least *ten* students in the institution, who *receive instruction free of expense*, under the provisions of an act of assembly. Provision is also made by the visitors and governors to receive in addition, one scholar from each county in the State.

The cabinet of minerals belonging to the college, consists of various and interesting specimens of ores and marls found within the borders of our own State, which have been collected and arranged by Mr. Ducatel, the distinguished professor who was recently at the head of that branch of science; also, some very valuable specimens of minerals and ores of other States and foreign countries. And valuable contributions are continued to be made from various quarters.

St. John's college stands on an eminence at the termination of Prince George street, and is a four-storied structure, including the basement, and has recently undergone considerable repairs. A more delightful situation was never appropriated than this for its purposes. It is situated on the banks of the Severn, within the limits of the city, commanding, in every point of view, the most interesting and beautiful objects. The adjacent country is open and healthy; the contiguous grounds are sufficiently extensive for the advantages of exercise and amusement; and the fabric contains a variety of spacious and convenient apartments for the accommodation of the professors and students.

The peculiar advantages to youth in being educated at this seminary, are numerous and evident; with respect to health, as far as a high and dry soil, with pure air, will contribute to its preservation, or restore it when impaired, few places can be put in competition with, and none can excel it. The sessions of the general assembly, and the meeting of the courts of appeals, chancery and county, are so obviously beneficial to those young men who may be called to the public service, or enter into the profession of the law, that no parent, especially a citizen of our State, should hesitate a moment to send his son, whom he desires to become eminent in any of the professions, to a place where he is the most likely to acquire those qualifications which will render him useful and distinguished as a statesman, or afford him the greatest chance of professional improvement.

Large cities often defeat the salutary purposes of education, by furnishing incitements to vice, and affording opportunities of concealment. Annapolis is happily free from these objections; and the discipline of this institution is such as to prevent the student from deviating from the path of rectitude, even if so inclined. The forming of manners, so essential to those who are intended for any public or private pursuit, will keep pace with the improvement of the intellect, and a youth when qualified to enter on the scene of action, will be enabled to perform his part with ease to himself and satisfaction to the observer.

If all the advantages mentioned are united in this institution, and which it is presumed no one will dispute, why, we may inquire, should the citizens of Maryland send their sons abroad to other seminaries, instead of patronizing an institution of our own? An institution, we will venture to assert, that has sent forth to the world, a constant and regular supply of alumni, who by their talents at the bar, in the sacred desk, and in our legislative halls, have proved themselves inferior to none from any other seminary in the Union.

The college green, in the revolutionary war, was used as the encampment of the French army; and also by the American troops assembled in the war of 1812. Traces of these encampments still remain, and render it an object of touching interest; parts of it exhibit mounds raised to those who died in service; and though 'no storied urn' designates the spot where the remains of any distinguished warrior repose—all being indiscriminately inhumed—yet the interest of their fate is undiminished by this circumstance, when we reflect that they died in the same glorious cause.

On the grounds east of the college, stands a large forest poplar, or 'American tulip tree,' the age of which is not known. It is highly probable that it formed a part of the forest which was growing when Annapolis was first settled by the puritans in 1649. This tree has been commemorated in verse by a distinguished graduate of St. John's, (the lamented Doctor John Shaw, who was a native of our city,) and is held to this day in great veneration by our citizens. But a short time since, it was accidentally set on fire. The occurrence excited as much interest in, and exertion on the part of our inhabitants to extinguish it, and save the old favourite tree from destruction, as if it had been one of the finest buildings of the town. It was truly gratifying to see the interest elicited and the delight manifested by many when the progress of the fire was arrested.

THE EPISCOPAL CHURCH

Is a large and commodious building,* and stands about two hundred yards west of the state-house. It is enclosed by a post and rail fence. Between the church and the enclosure, are arranged in a circular form, Lombardy poplars, which in the summer afford an agreeable shade. The interior of the church is plain and neat, and is capable of containing a numerous congregation. A large and fine toned bell hangs in the belfry, and is said to have been presented to the city by Queen Anne. It has an old but fine organ in the gallery. Fronting the reading-desk and pulpit, affixed to the wall, is a marble statue of chaste and beautiful sculpture, erected in memory of one of the Dulany family. In the church-yard are several sculptured tombs enclosed with iron railing, which contain the remains of the Tasker family. There is also a monument erected in memory of some of the members of the Carroll family.

* This church was erected soon after the American revolution. Its architect was Mr. Robert Key, long a worthy and respectable citizen of Annapolis.

THE ROMAN CATHOLIC CHAPEL

Is a small structure, and is situated on the Duke of Gloucester street. It was built mainly through the instrumentality of the venerable and generous Charles Carroll of Carrollton. It has been erected but a few years, and has a neat appearance outside. The interior is very appropriate, and the general arrangement is convenient and comfortable. It has a fine new organ in the gallery. Near the chapel is a house for the minister, which is one of a row of buildings that formerly stood there, then known as 'Mac Namara's row,' and is said to be one of the oldest houses in the city.

THE METHODIST CHURCH

Was built about twenty years ago, and is capable of accommodating a large congregation. This building is of plain structure, and is situated on the north side of the state-house circle. It is larger than the Roman chapel, but smaller than the episcopal church, its interior is like the outside, plain, but becomingly neat.

THE AFRICAN HOUSE OF WORHIP

Is situated on West street, in the suburbs of the city. It is of brick and but recently erected, large and commodious, and accommodates the coloured population of the place, who deserve great credit for their liberal contributions towards its erection.

THE FARMERS' BANK OF MARYLAND

Is situate at the corner of West street, fronting the church circle. It consists of one story, and is of singular form externally, though the interior, particularly the

21*

banking room, is well calculated for the purpose for which it is intended. It may be truly said of this institution, that it has ever been, and still is considered as sound and as safe as any other banking establishment in this country.

THE COURT-HOUSE

Is quite a modern edifice, and stands on the south-west of the church circle. As you enter there is a spacious hall, on each side of which are two commodious offices. The one on the right hand is occupied by the register of wills, the other by the clerk of the county. Immediately in the rear of the clerk's office, is the sheriff's, and at the end of the hall is the court room. This is a fine, spacious room, and well suited to the purposes to which it is appropriated. On the second floor are the jury rooms, surveyor's office, and rooms used by the commissioners of the county. The front roof of the building, compared with the rear, exhibits the appearance of wings. It is enclosed by a brick wall, surmounted by a neat wood railing.

THE CITY HALL

Is situate on Church street. It is a neat edifice, and contains a hall on the upper floor the whole length of the house, and is the place of meeting for the corporate authorities of the city. Rising from the roof is a belfry, and under the hall the fire engines and apparatus belonging the city are kept.

THE CITY HOTEL

Stands at the corner of Church and Conduit streets, and has been in the occupancy of several individuals since its establishment as such. The old building, as it is termed, originally belonged to, and was occupied by, Mr. Lloyd Dulany, as his residence. It is two stories high; the new building is three; and a large building of two stories has recently been added, extending back to the Duke of Gloucester street. The present worthy and enterprising proprietors have added greatly to its appearance and comfort. The court fronting the main building is tastefully embellished by neat enclosures and shrubbery. This structure, with its appendages, covers a large space of ground. It is an excellent establishment, and in every respect well calculated for the comfortable accommodation of travelers, and others, who make it a place of abode or resort.

THE BALL ROOM

Is on the Duke of Gloucester street, and is a spacious edifice. The dancing room is large and of elegant construction, and when illuminated, shows to great advantage; the walls are decorated by a full length likeness of Charles Lord Baltimore, and portraits of several of the former governors of Maryland. At the lower extremity is the supper room, which was formerly the revenue office of the province. At the upper end is a card room, for the use of the gentlemen who may choose to enjoy the 'circulation of the party-coloured gentry,' without having their attention diverted by the sound of the violin, and the evolutions of youthful performers.

This building was used as our legislative hall, during the erection of the present state-house.

THE THEATRE

Is also situated on the Duke of Gloucester street, and is of late construction. It is built of wood, and is rarely opened, not having votaries of the dramatic muse sufficient to sustain it even for a season.

THE GARRISON AT FORT SEVERN

Occupies an area of several acres, tastefully laid off. A substantial brick wall encloses in part the garrison, consisting of several handsome buildings; the river Severn encloses the residue. On approaching this establishment by water, your admiration is elicited by a romantic and picturesque landscape, ornamented by the dwellings, cottages, fort, trees and shrubbery.

There can be no site better suited for the purpose to which it is applied. Great labour has been bestowed in rendering it perfectly healthy. The quarters or barracks are preserved with all imaginable neatness, and whatever belongs to the soldiers' apartments is kept in the neatest order. The section of the town where the garrison is located was formerly much neglected, and had a very desolate appearance. Now the entire aspect of the ground is greatly changed and improved from the water's edge, where the fort stands, to the extent of the enclosures.

The main building, occupied by the commandant of the post, was erected by a Mr. Duff, (the architect of St. John's college,) and by him sold to Mr. Walter Dulany, who resided there for many years.

Governors of the Province and State of Maryland from the First Settlement in 1633 to 1840.

UNDER THE PROPRIETARY GOVERNMENT.

1633. Leonard Calvert.
1647. Thomas Greene.
1649. William Stone.
1654. Commissioners under Parliament.
1658. Josiah Fendall.
1661. Philip Calvert.
1662. Charles Calvert.
1676. Charles Lord Baltimore.
1678. Thomas Notley.
1681. Charles Lord Baltimore.
1715. John Hart.
1720. Charles Calvert.
1727. Benedict Leonard Calvert.
1732. Samuel Ogle.
1733. Charles Lord Baltimore.
1735. Samuel Ogle.
1742. Thomas Bladen.
1747. Samuel Ogle.
1753. Horatio Sharpe.
1769. Robert Eden.

UNDER THE ROYAL GOVERNMENT.

1689. Government seized by the crown of England.
1692. Lyonel Copley.
1694. Francis Nicholson.
1699. Nathaniel Blackiston.
1704. John Seymour.
1714. John Hart.

PRESIDENTS OF THE PROVINCE.

1703. Thomas Tench.
1709. Edward Lloyd.
1752. Benjamin Tasker.

UNDER THE STATE GOVERNMENT.

1776. Provisional Government.
1777. Thomas Johnson.
1779. Thomas Sim Lee.
1782. William Paca.
1785. William Smallwood.
1788. John Eager Howard.
1791. George Plater.
1792. Thomas Sim Lee.
1794. John H. Stone.
1797. John Henry.
1798. Benjamin Ogle.
1801. John Francis Mercer.
1803. Robert Bowie.
1806. Robert Wright.
1809. Edward Lloyd.
1811. Robert Bowie.
1812. Levin Winder.
1815. Charles Ridgely, of Hampton.
1818. Charles Goldsborough.
1819. Samuel Sprigg.
1822. Samuel Stevens, Jr.
1825. Joseph Kent.
1828. Daniel Martin.
1829. Thomas King Carroll.
1830. Daniel Martin.
1831. George Howard.
1832. James Thomas.
1835. Thomas W. Veazey.
1838. William Grason.

APPENDIX.

Letter from General Charles Lee to the Honourable Daniel of St. Thomas Jenifer, Esq., President of the Council of Safety of Maryland.

'WILLIAMSBURG, *May the* 6*th,* 1776.

'*Dear Sir,*—I find that I am extremely censured not only by your board, but by a multitude of others, for my letter to Mr. Purviance with respect to the seizure of Mr. Eden's person and papers—but I really think when the circumstances are explained, that the censure will appear unjust, and that I was neither violent, assuming nor precipitate. When the secretary of state's letter to your governor was put into my hands, I naturally concluded that could we possess ourselves of all Mr. Eden's papers, the whole machinations of the ministry might be discovered; that this discovery might enable us to prevent their effects, and perhaps defeat the whole plan. The possession of these papers could not be hoped for without previously securing his person, and to accomplish this, the utmost secrecy and expedition were necessary. Now, sir, as I imagined you had no troops at Annapolis to execute the purpose, (but in this I find I was mistaken,) and as I knew there were troops in readiness at Baltimore, and as there was no continental general or other officer in Maryland, Mr. Purviance, chairman of the committee, on the spot where I had conceived troops alone to be stationed, occurred to me as the only person to whom I could with propriety and effect make application. Had I known, sir, that a regiment or any troops were stationed at Annapolis, I should undoubtedly, sir, have addressed myself to you as president of the council of safety.

'It is said, sir, that Maryland was out of the district of my command; that consequently to intrude myself into the business and concerns of that province, was assuming and arrogant. I really conceive, sir, that when the safety or very being of the whole community appears at stake, the part I have acted in this affair cannot with justice be esteemed arrogance. I did not presume authoritatively to order, but as one servant of the public earnestly to entreat and consider another servant who alone appeared to me to have the means in his hands, to take a certain step of the best importance to the public cause. I must, therefore, repeat, sir, that my reason for addressing myself to Mr. Purviance, at Baltimore, proceeded entirely from my ignorance of there being any troops at Annapolis, and not (as I have been told has been thrown out) from any indifference in your virtue and decision. I suppose the committee of safety here viewed it in the same light, for I read my letter to them, and it was approved of. In times like these, sir, I conceive that when we have received sufficient evidences of any treasonable practices being carried on, and that when it appears to us that the immediate seizure of a particular traitor's person, may lead to discoveries on which the salvation of the State may depend; that when the utmost secrecy and expedition are necessary to the seizure of his person, it is the duty of a good citizen not to delay a single instant, if a single instant's delay may prevent the execution. This was the manner I thought it my duty to proceed in the case of Mr. Wormley. On the discovery of his correspondence with the enemy, I gave orders for the security of his person and papers, and then referred the affair to the proper tribunal, the committee of safety. The measure was so far from giving umbrage or creating jealousy, that it met with their unanimous approbation. If this method is proscribed at a juncture like the present, the great check on dangerous correspondence and conspiracies will be taken off; if councils are to be held previously to the seizure of any traitor's person or papers, notwithstanding the strongest evidences against him, I am much mistaken if every traitor does not slip through your hands.

'I must now, sir, conclude, with assuring you, and the respectable body over which you preside, that if they suppose me capable of aiming or wishing to extend the military authority, or trespass on the civil, they do me the most cruel injustice. Although I was bred in the army, I thank God the spirit and principles of the citizen were ever predominant, and I solemnly declare that if I thought it possible I should ever be so far intoxicated by military command, as to harbour a wish injurious to the civil supremacy in all things, I would now, whilst I retain my senses, beg leave to divest myself of my present office, and serve as a volunteer in the glorious cause in which I have embarked my person, fortune and reputation. What I did in this affair, I did in the character of a common zealous member of the community, not of an officer; what appeared irregular or offensive in the mode, I hope I have explained to your satisfaction, and I entreat that it may be entirely attributed to a mistake for which I am heartily concerned, as it has prejudiced me in the opinion of men whose esteem I am most ambitious of obtaining.

'I am, dear sir, your most obd't, humble serv't,

'CHARLES LEE.

To Daniel of St. Thomas Jenifer, Esq.
President of the Council of Safety of Maryland.'

APPENDIX.

Letter from the Honourable John Hancock to the Honourable Convention of Maryland.

'PHILADELPHIA, *June 4th*, 1776.

'*Gentlemen,*—Our affairs are hastening fast to a crisis; and the approaching campaign will, in all probability, determine forever the fate of America.

'Such is the unrelenting spirit which possesses the tyrant of Britain and his parliament, that they have left no measure unessayed that had a tendency to accomplish our destruction.

'Not satisfied with having lined our coasts with ships-of-war, to starve us into a surrender of our liberties, and to prevent us from being supplied with arms and ammunition, they are now about to pour in a number of foreign troops, who from their want of connections, and those feelings of sympathy which frequently bind together the different parts of the same empire, will be more likely to do the business of their masters without remorse or compunction.

'By the best intelligence from Canada, it appears that our affairs in that quarter wear a melancholy aspect. Should the Canadians and Indians take up arms against us, (which there is too much reason to fear,) we shall then have the whole force of that country to contend with, joined to that of Great Britain, and all her foreign auxiliaries. In this situation what steps must we pursue? The continental troops alone, are unable to stem the torrent; nor is it possible at this day to raise and discipline men ready to take the field by the time they will be wanting.

'From the secrecy with which the ministry carry on their machinations, we neither know their views, or how near our enemies may be. Perhaps at this moment they are landing on some part of our country.

'In this difficult and trying situation of our affairs, the congress have come to the enclosed resolves, which I have it in command to transmit you by express, containing matters of the greatest importance, and to which I beg leave to request your attention. You will there find the congress have judged it necessary to call upon the militia at this alarming crisis.

'Should the united colonies be able to keep their ground this campaign, I am under no apprehensions on account of any future one. We have many disadvantages at present to struggle with, which time and progress in the art of war will remove.

'But this circumstance should rouse us to superior exertions on the occasion.

'The militia of the united colonies are a body of troops that may be depended upon.

'To their virtue, their delegates in congress now make the most solemn appeal.

'They are called upon to say, whether they will live slaves or die freemen. They are requested to step forth in defence of their wives, their children, their liberty and every thing they hold dear. The cause is certainly a most glorious one, and I hope every man in the colony of Maryland is determined to see it gloriously ended, or to perish in the ruins of it.

'In short, on your exertions at this critical period, together with those of the other colonies in the common cause, the salvation of America now evidently depends.

'Your colony, I am persuaded, will not be behind hand. Exert, therefore, every nerve to distinguish yourselves. Quicken your preparations, and stimulate the good people of your government, and there is no danger, notwithstanding the mighty armament with which we are threatened, but they will be led on to victory, to liberty, and to happiness

'I have the honour to be, with great respect, gentlemen, your most obedient and very humble servant,

'JOHN HANCOCK, *President.*
'*The Honourable the Convention of Maryland.*'

Letter from John Hancock, Esquire, President of Congress, to the Honourable Convention of Maryland.

'PHILADELPHIA, *July 8th*, 1776.

'Gentlemen,—Although it is not possible to foresee the consequences of human action, yet it is nevertheless a duty we owe ourselves and posterity, in all our public councils, to decide in the best manner we are able, and to trust the event to that Being, who controls both causes and events, so as to bring about his own determinations.

'Impressed with this sentiment, and at the same time fully convinced that our affairs may take a more favourable turn, the congress have judged it neccessary to dissolve all connection between Great Britain and the American Colonies, and to declare them Free and Independent States, as you will perceive by the enclosed declaration, which I am directed by congress to transmit to you, and to request you will have it proclaimed in your colony, in the way you shall think most proper.

'The important consequences to the American States from this Declaration of Independence, considered as the ground and foundation of a future government, will naturally suggest the propriety of proclaiming it in such a manner, as that the people may be universally informed of it.

'I have the honour to be, gentlemen, your most obedient and very humble servant,

'JOHN HANCOCK, *President.*

'*The Hon'ble Convention of Maryland.*'

Letter from Colonel Smallwood to the Hon'ble Matthew Tilghman, Esq. President of the Convention of Maryland.

'CAMP OF THE MARYLAND REGULARS,
HEAD-QUARTERS, *October 12th,* 1776.

'*Sir,*—Through your hands I must beg leave to address the honourable Convention of Maryland, and must confess, not without an apprehension, that I have incurred their displeasure for having omitted writing when on our march from Maryland for New York, and since our arrival here. Nor shall I in a pointed manner urge any thing in my defence, but leave them at large to condemn or excuse me, upon a presumption, that should they condemn, they will at least pardon, and judge me perhaps less culpable, when they reflect, in the first instance, on the exertions necessary to procure baggage wagons, provisions and house room for seven hundred and fifty men, marched the whole distance in a body, generally from fifteen to twenty miles per day, as the several stages made it necessary. And in the latter, I trust they will give some indulgence for this neglect, for since our arrival at New York, it has been the fate of this corps to be generally stationed at advanced posts, and to act as a covering party, which must unavoidably expose troops to extraordinary duty and hazard, not to mention the extraordinary vigilance and attention in the commandant of such a party, in disposing in the best manner, and having it regularly supplied, for here the commanders of regiments, exclusive of their military duty, are often obliged to exert themselves in the departments of commissary and quarter-master-general, and even directors of their regimental hospitals.

'Perhaps it may not be improper to give a short detail of occurrences upon our march to Long Island, and since that period.

'The enemy, from the 21st to the 27th of August, were landing their troops on the lower part of Long Island, where they pitched a large encampment, and ours and their advanced parties were daily skirmishing at long shot, in which neither party suffered much.

'On the 26th the Maryland and Delaware troops, which composed part of Lord Sterling's brigade, were ordered over.

'Col. Haslet and his lieut. col. Bedford, of the Delaware battalion, with lieut. col. Hare and myself, were detained on the trial of lieut. col. Zedwitz, and though I waited on general Washington, and urged the necessity of attending our troops, yet he refused to discharge us, alledging there was a necessity for the trials coming on, and that no other field-officers could be then had.

'After our dismission from the court martial, it was too late to get over, but pushing over early next morning, found our regiment engaged. Lord Sterling having marched them off before day, to take possession of the woods and difficult passes between our lines and the enemy's encampment; but the enemy the over night had stole a march on our generals, having got through those passes, met and surrounded our troops on the plain grounds, within two miles of our lines. Lord Sterling drew up his brigade on an advantageous rising ground, where he was attacked by two brigades in front, headed by the generals Cornwallis and Grant, and in his rear the enemy's main body stood ready drawn up to support their own parties and intercept the retreat of ours. This excellent disposition and their superior numbers, ought to have taught our generals there was no time to be lost in securing their retreat, which might at first have been effected, had the troops formed into a heavy column and pushed their retreat, but the longer this was delayed, it became the more dangerous, as they were then landing more troops in front from the ships.

'Our brigade kept their ground for several hours, and in general behaved well, having received some heavy fires from the artillery and musquetry of the enemy, whom they repulsed several times; but their attacks were neither so lasting or vigorous as was expected, owing, as it was imagined, to their being certain of making the whole brigade prisoners of war; for by this time they had so secured the passes on the road to our lines, (seeing our parties were not supported from thence, which indeed our numbers would not admit of,) that there was no possibility of retreating that way. Between the place of action and our lines there lay a large marsh and deep creek, not above eighty yards across at the mouth, (the place of action upon a direct line, did not exceed a mile from a part of our lines,) towards the head of which creek there was a *mill and bridge*, across which a certain col. Ward, from New England, (who is charged with having acted a bashful part that day,) passed over with his regiment and then burnt them down, though under cover of our cannon, which would have checked the enemy's pursuit at any time, otherwise this bridge might have afforded a secure retreat. There then remained no other prospect but to surrender or attempt to retreat over this marsh and creek at the mouth, where no person had ever been known to cross. In the interim, I applied to general Washington for some regiments to march out to support and cover their retreat, which he urged would be attended with too great risk to the party and the lines; he immediately afterwards sent for and ordered me to march down a New England regiment, and captain Thomas' company, which had just come over from York, to the mouth of the creek, opposite where the brigade was drawn up, and ordered two field pieces down, to support and cover their retreat, should they make a push that way. Soon after our march, they began to retreat, and for a small time the fire was very heavy on both sides, till our troops came to the marsh, where they were obliged to break their order, and escape as quick as they could to the edge of the creek, under a brisk fire, notwithstanding which they brought off twenty-eight prisoners.

'The enemy taking advantage of a commanding ground, kept up a continual fire from four field pieces, which were well served and directed, and a heavy column advancing on the marsh must have cut our people off, their guns being wet and muddy, not one of them could have fired; but having drawn up the musquetry and disposed of some riflemen conveniently, with orders to fire on them when they came within shot; however, the latter began their fire rather too soon, being at two hundred yards distance, which, notwithstanding, had the desired effect, for the enemy immediately retreated to the fast land, where they continued parading within six hundred yards, till our troops were brought over; most of those who swam over, and others who attempted to cross before the covering party got down, lost their arms and accoutrements in the mud and creek, and some poor fellows their lives, particularly two of the Maryland, two of the Delaware, one of Astley's Pennsylvania, and two Hessian prisoners, were drowned.

'Thomas' men contributed much in bringing over this party—have enclosed a list of the killed and missing, amounting to 256, officers included. It has been said the enemy during the action also attacked our lines, but this was a mistake; not knowing the ground, one of their columns advanced within long shot, without knowing they were so near, and upon our artillery and part of the musquetry's firing on them, they immediately fled.

'The 28th, during a very hard rain, there was an alarm that the enemy had advanced to attack our lines, which alarmed the troops much, but was without foundation.

'The 29th, it was found by a council of war, that our fortifications were not tenable, and it was therefore judged expedient that the army should retreat from the island that night; to effect which, notwithstanding the Maryland troops had had but one day's respite, and many other troops had been many days clear of any detail of duty, they were ordered on the advanced post at fort Putnam, within 250 yards of the enemy's approaches, and joined with two Pennsylvania regiments on the left, were to remain and cover the retreat of the army, which was happily completed under cover of a thick fog and a southwest wind, both which favoured our retreat, otherwise the fear, disorder, and confusion of some of the eastern troops, must have retarded and discovered our retreat, and subjected numbers to be cut off.

'After remaining two days in New York, our next station was at Harlaem, nine miles above, at an advanced post opposite to Montresore's and Bohana's islands, which in a few days the enemy got possession of without opposition, from the former of which we daily discoursed with them, being within two hundred yards, and only a small creek between.

'It being judged expedient to abandon New York and retreat to our lines below fort Washington, the military stores, &c. had been removing some days, when on the 15th September, the enemy effected a landing on several parts of the island below, and it is cutting to say, without the least opposition.

'I have often read and heard of instances of cowardice, but hitherto have had but a faint idea of it till now. I never could have thought human nature subject to such baseness. I could wish the transactions of this day blotted out of the annals of America. Nothing appeared but flight, disgrace and confusion; let it suffice to say that 60 light infantry upon the first fire put to flight two brigades of the Connecticut troops—wretches who, however strange it may appear, from the brigadier-general down to the private sentinel, were caned and whipped by the generals Washington, Putnam and Mifflin, but even this indignity had no weight, they could not be brought to stand one shot. General Washington expressly sent and drew our regiment from its brigade, to march down towards New York, to cover the retreat and to defend the baggage, with direction to take possession of an advantageous eminence near the enemy, upon the main road, where we remained under arms the best part of the day, till Sargent's brigade came in with their baggage, who were the last troops coming in, upon which the enemy divided their main body into two columns, one filing off on the North river, endeavoured to flank and surround us; we had orders to retreat in good order, which was done, our corps getting within the lines a little after dusk.

'The next day about 1000 of them made an attempt upon our lines, and were first attacked by the brave col. Knolton, of New England, who lost his life in the action, and the third Virginia regiment, who were immediately joined by three independent companies under major Price, and some part of the Maryland flying camp, who drove them back to their lines, it is supposed with the loss of 400 men killed and wounded; our party had about 100 killed and wounded, of the former only 15. Since which we have been viewing each other at a distance, and strongly entrenching, till the 9th October, when three of their men-of-war passed up the North river, above King's bridge, under a heavy cannonade from our batteries, which has effectually cut off our communication by water, with Albany.

'I must now break off abruptly, being ordered to march up above King's bridge, the enemy having landed 6000 men from the sound on Frog's Point; 50 ships have got up there, landing more troops; there is nothing left but to fight them; an engagement is generally expected, and soon. Have enclosed a copy of a general return of the battalion, and Veazey's company, being all the troops I marched from Maryland, with the accoutrements and camp equipage, taken in Philadelphia, to be rendered the congress, together with our weekly general return.

'The independents are about their returns of arms, accoutrements and camp equipage, brought by them from Maryland, but not having time to finish, they must hereafter be returned to the council of safety.

'We have upwards of 300 officers and soldiers of the Maryland regulars, very sick, which you will observe by the return, and I am sorry to say, it's shocking to humanity to have no more care taken of them; this must hurt the service upon the new establishments. Majors Price and Gist, and capt. Stone, are in the Jerseys, very sick, and col. Ware and myself are very unfit for duty, though we attend it; many more officers are very unwell.

'I am, very respectfully, your obedient and very humble servant, W. SMALLWOOD.'

Letter from General Washington to Thomas Johnson, Esq., Governor of Maryland.

'HEAD-QUARTERS, VALLEY FORGE, 17th May, 1778.

'*My Dear Sir*,—From a number of concurring circumstances, there is reason to believe that the enemy mean to evacuate Philadelphia.

'It is necessary, therefore, to draw together as great a force as can be provided for, with the utmost expedition. But as several of our out-posts, covering magazines and the like, cannot be recalled without a body of militia to act in their room, I am obliged to request of the neighbouring States a reinforcement for this and other purposes. The requisition of congress extends to 5000 militia from the Jerseys, Pennsylvania and Maryland.

'A large compact body of regulars are wanted, and several valuable intentions to be attended to at the same time.

'General Smallwood, who lays at Wilmington, covers a quantity of stores at the head of Elk. If he is withdrawn, the enemy may destroy our magazine at that place.

'I would imagine that five hundred militia of your State would be a sufficient security, and proper restraint upon the enemy on that quarter. I would, therefore, beg of you to embody and send forward five hundred of your militia, equipped, and the most contiguous to the head of Elk. You may probably find it most convenient to send them by companies.

'The most expeditious way is certainly the best, and the sooner they get to the head of Elk, the sooner shall I have it in my power to recall the garrison from Wilmington, and complete such a body of continental troops as may enable me to act according to conjunctures.

'I rely upon your particular assistance on this critical occasion, and am,

  'Dear sir, with respect and esteem,

    'Your ob't and very humble servant,

           'Go. Washington.

'*His Excellency Thomas Johnson,*

 '*Governor, &c. Maryland, at Annapolis.*'

Letter from General Washington to Daniel of St. Thomas Jenifer and William Fitzhugh, Esquires.

  'Head-Quarters, Middlebrook, 10*th April,* 1779.

'*Gentlemen,*—I have been duly honoured with your letter of the 26th ultimo and its enclosures.

'The length of time in which the rank has been fluctuating and undecided, by producing, in some measure, a number of claims, gives apprehension of complaint, from whatever mode may be now adopted for determining the several disputes.

'However, to afford the utmost latitude for their consideration, I have ordered a board of general officers to sit, to hear and report on respective claims, precedencies, and the rank of the whole line, which I hope will enable me to complete a final arrangement, as much as possible to the general satisfaction.

'The officers cannot but be pleased in the provision which you have made them, not only for the prospect of ease which it promises, but that honourable distinction of past services, when they shall resume the happy character of citizen.

'I am, gentlemen, with the greatest regard, your most obedient and humble servant, G. Washington.

 (*Public service.*)

'*Daniel of St. Thomas Jenifer, Esq., President of the Senate, and William Fitzhugh, Esq., Speaker of the House of Delegates, at Annapolis.*'

Letter from General Washington to Governor Lee.

'Head-Quarters, Morristown, 24th *January*, 1780.

'*Sir*,—I have been honoured with your excellency's letter of the 26th December, and its inclosures. The immediate attention of government to the distresses of the army, and the effectual assistance promised from the operation of the act, cannot but claim the acknowledgments of every good citizen.

'I flatter myself from your exertions, and those of the other States from which we derive our supplies, that we shall not again experience a like evil.

'I have the honour to be, &c.

'G. Washington.

'*Thomas Sim Lee, Esq. Governor, &c. at Annapolis.*'

Letter from the same to the same, dated

'*February* 19*th*, 1780.

'*Sir*,—About the latter end of December last, I had the honour to receive a letter from his excellency governor Johnson, dated the 27th October, in which he proposes an arrangement for the three companies of artillery, belonging to the State of Maryland, and asks my opinion upon it. As general Knox, being at the head of the artillery, is consequently best acquainted with its interior circumstances, and can best judge of the operation of any arrangements which might take place, I communicated the letter to him to know his sentiments. His answer you will find in the enclosed extract. I beg leave to add that the mode he recommends appears to me well calculated to do justice to the State, to the officers of the three companies, and to promote the general good of the service.

'It is essential to have the corps that compose the army upon our formation, regulated by general principles. The contrary is productive of innumerable inconveniences.

'This makes me wish the idea of erecting the four companies into a separate corps under the command of a major, may be relinquished.

'If the plan now proposed is agreeable to the views of the State, I shall be happy its intentions may be signified as speedily as possible to congress, that the incorporation and arrangement may be carried into execution.

'I have the honour, &c.

'G. WASHINGTON.'

Letter from the same to the same, dated
'*March 26th*, 1780.

'*Sir*,—Your excellency will have received, I presume, before this, a transcript of an act of congress of the 25th of last month, calling on the several States for specific quantities of provisions, rum and forage for the army, and directing the articles of supplies to be collected and deposited at such places in each of the States as should be judged most convenient by me. In the case of a defensive war like ours, which depends almost wholly on the movements and operations of the enemy, it is difficult, if not impracticable, to fix on places of deposite for stores, which may not be rendered improper by subsequent events, and all we can do upon such occasions, is to collect them where it shall appear from a comparative view of circumstances, that they will be probably secure, and most likely to facilitate the purposes intented. I have considered the point with respect to the supplies required of your State, and I beg leave to inform your excellency, that it appears to me, that they should be deposited in the following places, and in the proportions set against each respectively, viz:

	Barrels Flour.	Tons Hay.	Bushels Corn.
Head of Elk,	14,000	140	52,152
Baltimore,	3,000	30	2,000
George Town,	3,000	30	2,000
	20,000	200	56,152

'As to the beef, the time and place of delivery, and the proportion from time to time, must of necessity be governed by the occasional requisitions of the commissary-general.

'I have the honour to be, &c.

'G. WASHINGTON.'

Letter from General Washington to Philip Schuyler, John Matthews, and Nathaniel Peabody, Committee of Congress.

'HEAD-QUARTERS, SPRINGFIELD, *June* 11*th*, 1780.

'*Gentlemen,*—It appears to me to be a very eligible step, at the present juncture, to reiterate our instances with the several States, to engage them to press the measures recommended in your former letter. Not only the time is sliding away very fast, every moment of which ought to be improved for the intended co-operation, but the movements of the enemy demand every exertion in our power for the purpose of defence.

'There can now remain no doubt that Charleston and its garrison have fallen. There is every reason to believe that Sir Henry Clinton, with the whole or the greatest part of his force will shortly arrive at New York.

'The expectation of the French fleet and army, will certainly determine the enemy to unite their forces. General Knyphausen still continues in the Jerseys, with all the force which can be spared from New York; a force greatly superior to ours.

'Should Sir Henry join him, the superiority will be decided, and equal to almost any thing the enemy may think proper to attempt. It is true they are at this time inactive, but their continuance where they are, proves that they have some project of importance in contemplation. Perhaps they are only waiting till the militia grow tired and return home, (which they are doing every hour) to prosecute their designs with less opposition.

'This would be a critical moment for us. Perhaps they

are waiting the arrival of Sir Henry Clinton, either to push up the North river against the highland posts, or to bend their whole force against this army. In either case the most disastrous consequences are to be apprehended. You, who are well acquainted with our situation, need no arguments to evince the danger.

'The militia of this State have run to arms, and behaved with an ardor and spirit of which there are few examples.

'But perseverance in enduring the rigors of military service, is not to be expected from those who are not by profession obliged to it.

'The reverse of this opinion has been a great misfortune in our affairs, and it is high time we should recover from an error of so pernicious a nature. We must absolutely have a force of a different composition, or we must relinquish the contest.

'In a few days we may expect to have to depend almost wholly on our continental force, and this (from your own observation) is totally inadequate to our safety. The exigency calls loudly upon the States to carry all the recommendations of the committee into the most vigorous and immediate execution, but more particularly that of completing our battalions by a draft, and with all the expedition possible.

'I beg to advise that these ideas be all clearly held up to the States. Whatever inconvenience there may be in diffusing the knowledge of our circumstances, delicate as they are, there is, in my opinion, more danger in concealing than disclosing them.

'I have the honour to be, with perfect respect and esteem, gentlemen, your most obedient and humble ser'vt,

'GEO. WASHINGTON.

'*Committee of Congress for Co-operation.*'

APPENDIX.

Letter from General Washington to the Committee of Congress for Co-operation.

'HEAD-QUARTERS, SPRINGFIELD, *June* 12*th*, 1780.

'*Gentlemen,*—I have received information, which though not official, I deem authentic, that some of the States have taken up the measure of augmenting their battalions by draft, on a less extensive footing than was urged in your circular letter of the 23d of May. Though I wish to pay in every instance, implicit deference to the determination of the respective States, I think it my duty, in the present crisis, once more to declare with freedom, that I conceive the measure of filling our battalions to their full complement, fundamental to a co-operation on a large scale, that any thing short of this, will infallibly compel us to confine ourselves to a mere defensive plan, except as to some little partial indecisive enterprize against remote points, and will of course disappoint the expectations of our allies, and protract the war.

'The force which has been stated as necessary, is as small as can give us any prospect of a decisive effort. If it is not furnished, we must renounce every hope of this kind.

'It remains with the States to realize the consequences.

'I have the honour to be, with the greatest respect and esteem, gentlemen, your most obedient servant,

'GO. WASHINGTON.

'*The Committee of Co-operation.*'

Letter from General Washington to the Committee of Congress.

'HEAD-QUARTERS, ROCKAWAY, 23*d June,* 1780.

'*Gentlemen,*—The enemy are now in full force, bending their march towards Morristown, and by my last advices had advanced beyond Springfield. They were vigorously opposed by our advanced corps. But what could the valour of a handful do against so infinite a superiority of numbers?

'The enemy can effect any particular object they may attempt. Besides the army, they can have no other in this State, than our stores, as we cannot defend them, we must endeavour to remove them.

'I am so entirely engaged in attention to our military operations, that I must entreat you to write to the executives of Pennsylvania and Jersey, pressing them to bring out all the wagons they can to our relief. An application has been already made to Pennsylvania for two hundred and fifty wagons, they ought to be instantly furnished.

'But we do not know what may be the ultimate designs of the enemy, all we know is, that they are very strong, and that we are very weak.

'I beg leave to recommend that the States may be again called upon to redouble their exertions, to comply with the demands that have been already made upon them.

'It is essential to our immediate safety, to say nothing of the expected co-operation. If she means to be free, this is the moment for America to exert herself.

'With every sentiment of esteem, I have the honour to be, gentlemen, your most obedient, humble servant,

'Go. Washington.

'*Hon'ble Committee of Co-operation.*'

Letter from General Washington to the Committee of Congress.

'Head-Quarters, *July* 13*th*, 1780.

'*Gentlemen,*—We have received intelligence through different channels, from New York, that the Gaudeloupe had arrived there on Sunday morning, and brought an account that she had fallen in with a large French fleet, consisting of several sail of the line, and a number of transports, between the capes of Virginia and Delaware. This intelligence has every appearance of authenticity, and if true, the arrival of the fleet on the coast may be instantly looked for. This indeed must be the case, at any rate, from the time they are said to have sailed.

'It cannot be too much lamented, that our preparations are still so greatly behind hand. Not a thousand men, that I have heard of, have yet joined the army; and in all probability, the period for commencing our operations is at hand.

'I am happy to learn that a spirit of animation has diffused itself throughout the States, from which we may expect the happiest consequences. But the exigency is so pressing, that we ought to multiply our efforts to give new activity and despatch to our measures; levying and forwarding the men, providing the supplies of every sort required: forage and transportation demand particular attention.

'After what has been preconcerted with the honourable, the congress, after two months previous notice of the intended succour, if our allies find us unprepared, and are obliged to wait several weeks in a state of inaction, it is easy to conceive how unfavourable the impressions it will make of our conduct. Besides this, the season is exceedingly advanced. A decisive enterprize, if our means are equal to it, will not permit us to lose a moment of the time left for military operations, which if improved with all the vigour in our power, is less than were to be wished for an undertaking of so arduous and important a nature; so much is at stake; so much to be hoped; so much to be lost; that we shall be inexcusable if we do not employ all our zeal and all our exertion.

'With the highest respect and esteem, I have the honour to be, gentlemen, your most obedient and humble servant,

'Go. WASHINGTON.

'*The Committee of Co-operation.*'

Letter from General Washington to Governor Lee, of Maryland, dated

'July 26, 1780.

'*Sir,*—I have been honoured with your excellency's favour of the 10th, enclosing copies of the several laws passed by the legislature of your State, for procuring the supplies of men, provisions and carriages, required by the Honourable Committee of Co-operation in conjunction with me.

'The readiness with which these laws were passed, and the pointed attention which your excellency seems determined to pay to the due execution of them, are happy presages that they will be speedily and fully carried into effect.

'I have the honour to be, &c.

'Go. Washington.'

Letter from General Washington to the Committee of Congress.

'Head-Quarters, Orangetown, 17th *August*, 1780.

'*Gentlemen,*—We are now arrived at the middle of August, if we are able to undertake any thing in this quarter this campaign, our operations must commence in less than a month from this, or it will be absolutely too late. It will then be much later than were to be wished, and with all the exertions that can be made, we shall probably be straitened in time.

'But I think it my duty to inform you, that our prospects of operating diminish in proportion as the effects of our applications to the respective States unfold; and I am sorry to add, that we have every reason to apprehend, we shall not be in a condition at all to undertake any thing decisive.

'The completion of our continental battalions to their full establishment of five hundred and four, rank and file, has been uniformly and justly held up as the basis of offensive operations.

APPENDIX. 273

'How far we have fallen short of this, the following state of the levies received, and of the present deficiencies, will show.

'By a return of the 16th instant we had received from

New Hampshire,	457
Massachusetts,	2,898
Rhode Island,	502
Connecticut,	1,356
New York,	283
New Jersey,	165
Pennsylvania,	482
Rank and file,	6,143

'The deficiencies of the battalions from a return of the 12th, allowing for the levies since arrived, to the 16th,

Of New Hampshire, three battalions,	248
Of Massachusetts, including Jackson's adopted, 16 battalions,	3,514
Of Rhode Island, 2 battalions,	198
Of Connecticut, including Webbs' battalion adopted, 9 battalions,	1,866
Of New York, 5 battalions,	1,234
Of New Jersey, 11 battalions,	2,768
Rank and file,	10,397

'If the amount of these deficiencies and the detached corps, necessarily on the frontier, and at particular posts, be deducted, and a proper allowance made for the ordinary casualties, and for the extra calls upon the army for wagoners, artificers, &c. it will be easy to conceive how inadequate our operating force must be to any capital enterprize against the enemy. It is indeed barely sufficient for defence.

'Hitherto all the militia for three months, that have taken the field under my orders, have been about 700 from New Hampshire, 1,700 from Massachusetts, 800 from New York, 500 from New Jersey.

'A part of the eastern militia has been detained to assist our allies at Rhode Island, and will shortly march to join the army.

'But from all the information I have, the number of militia will fall as far short of the demand as the continental troops; and from the slow manner in which the latter have for some time past come in, I fear we have had nearly the whole we are to expect.

'In the article of provisions, our prospects are equally unfavourable. We are now fed by a precarious supply from day to day.

'The commissary, from what has been done in the several States, so far from giving assurances of a continuance of this supply, speaks in the most discouraging terms, as you will perceive by the enclosed copy of a letter of the 15th instant, in which he proposes sending back the Pennsylvania militia, who were to assemble at Trenton the 12th, on the principle of a failure of supplies.

'As to forage and transportation, our prospects are still worse. These have lately been principally procured by military impress, a mode too violent, unequal, oppressive, and consequently odious to the people, to be long practised with success.

'In this state of things, gentlemen, I leave it to your own judgment to determine how little it will be in my power to answer the public expectations, unless more competent means can be, and are, without delay, put into my hands.

'From the communications of the general and admiral of our allies, the second division, without some very unfortunate contrariety, will in all probability arrive before the time mentioned as the ultimate period for commencing our operations.

'I submit it to you whether it will not be advisable immediately to lay before the several States, a view of our circumstances at this juncture, in consequence of which they may take their measures.

'I have the honour to be, with the greatest respect and esteem, gentlemen, your most obedient servant,

'Go. Washington.

'*The Honourable the Committee
of Congress for Co-operation.*

'N. B. The returns of the Rhode-Island recruits, is to the last of July. More may have since joined.

'There is a body of Connecticut State troops and militia, stationed on the Sound, employed in preparing fascines.'

Letter from General Washington to George Plater, Esq., President of the Senate, and William Bruff, Speaker of the House of Delegates of Maryland, dated

'*February 9th*, 1781.

'*Gentlemen*,—I am honoured with your favour of the 27th ultimo. As the troops of Maryland compose part of the southern army now under the immediate command of major-general Green, I think there would be an impropriety (as it may interfere with the arrangements of that army) to give general Smallwood directions to remain in Maryland for the purposes you mention; but if his doing this is not incompatible with the orders or views of general Green, I have no objection to his remaining in that State till application can be made to general Green, who I make no doubt will acquiesce in a measure which seems calculated for the public good, if general Smallwood's services from the army can be dispensed with.

'I have the honour to be, &c.

'Go. Washington.'

Letter from General Washington to Governor Lee, dated
'*June* 7, 1781.

'*Sir*,—By a resolve of congress of 31st May, two battalions of infantry and a corps of horse, consisting of sixty-four dragoons, are required of the State of Maryland, to serve for three months from the time of their respectively rendezvousing at the place or places directed by me.

'Your excellency has no doubt been made acquainted that the aforegoing requisition is founded upon the alarming progress which the enemy are making in Virginia.

'You will be pleased, therefore, to give orders to the officers commanding the respective corps, to march by detachments as they are raised and equipped, to whatever place may be the head-quarters of the American army in Virginia or Maryland, (should the enemy have advanced into that State,) and take their further commands from the general or other commanding officer.

'I need but refer your excellency to the circular letter of the president of congress, of the 1st inst., for the reasons which ought to influence the exertions of your State, most particularly at this moment.

'I have the honour to be, &c.

'Go. Washington.'

Extract of a letter from General Washington to Governor Lee, dated

'10th *July,* 1781.

'I have the honour to acknowledge the receipt of your excellency's favour of the 29th June. It is with very great satisfaction I observe the proceedings of the general assembly of your State, which you have been pleased to communicate to me.

'The exertions of that legislature have heretofore been laudable, and I am exceedingly glad to see the same spirit still prevailing. G. Washington.'

Letter from General Washington to Governor Lee.

'Head-Quarters, Chatham, 27th *August,* 1781.

'*Sir*—Official accounts which I have received, giving me reason to expect the arrival of a powerful fleet of our allies very soon in the Chesapeake, if not already there; this expectation, together with some other circumstances not necessary at present to detail to your excellency, have induced me to make a total alteration in the concerted operations of this campaign. In consequence, I am now marching a very considerable detachment from the American army, with the whole of the French troops, immediately to Virginia.

'As our hopes of success against lord Cornwallis, in a great measure depend on the despatch and celerity of our movements, I have to request in the most earnest manner, all the aid and assistance from your excellency, which we may have occasion for, and that may be in your power to afford us.

'Among these the means of transportation from the head of Elk to the point of operation, will be among the most essential. All the water craft that can be procured suitable for the transportation of our army, with their artillery, baggage, stores, &c., will be needed, and should be ready at the head of Elk, by the 8th of September; a quantity of forage will also be necessary for the cattle which will unavoidably attend the army. As I shall probably be disappointed of a quantity of salted provisions, which cannot with safety be conveyed from the eastern States, I must beg your excellency to pay particular attention to that article, if any is to be obtained in your State. Other aids, as well in provisions as other articles, will probably be needed, which cannot at this moment be particularly specified.

'I communicate my intentions to your excellency, and have the fullest confidence that I shall receive every aid and assistance that is in your power, towards their execution.

'I expect to have no occasion to call on you for the aid of men, further than your State troops which are ordered to be raised, and which I hope you have already completed.

'Mr. Robert Morris will have the principal agency in procuring the water craft mentioned; perhaps nothing more will be expected from your excellency in that article, than to afford Mr. Morris every aid which he may stand in need of, from government, in their procurement. This, I am persuaded, you will do with readiness and decision.

'The moment is critical—the opportunity is precious—the prospect is most happily favourable. I hope that no supineness or want of exertion on our own part, may prove the means of a fatal disappointment.

'I have the honour to be, with great sincerity of esteem and regard, your excellency's most obedient and humble servant,   Go. Washington.

'P. S. Our forage will be principally wanted at the head of Elk, and from thence on the route to Georgetown.

'*To his Excellency Governor Lee, of Maryland.*'

Letter from General Washington to Governor Lee.

'Mount Vernon, 11*th September*, 1781.

'*Sir*,—I intended on passing through Maryland, to have done myself the pleasure to have called on your excellency, but circumstances pressing upon me, as I advanced on my march, and time slipping too fast from me, I found a necessity of getting on with that rapidity as has obliged me to proceed without calling at Annapolis.

'I am exceedingly pleased to find, as I passed through your State, that a spirit for exertion prevails universally in such manner as gives me the happiest prospects of receiving very effectual support from you.

'Great attention is necessary to be given to the article of supplies. I mention this circumstance, as I am just informed from below, that the army is in distress at this moment for want of provisions, particularly flour; let me entreat your excellency to give every, the most expeditious relief on this head that is within your power.

'With very great regard and esteem, I have the honour to be your excellency's most obedient and most humble servant, Go. WASHINGTON.

'*His Excellency Governor Lee.*'

Letter from General Washington to Governor Lee.

'HEAD-QUARTERS, WILLIAMSBURGH, 15*th* Sept., 1781.

'*Sir*,—Your excellency has been informed, on hearing the French fleet had sailed from the capes, I had given orders to the troops which were embarked, to stop their proceedings. I am now happy to be able to inform your excellency, that the Count De Grasse is returned to his former station at Cape Henry, having driven the British fleet from the coast, formed a junction with the squadron of the Count De Barris, and captured two British frigates. The bay being thus secure, I have given orders for the troops to proceed with all possible despatch to the point of operation.

'I am distressed, my dear sir, to find on my arrival at Williamsburgh, that the supplies for the army here, are not in that desirable train that could be wished; they have already experienced a want of provisions, and are greatly apprehensive for the prospect in future, particularly in the article of bread; all the flour within your reach should be immediately forwarded down, which may, I think, be speedily done, now that the navigation of the bay is secured. I beg, sir, that not a moment may be lost in furnishing us with every supply within your power.

'Happily if the fleet will remain with us, our prospects of success are most promising, if we are not wanting in our own exertions.

'An army cannot be kept together without supplies; if

these fail us, our operations must cease, and all our highest hopes will vanish into disappointment and disgrace.

'With great regard and esteem, I have the honour to be your excellency's most obedient servant,

'Go. Washington.

'P. S. If your excellency can assist us in procuring some axes and hatchets, and entrenching tools of all kinds, it will be a great advantage.

'We shall have much occasion for tools of this sort, and I find almost a total want here, and it will be difficult to make a collection from a small compass.

'*To his Excellency Governor Lee.*'

Letter from General Washington to Governor Lee.
'Head-Quarters, before York, *October* 12*th*, 1781.

'*Sir,*—I was yesterday honoured with your excellency's favour of the 3d. Give me leave to return you my sincerest thanks for your exertions on the present occasion.

'The supplies granted by the State are so liberal, that they remove every apprehension of want. Col. Blaine has gone himself over to the eastern shore, to see that the cattle from thence are brought down to the proper landing, where they will be slaughtered, and the meat sufficiently salted to be transported by water.

'Proper measures have been taken by the commissaries, to receive the cattle of the western shore, and to have them driven by land.

'Arrangements have also been made to send up the craft for flour, as fast as they discharge their lading of stores.

'I will desire col. Stewart to send up all the empty flour barrels that can be made of further use.

'We opened our first parallel on the night of the 6th, and established it completely with a loss too trifling to mention.

'Our shells have done considerable damage in the town, and our fire from the cannon has been so heavy and well directed against the embrazures of the enemy's works, that they have been obliged during the day to withdraw their cannon and place them behind their merlins.

'The Charon, of 44 guns, and two large transports, have been burnt by hot balls. The guns and stores had been previously taken out of the frigate. We last night advanced our second parallel within 300 yards of the enemy's works, without the least annoyance from them. Lord Cornwallis' conduct has hitherto been passive beyond conception; he either has not the means of defence, or he intends to reserve himself until we approach very near him. A few days must determine whether he will or will not give much trouble.

'I have the honour to be, with great respect, your excellency's most obedient servant,   Go. Washington.

'*His Excellency Governor Lee.*'

Extract of a letter from General Washington to Governor Lee, dated

'*October,* 1781.

'My present engagements will not allow me to add more than my congratulations on the happy event, (alluding to the surrender of the British army at York,) and to express the high sense I have of the powerful aid which I have derived from the State of Maryland, in complying with my every request to the executive of it.

'Go. Washington.'

Letter from General Green to Governor Lee.

'HEAD-QUARTERS, SOUTH CAROLINA,
December 20*th*, 1782.

'*Sir*,—The evacuation of Charleston, so long expected, took place on the 14th instant. It is an event of great moment to America in general, and of the last importance to the southern States in particular.

'I beg leave to congratulate your excellency on the happy consequences that are likely to flow from it. It puts a period (at least for a time) to the distresses of a worthy people, and will give them an opportunity to recover from those misfortunes which the nature of the war inevitably exposed them to. Government will be at leisure to examine its state and condition, and society, so long disturbed by discordant interests, will combine its views and objects, and the people be induced to unite in their exertions to prevent a return of those difficulties under which they have so recently smarted.

'I have the honour to be, with great respect and esteem, your excellency's most obed't and most humble ser'vt,

'NATH. GREENE.

'*His Excellency Governor Lee, Maryland.*'

Letter from Colonel Armand to the Governor of Maryland.*

'MAHALISTER, IN PENNSYLVANIA, *December* 28*th*, 1783.

'*Sir*,—After having passed through the State over which you preside, I conceive it of my duty to express to your excellency the thanks of the legion under my command, and mine in particular, for the friendly dispositions and behaviour of the Marylanders towards us. The town of Frederick, in which we have made the longest station, has more particularly evidenced to us the worthy and high character of that country. Permit me to add here, that

* William Paca.

where people are sensible as those, of the rights of military men to their attention and care, they do deserve having respectable troops as the Maryland line—and do create in others, wishes for the opportunity to serve them.

'I am, with great respect, your excellency's very—the most obedient, humble servant,

'ARMAND MQIS. LA ROUERIE.

'*His Excellency the Governor*
   of the State of Maryland, Annapolis.'

THE END.

www.ingramcontent.com/pod-product-compliance
Lightning Source LLC
Chambersburg PA
CBHW062004220426
43662CB00010B/1229